HIDDEN LIVES

British Library Lansdowne MS 383, fol. 165v; see p. vi

HIDDEN LIVES
THE NUNS OF
SHAFTESBURY ABBEY

WILLIAM SMITH

THE HOBNOB PRESS

First published in the United Kingdom in 2020

by The Hobnob Press,
8 Lock Warehouse, Severn Road, Gloucester GL1 2GA
www.hobnobpress.co.uk

in association with Shaftesbury Abbey Museum
and Garden,
Park Walk, Shaftesbury SP7 8JR,

a joint undertaking gratefully acknowledged by the author.

British Library Cataloguing in Publication Data
A catalogue record for this book is available from the British Library

ISBN 978-1-906978-92-1

Typeset in Baskerville 11/14 pt.
Typesetting and origination by John Chandler

Contents

Illustrations   vi
Dedication   vii
Abbreviations   viii
Preface and Acknowledgements   ix

The Abbey and its Nuns
    Pre-Conquest   1
    Post-Conquest   14
    St Anselm and the Nuns of Shaftesbury   16

The Abbesses
    Emerging from the Shadows   23
    A Group of Feudal Dames   24
    At the King's Will Their Manner of Appointment   25
    Their Sisters in Christ   33

Dissolution
    From the Cloister into the World   36

Appendix: Shaftesbury Abbesses and known Nuns from the
    Abbey's Foundation to its Dissolution   38

Bibliography
    1 Primary sources (Original)   112
    2 Primary sources (Printed)   113
    3 Secondary sources (Books, articles, catalogues,
    dictionaries, and other reference works)
        1 Printed   121
        2 Online   132

Index   135

Illustrations

Front cover image
Virgin and Child enthroned in an architectural setting, from the Shaftesbury Psalter, 1125/1135? x 1150. The female suppliant in the lower left corner may represent an abbess or a nun.
British Library Lansdowne MS 383, fol. 165v
© British Library Board. All rights reserved/Bridgeman Images.

Frontispiece
Christ in Majesty nimbed and seated on a rainbow within a mandorla surrounded by symbols of the four Evangelists, from the Shaftesbury Psalter. The richly dressed female suppliant in the lower margin may represent an abbess, or a secular owner, who may have commissioned the manuscript for personal use. It has been suggested that the suppliant may be Adeliza of Louvain (d. 1151), second queen consort of Henry I, for whom the Psalter was possibly made after Henry's death in 1135. In any event, the calendar, litany and some of the prayers in the Psalter indicate a Shaftesbury association, even though it may not have been originally intended for use there.
British Library Lansdowne MS 383, fol. 14v
© British Library Board. All rights reserved/Bridgeman Images.

for HELEN

… voi mi levate sì, ch'i' son più ch'io.
Dante, *Paradiso,* XVI. 18.

Abbreviations

Note: The following non-bibliographical abbreviations are used in this work: Aug., Augustinian; Ben., Benedictine; bl., blessed; Brig., Brigettine; Cist., Cistercian; Clun., Cluniac; conf., confirmed; d., died; el., elected; *fl.*, *floruit*; Font., Fontevraud (or Fontevrault), Order of; occ., occurs; Prem., Premonstratensian; roy. ass., royal assent; *s.*, *sæculum* (used as shorthand in dates, as, for example, *s.* x, tenth century); temps., temporalities. Periods shortly before or after a particular date are indicated by - or + (e.g. -4 October 1291). Expansions of manuscript name and Latin word contractions are indicated by italics.

Preface and Acknowledgements

The long history of women's monasticism in Dorset is distinguished by its association with royalty. Three of its five medieval nunneries (four pre-Conquest), Shaftesbury, Wimborne, and the Cistercian Tarrant Keyneston were the burial places of monarchy, while the other two, Horton and Wareham, may well have had regal connections yet to be established. Of the four Anglo-Saxon foundations, Shaftesbury Abbey alone survived the Conquest to become the richest and most important nunnery of its Benedictine order in England. With most of its landed property extending throughout northern and central Dorset and southern Wiltshire, its gross annual income at the time of its suppression in 1539 made it second only in wealth and status to Henry V's Brigettine foundation of Syon in Middlesex. Shaftesbury's post-Conquest continuation was made possible by its beneficial associations with the West Saxon and English ruling dynasties, which, from the reign of the abbey's founder Alfred the Great, generously endowed this royal nunnery with the considerable estates it succeeded in maintaining throughout its history. By contrast, Dorset's three other pre-Conquest nunneries, Wimborne, Horton and Wareham, had disappeared by the early eleventh century, when they were succeeded by male religious communities. The reasons for this are not entirely clear, but economic decline, perhaps due to steadily diminishing endowments caused by the disintegration of formerly large royal estates, has been suggested as a principal cause. Shaftesbury's wealth and prestige were also enhanced by its status as a prominent regional centre of pilgrimage, which sought to promote the cults of its two royal saints, the murdered adolescent King Edward the Martyr (d. 978), the abbey's co-titular, and his grandmother Ælfgifu (d. 944), both of whose relics were enshrined and venerated there.

Long the interest of historians and archaeologists, much has been written about Shaftesbury Abbey, but very little about the nuns themselves. These *cloîtrées*, from young to old, whose routine and hidden lives governed daily by the precepts of the *Rule* of St Benedict and the monastic *horarium* with its liturgical cycle of mass and office, made up the often neglected living and spiritual history of this great foundation. This work has for its focus these forgotten women, retrieving their names from sometimes sparse historical sources, which can only ever tell a limited story, and that usually from an official rather than a human aspect, but which must nevertheless remain our starting-point. While this study falls short of a full prosopography, an attempt has been made to identify and describe its subjects from the monastery's foundation in the late ninth century to its dissolution in the sixteenth, a period of six and a half centuries. In the end, however, one is aware that there is still very much more to be discovered, particularly when investigating the less well documented early medieval period, when anonymity will continue to prevail. As a tentative beginning, it is hoped that this book will stimulate further studies, not just for Shaftesbury itself, complementing what has now been brought to light, but also for other communities of medieval religious women, whose lives and identities will otherwise remain lost forever in the dim recesses of the vanishing past.

In concluding this work, my thanks are due to my wife Helen for tirelessly reading and commenting on its revisions; to Peter Waterman and the staff of Warminster library for their cheerful and unflagging help in obtaining sometimes difficult resources; to Dr Anne Dutton and Emily Naish of Salisbury Cathedral library and archives for access to the Dean and Chapter collections; and to the staff of the Wiltshire and Swindon History Centre for their interest and help. I am especially grateful to Claire Ryley of Shaftesbury Abbey Museum and Garden for obtaining the images, and the British Library Board/ Bridgeman Images for licensing their use; and to Dr John Chandler FSA (himself the author of a very good book on Shaftesbury Abbey) of The Hobnob Press, Gloucester, for kindly accepting this work for publication, and for skilfully and patiently bringing it to fruition.

WILLIAM SMITH

The Abbey and its Nuns

Pre-Conquest

Piously founded by one monarch and peremptorily suppressed by another six and a half centuries later, the Benedictine Abbey of St Mary and St Edward at Shaftesbury was the wealthiest and most important nunnery of its order in England until its dissolution in 1539.[1] According to a generally accepted tradition, it was established in the late 880s, perhaps in or around 888, by King Alfred the Great,[2] who bestowed on it one-sixteenth of his royal revenues, appointing his second eldest daughter Æthelgifu as its first abbess. Alfred's biographer Asser describes Æthelgifu as 'devoted to God through her virginity, subject and consecrated to the rules of monastic life'.[3] Her age at the time of appointment is unknown, nor perhaps is it material, if in the manner of her time she had been well prepared for this demanding position. It is possible that she had served her earlier vocation as a novice or professed nun in another Wessex religious

1   *Monasticon* 2, 471–88; *VCH Dorset* 2 (1908), 73–9; Power, 2, 30, 146, 181, 186, 188–9, 198–9, 238, 243, 338–9 *et passim*; Sydenham; Murphy, 40–53; Smith, 3–18; Bettey 1992, 3–11; Kelly, xiii–xv; Keynes 1999, 17–72; Foot 2000 1, 2–3, 6, 11–13, 15, 70, 76, 82, 86, 136–8 *et passim*, and especially 2, 165–77; Chandler; Yorke 2003, 76, 81–3, 111, 158 *et passim*. In gross annual income Shaftesbury, £1324, was second only to Syon Abbey (Middlesex, Brig.), £1943 (Power, 2).

2   Keynes 1999, 37–41. John of Worcester (*Chronicle* 2, 328–29 [(ix) 909]) and Simeon of Durham (2 *Historia regum*, 119), the former following Asser, give the year as 887 (Asser, 85 [98. 1–3]) and 888 (so *Monasticon* 2, 473a, and also Murphy, 40, 50) respectively. Earlier and later dates occur in *Annales monasterii de Wintonia* [Winchester], 872, and *Annales monasterii de Waverleia* [Waverley], 896 (*AM* 2, 10, 163), though these are not generally accepted.

3   ... *monasticæ vitæ regulis, devota Deo virginitate, subiuncta et consecrata* (Asser, 58 [75. 9–10]). Asser's *Life of King Alfred* was written in 893.

foundation, where she might have 'entered the service of God'[1] from childhood, perhaps as an oblate.[2] Wareham,[3] an ancient *monasterium sanctimonialium* within a fortified settlement (*castellum*) mentioned by Asser has been proposed,[4] and also Wimborne,[5] a double house in the early Frankish style established by St Cuthburh (Cuþburh, Cuðburh, Cuthburg, Cuthburga), a sister of King Ine of Wessex, in 718,[6] as recorded by the *Anglo-Saxon Chronicle*.[7] Wilton is another possibility,[8] with the topography of the town centre suggesting the existence of an early minster on the site later occupied by the now largely ruined parish church of St Mary.[9] This foundation was in the proximity of the former royal residence (*villa regalis*), whose memory the name

1   ... *divinum subiit servitium* (Asser, 58 [75. 10]).

2   The custom of oblating children to religious houses is discussed by Knowles 2004, 9–10, 212, 418–22, 634–5.

3   Keynes 1999, 41, with n. 58.

4   ... *castellum, quod dicitur Werham* (Asser, 36 [49. 4]; RCHM *Dorset*: 2 *South-East*, pt. 2, 322–4; see also *infra* p. 12 n. 2). The nunnery, possibly founded in the late seventh century and evidently important in its day, did not survive the Conquest (Foot 2000 1, 15, 48, 77, 86, 151, 154–7, 159, 162 *et passim*, and especially 2, 197–204). Another religious community, replacing a college of secular canons subsequently settled there, was established in the same place (perhaps the early minster later serving as the parish church of Lady St Mary) *c.*1150 as a dependent priory (Ben.) of Lire in Normandy and suppressed in 1414 as an alien house, when its lands were bestowed by Henry V on the Carthusian priory he founded at Sheen in Surrey (*VCH Dorset* 2, 121–2; RCHME *Dorset* 2, pt. 2, 304a).

5   Keynes 1999, 41, with n. 58. For Wimborne, which had become a college of secular canons by the time of the Conquest, see *Monasticon* 2, 88–9; *VCH Dorset* 2, 107–13; Coulstock, 7–41 (Chs. I–III); Foot 2000 1, 15, 22, 26, 30, 39, 41, 44, 48, 53, 77, 86 *et passim*, and especially 2, 233–7; and Keen, 'Dorset', 227, 230, 238, 242.

6   *GP* 1, 569 (v. 225. 6), with note *GP* 2, 279; *GR* 1, 52–3 (ii. 36. 1), with note *GR* 2, 35.

7   *ASC* A, E 718.

8   Yorke 2003, 76.

9   Haslam, 'Wiltshire', 123, 125; Pevsner & Cherry, 579. St Mary's was partly demolished following the building of the new Italianate style parish church of St Mary and St Nicholas in 1845.

of the town's Kingsbury Square now perpetuates.[1] According to later medieval Wilton tradition, King Egbert (Ecgberht) of Wessex (reigned 802-39) founded a house for thirteen women near there from a former chantry in 830.[2] The same tradition also relates its subsequent incorporation with another house for thirteen women supposedly established by King Alfred in 890.[3] Dedicated like its predecessor to St Mary,[4] the new convent is believed to have been located on the site of the old royal palace away from the original minster and styled an abbey.[5] The earliest surviving pre-Conquest references to a religious foundation at Wilton, however, date from the mid-tenth century.[6] This may suggest that Alfred's reputed nunnery was subsequently refounded by his son Edward the Elder (king of the Anglo-Saxons, reigned 899-924), when it was moved again to another site just east of the town. [7] An expanding borough may have been the reason for relocation, though equally the convent may have sought new premises in order to accommodate growing numbers of nuns during this period. In any event, Wilton Abbey was to remain here until its demolition in the mid-sixteenth century to make way

1   Haslam, 'Wiltshire', 123, 125. Another clue to the existence of a former religious house in the vicinity is found in the name of Minster Street, the main access to Kingsbury Square from the east.

2   Horstmann, 4, vv. 130–53; *VCH Wiltshire* 3 (1956), 231a.

3   Horstmann, 14, vv. 598 ff. *VCH Wiltshire* 3, 231b, is dismissive of this tradition through apparent lack of evidence, though it deserves consideration. William of Malmesbury is reticent about the origins of Wilton Abbey, devoting most of his narrative instead to the story of St Edith (Edgitha) of Wilton drawn from Goscelin's *Vita S. Edithæ* (*GP* 1, 296–301 (ii. 87. 2–10), with notes *GP* 2, 134–6; *GR* 1, 402–5 (ii. 218–19), with notes *GR* 2, 205–6). For Wilton Abbey, see *Monasticon* 2, 315–32; Power, 2–3, 54, 105 146, 172, 185–6, 188–9, 350 *et passim*; *VCH Wiltshire* 3, 231–42; Foot 2000 1, 1–2, 4, 6, 11–13, 94–5, 137, 159–61 *et passim*, and especially 2, 221–31.

4   Haslam, 'Wiltshire', 123

5   Ibid., citing Richard Colt Hoare, *History of Modern Wiltshire* (London: John Nichols & Son, 1825) 2, pt. 1, 78.

6   Foot 2000 1, 160, and 2, 221.

7   Haslam, 'Wiltshire', 123, with plan (no. 52), 126, showing the situation of the abbey in relation to the early tenth-century *burh*; cf. also Foot 2000 1, 160.

for Wilton House,[1] which has been the family seat of the earls of Pembroke for nearly five hundred years.

The interest of the West Saxon ruling dynasty in nunneries, both as a means of promoting monastic ideals for women as well as maintaining the cult of the royal dead, was to continue with the creation of further female religious houses. These were established at Winchester (the Nunnaminster) by Alfred's consort[2] Ealhswith shortly before or after 899,[3] and, according to one of the more reliable

1   Briefly described by Pevsner & Cherry, 580–6; see also note to *Wiltunense cenobium* in *GP* 2, 134–5. Most of the nunnery is buried under Wilton House, which makes archaeological investigation difficult, if not impossible, but part of the claustral range is believed to lie beneath the dining room.

2   In accordance with the custom of the time Ealhswith was never styled 'queen' (*cuen, cwene, regina*), but always as wife or consort of the king (*coniux/coniunx regis, regia coniux/coniunx*): Asser, 11 (13. 12–15); Birch, 57; Keynes & Lapidge, 71, 235–6 n. 28; Ridyard, 234; Keynes 1996, 94b, fol. 26r. The status of *coniux/coniunx* gradually changed during the tenth century, when *regina* starts to appear regularly (Keynes & Lapidge, 235–6 n. 28). King Edgar (reigned 959 (crowned 973)–975, ruling in Mercia and the Danelaw 957–9), for example, is recorded as taking Ælfthryth for his queen (*Her on þissum geare Eadgar cyning genam ælfðryðe him to cwene, ASC* D 965). In one section of the *Regularis Concordia* (2 [c.3]), however, Ælfthryth, named as 'protectress and fearless guardian of the communities of nuns' (*sanctimonialium mandras ut impauidi more custodis defenderet*; see also Meyer 1977, 54), is styled *coniux*, though this appears to be the equivalent of *regina* occurring elsewhere in the *Concordia*. John of Worcester (d. *c*.1140) inaccurately styles Ealhswith *regina* [see *infra* n. 3].

3   *Monasticon* 2, 451–8, at 451a; *VCH Hampshire* 2 (1903), 122–6, at 122, with n. 1; Biddle, 127–8, 134 ('The Nunnaminster was refounded by Æthelwold early in 964, at about the same time as the reformation of New Minster ... Nothing else is known of how this house fared under reform, except that it shared in the general adjustment, enlargement, and enclosure of the lands of all three monasteries [Old Minster, New Minster and Nunnaminster] by which Æthelwold sought to reduce disputes and to provide a more secluded setting for their reformed monastic life' [for Æthelwold, see *infra* p. 48 n. 4]); Ridyard, 32, 34, 97–8; Coldicott, 2–5; Foot 2000 1, 2, 6, 50, 86, 91, 93, 97, 103, 159–61 *et passim*, and especially 2, 243–52; Foot 2011, 45; Costambeys, 'Ealhswith'. John of Worcester (*Chronicle* 2, 360–1 [(vi) 927 *sub anno* 905]) describes Ealhswith as 'Christ's devout follower' (*religiosa Christi famula Ealhsuuiþa regina*). Although the foundation is commonly attributed to Ealhswith, Alfred is likely to have been involved in, if not initiating, its early planning.

foundation traditions known to William of Malmesbury, Romsey, by
King Edgar in 967.[1] Edgar's grandfather Edward the Elder appears
to have begun the family association with Wilton, where his second
wife Ælfflæd (Elffled)[2] seems to have retired, perhaps as a lay sister,
on the dissolution of her marriage around 917.[3] Three of Edward's
eight daughters also pursued religious vocations,[4] two, Eadflæd[5] and
Eadburh (Eadburg, Eadburga)[6] becoming consecrated nuns at Wilton

> After Ealhswith's death the nunnery is likely to have been completed by
> her son Edward the Elder (Foot 2000 1, 160). The *Anglo-Saxon Chronicle*
> variously assigns the date of Ealhswith's death to 902 (C) and 905 (D),
> indicating that John of Worcester followed the latter.

1   *GP* 1, 276–7 (ii. 78. 7), with note *GP* 2, 119–120. William, however, may
    be referring to its re-establishment with Merewenna as first abbess (*ODS*,
    367a, art. 'Merewenna') as recorded by John of Worcester, who names
    Edward the Elder as founder (*Chronicle* 2, 416–19 [(xxxi) 989 *sub anno*
    967]), though this tradition appears doubtful and confused (Foot 2000
    2, 149–51). From the brevity of his description it is thought unlikely that
    William ever visited Romsey. For the pre-Conquest abbey, see *Monasticon*
    2, 506–10, at 506a; *VCH Hampshire* 2, 126–32, at 126; Liveing, 11–15,
    35–9; Foot 2000 1, 6, 13, 92–3, 159–61 *et passim*, and especially 2, 149–
    55.

2   PASE (Ælfflæd 10); *GR* 1, 198–201 (ii. 126. 1–2); Foot 2011, 11–12, 37,
    44, 57, 75, 122–3. Meyer 1977, 47, suggests that Ælfflæd retired to the
    Nunnaminster, Winchester. Ælfflæd, who died in the mid-tenth century,
    was a benefactor of Glastonbury Abbey, and is likely to have shown an
    interest in the early stages of the monastic reform movement. (ibid., 46–
    7).

3   Foot 2000 1, 141, 165, 180–1. There are indications that Edward put
    Ælfflæd out of the way in order to marry his third wife, Eadgifu (Foot
    2011, 57).

4   Most of the others (Æthelstan's half-sisters) married into Continental
    royal or noble houses (*GR* 2, 109–10; Foot 2011, 44–52, especially 51,
    where it is convincingly argued that Edward had eight daughters rather
    than nine).

5   PASE (Eadflæd 4); *GR* 1, 198–201 (ii. 126. 2); Foot 2000 1, 2–3, 141,
    165, and 2, 226; Foot 2011, 45. See also *infra* p. 6 n. 2.

6   PASE (Eadburg 8); Foot 2000 1, 180, and 2, 244–5; Foot 2011, 45, 124,
    184. For Eadburh (Eadburg) *sancta* (*festum* 15 June), see *GP* 1, 275–6 (ii.
    78. 3–6), 455 (iv. 162) with notes *GP* 2, 118–19, 212; *GR* 1, 200–1 (ii.
    126. 3), 400–3 (ii. 217), with note *GR* 2, 204–5; Liebermann, 15 [33];
    Birch, 93; Ridyard, 17–37, 96–139, 144, 235, 237, 253–308 (255–308

and the Nunnaminster respectively, while another, Æthelhild,[1] was a
lay sister or perhaps recluse at Wilton, where she ended her days and
was buried next to her mother Ælfflæd and sister Eadflæd.[2] Wilton
Abbey received donations of land during Æthelstan's reign (925-39),[3]
one, in 937, for the remission of his sins as well as those of his sister
Eadflæd,[4] increasing its endowments and aligning its interests more
closely with the West Saxon royal house in the manner of Shaftesbury.[5]

Both Wilton and Shaftesbury had features in common besides
their nunneries, each being a royal *burh* (fortified settlement) with
a mint by the late ninth century.[6] The fortification of Wilton was
undertaken early by Alfred following his defeat there by the Vikings
within a month of his accession in April 871.[7] The continuing
Scandinavian threat to this vulnerable, low-lying township is likely to
have raised concerns about the safety and upbringing of his young
daughter Æthelgifu,[8] who may initially have been entrusted to the
care of an established religious foundation there appropriate for the
purpose, assuming the existence of one in Wilton at this period. Over

is an edition of the twelfth-century *Vita Sancte Edburge* by Osbert of Clare
from *Ob* MS Laud. misc. 114, fols. 85–120), 309–10; Keynes 1996, fol.
38v; Foot 2000 1, 141, 180; Blair, 526–7; Yorke, 'Eadburh'.

1   *GR* 1, 198–201 (ii. 126. 2).

2   Ibid., where Eadflæd and Æthelhild are described as *celibatum Deo
    uouentes, Edfleda in sacrato Ethelhilda in laico tegmine, terrenarum nuptiarum
    uoluptatem fastidiere.* See also Foot 2000 1, 1–4, 33, 136, 141, 165, 181;
    Foot 2011, 45. According to *LMH*, 112, however, Eadflæd (as Elfleda)
    sancta was buried at Romsey, though Æthelhild (as Etheltilda) is said to
    rest at Wilton (ibid.).

3   *VCH Wiltshire* 3, 231b.

4   Foot 2011, 45.

5   Foot 2000 2, 223. Shaftesbury also received gifts of land from Æthelstan
    around this time, at Fontmell and Tarrant Hinton in Dorset in 932 and
    935 (Kelly, nos. 8 and 9).

6   For the mints, see Haslam, 'Wiltshire', 124, 128 (Wilton), and Keen,
    'Dorset', 239–42 (Shaftesbury).

7   *ASC* A, E 871; Stenton, 250; Abels, 137–8, 140.

8   If Æthelgifu was born in the early 870s (Keynes 1999, 41), she would
    have been very young at the time of Alfred's Wilton campaign, perhaps
    no more than one or two. Her mother Ealhswith married Alfred in 868
    (Asser, 24 [29]; Keynes & Lapidge, 77; Abels, 120).

a century later this threat was still very real, when, in 1003, Swein Forkbeard, king of Denmark,[9] 'led his raiding-army into Wilton, and ravaged and burnt the town' before continuing his destructive path to nearby *Searbyrig* and returning to his ships to depart for further depredations upcountry.[10] Æthelgifu's later removal to the security of the less accessible hilltop *burh* of Shaftesbury when she was of suitable age (presumably of adolescent years) may therefore be understood in this light, besides the continuing tradition of the West Saxon ruling house of promoting monasticism for royal and aristocratic women, commonly daughters and widows.[11]

Situated high above sea level on a precipitous, projecting greensand spur commanding extensive southerly and westerly views of Dorset across the Blackmore Vale and beyond to the coastal plains of the English Channel, Shaftesbury was an ideal location for a nunnery under the direct protection of a fortress. Local tradition recorded by William of Malmesbury in the early twelfth century from an ancient stone inscription in the abbey chapter house originally from the borough wall relates that Alfred established the town in 880,[12]

9   Swein, whose Old Norse sobriquet was *Tjúguskegg*, was king of Denmark from 987 to 1014, ruling as king of England for the last two years of his reign (*GR* 1, 300–3 (ii. 176–177. 3), 308–11 (ii. 179. 1–2), with notes *GR* 2, 160–3). His son Cnut was king of England (1016–35), Denmark (1019–35) and Norway (1028–35).

10 *ASC* E, F 1003 (E, *þa lædde he his here into Wiltune. 7 hi ða burh gehergodon 7 forbærndon*). *Searbyrig* (the Roman *Sorviodunum*, a place-name preserving an early British element) was the *burh* known later as Old Sarum lying east of the present city of Salisbury (New Sarum), which was established during the early thirteenth century, when the see was moved there from Old Sarum.

11 Widows were highly esteemed in Anglo-Saxon England, living a respectable life under the direct protection of the king, with legal rights and social privileges often denied to other women (Meyer 1977, 35–6). This gave them 'a greater opportunity to express their piety and devotion in visible terms' (ibid., 36), as exemplified by the royal widow Eadgifu (5) in her support of the monastic reforms of Dunstan and Æthelwold.

12 *GP* 1, 292–3 (ii. 86. 1), with note *GP* 2, 130; RCHME *Dorset 4 North*, 57. William begins his account of Shaftesbury by describing it as a town (*uicus*), which is said to have been a city at one time (*quondam urbs*). See also Keynes 1999, 38. John of Worcester derived this foundation date from William's account (*Chronicle* 2, 314–15 [(ii) 902 *sub anno* 880, with n. 5]). William's affectionate recollection of the nuns of Shaftesbury (...

perhaps meaning that he enhanced the fortifications of an already existing settlement. From its location Shaftesbury may be seen as one of an almost straight line of *burhs* extending from Pilton (*Pilletune*) in north Devon to Southampton (*Hamtun*) and further along the south coast before eventually reaching Hastings (*Hæstingaceaster*) in Sussex at its eastern limit.[1] It would thus have formed an important central link in this long line of defence (itself part of a wider network of fortifications across southern England), extending over two hundred miles with strategic oversight of this region of lower middle Wessex. Away to the west on the inaccessible Somerset marshes lay Alfred's fortress of Lyng,[2] which provided a refuge and centre of operations during his campaign against the Vikings,[3] and which subsequently protected a monastery of foreign monks on the nearby island of

---

quod eo loci multus deuotarum Deo feminarum chorus, claritate religionis terras istas irradians, etiam ipsa prestringit sidera ...), whom he may have visited during his travels, is well known (*GR* 1, 266–9 [ii. 163], 404–5 [ii. 219], with note *GR* 2, 145).

1   Forming part of the Burghal Hidage from the record of them compiled in Edward the Elder's reign (899–924) for the purpose of assigning taxes (assessed on hides of land) for their maintenance (Keynes & Lapidge, 24, 193–4, 339–41; Stenton, 264–5), there were over thirty such fortifications established by Alfred throughout southern England. The line extending from Pilton to Hastings may be clearly traced on the Ordnance Survey map *Britain Before the Norman Conquest*, South Sheet (Southampton: HMSO, 1973). For the Alfredian *burh* of Pilton, see Haslam, 'Wiltshire', 127, and 'Devon', 251, 262. Shaftesbury, which was also included in the Burghal Hidage, was assessed at 700 hides sufficient to maintain a garrison of 700 men (Keynes & Lapidge, 193; Keynes 1999, 39).

2   The *burh* was constructed in the year 878, according to Asser (44 [55. 1–3]), who merely mentions a fortification (*arcem*) built at Alfred's command near Athelney, but the reference is clearly to Lyng. John of Worcester relates that Athelney (without mentioning the monastery) was established by Alfred in 882 (*Chronicle* 2, 316–17 [(iiii) 904 *sub anno* 882]; cf. *GR* 1, 190–1 [ii. 122. 3]). For Lyng, a Burghal Hidage *burh*, see Aston, 'Somerset', 168–71, 183–5 (with plan (Fig. 67), showing the east and west parts of Alfred's fortification in relation to Athelney Abbey), 196–9.

3   Abels, 156–7, 272, 323.

Athelney,[1] some of Gallic origin,[2] established around the same time as Shaftesbury.[3] Asser's remark about a number of monasteries of his time not consistently observing the monastic rule may be taken to suggest that Alfred's aim in founding these two houses was to create exemplary establishments,[4] where a uniformly regulated religious life by both men and women would be diligently observed and eventually followed by other Wessex foundations. A new beginning was perhaps in mind rather than a systematic attempt to reform declining existing insitutions,[5] which was not undertaken during this period. Their establishment may be best understood, however, as acts of piety by

1 Asser describes the religious as *diversi generis monachos*, 'monks of various nationalities' (79–80 [92. 16, 93. 18]) and *ultramarinos presbyteros quosdam et diaconos*, 'certain priests and deacons from across the sea' (81 [94. 3–4]; see also Keynes & Lapidge, 103). The first abbot was John the Old Saxon (... *Iohannem, presbyterum et monachum scilicet Eald-saxonum genere* (Asser, 81 (94. 1–2); *GR* 1, 190–1 [ii. 122. 3]), against whose life a nearly successful attempt was made by two of his Gallic monks (Asser, 82–3 [96]).

2 ... *etiam quamplurimos eiusdem gentis Gallicæ* (Asser, 81 [94. 5–6]).

3 Athelney may have been the earlier foundation, since it is mentioned first by Asser (79–80 [92. 7–17]), being later intentionally complemented by a house for women at Shaftesbury (ibid., 85 [98. 1–7]). The monastic church at Athelney, accessible only by boat from Lyng, or the causeway (*pontem*) set up between two fortifications (Asser, 80 [92. 10–13]), is said by William of Malmesbury to be small and on a confined site, as might be expected in this still regularly inundated area, and the monks few in number and poor (... *monachi pauci numero et pauperes...*), *GP* 1, 313 (ii. 92. 1, 3), with notes *GP* 2, 144–5. The monastery, though small, survived until early 1539 (*GP* 2 144 (note on *GP* 1 (ii. 92. 2), with references); *Monasticon* 2, 402–9; *VCH Somerset* 2 (1911), 99–103; Bettey 1989, 84–5, 182 Appendix XII).

4 ... *quamvis perplurima adhuc monasteria in illa regione constructa permaneant, nullo tamen regulam illius vitæ ordinabiliter tenente* ... (Asser, 80–1 [93. 8–11]). Asser does not enlarge upon *in illa regione*, but taken in the context of the foundation of Athelney just described it would appear to refer to Somerset or the wider West Country, in which Shaftesbury was situated. He mentions a number of monasteries that had survived into the late ninth century, naming in particular Wareham (Asser, 36–7 [49]), and Congresbury and Banwell (ibid., 68 [81]) in Somerset, some or all of which were supported financially by Alfred. Athelney and Shaftesbury would therefore have been the latest additions to these.

5 *Regularis Concordia*, Introduction, x.

Alfred, a demonstration of his religious and charitable concerns, rather than a specific interest in monastic revival in Wessex in the manner of the earlier Carolingian reforms on the Continent or of those in England during the following century.[1] The foundation of Athelney would then represent a gesture of profound gratitude for his deliverance from the Vikings against seemingly overwhelming odds,[2] while its female complement, Shaftesbury, was intended as a refuge for noble women serving God in peace and security in obedience to the king's young daughter appointed as abbess.[3] Such acts were characteristic of Alfred, ever mindful of 'what was most essential for his soul, among his other good deeds performed by day and night, on which he concentrated attentively and fully', according to Asser.[4] Beyond this, his main purpose, with the support of such *eruditi* as Grimbald and Asser attending his court,[5] was the revival of religious life and learning in his kingdom (undoubtedly influenced by earlier Carolingian achievements in this respect) after a century of foreign invasions by encouraging Latin scholarship and promoting literacy in the Anglo-Saxon language to enable 'all [to] understand certain books, which are the most necessary for all men to know'.[6] These included Alfred's translations of St Gregory's *Pastoral Care* (*Regula Pastoralis*),[7] Boethius's *On the Consolation of Philosophy* and St

1   Keynes 1999, 39–40.

2   Keynes & Lapidge, 36; Keynes 1999, 39–40; Yorke 2003, 111.

3   Keynes & Lapidge, 36; Keynes 1999, 40.

4   … *de necessitate animæ suæ solito cogitaret, inter cetera diuturna et nocturna bona, quibus assidue et maxime studebat* (Asser, 79 [92. 4–5]).

5   *GR* 1, 190–1 (ii. 122. 3–4), with notes *GR* 2, 99–100; Abels, 222–5; Wormald, 'Alfred', under *The reading and writing of books*.

6   Keynes & Lapidge, 126 (from the Prose Preface to St Gregory's *Pastoral Care*). By 'all' Alfred means 'all the free-born young men now in England, who have the means to apply themselves … [and] may be set to learning … until the time that they can read English writings properly' (Keynes & Lapidge, 126). Alfred's bishops may also have been involved in the task of translating and disseminating vernacular texts (ibid., 296 n. 13).

7   *GR* 1, 192–3 ([ii. 123. 1–3], with note on 123. 2–3, *GR* 2, 104–5); Abels, 219–21, 231–3, 236–7, 241–2 *et passim*; Keynes 1999, 30–1. The *Pastoral Care* is edited by Henry Sweet, *King Alfred's West-Saxon Version of Gregory's Pastoral Care*, 2 vols., EETS Original Series 45, 50 (London: Kegan Paul, Trench, Trübner & Co., and Oxford University Press, 1871–2, reprinted

Augustine's *Soliloquies*,[1] which, 'turned into the language that we can all understand',[2] were copied and circulated.[3] A full prose translation of the Psalms was also intended, but this was apparently thwarted by Alfred's death.[4] This great religious and literary revival stimulated church building and the visual arts, such as manuscript illumination, metalwork and stone carving, achieving what may fairly be described as a cultural renaissance made all the more distinctive by Alfred's own part in it.[5]

Asser's statement that the nunnery at Shaftesbury was established 'by the east gate' (*iuxta orientalem portam*) of the *burh* may suggest a situation within rather than beyond its walls,[6] though it has been proposed that these lay to the west of the abbey,[7] thereby excluding it from their protection. The former location would have

1909).

1   Abels, 220–2, 232–6, 239–42 *et passim*; Keynes 1999, 30–1. William of Malmesbury includes the *Pastoral Care* and *On the Consolation of Philosophy* in his list of Alfred's translations (*GR* 1, 190–3 [ii. 122. 4, 123. 1]), but omits the *Soliloquies* (see note to 123.1, *GR* 2, 102–4). The translations of Orosius and Bede noted by William are no longer attributed to Alfred (*GR* 2, 102; Abels, 236; Wormald, 'Alfred', under *The reading and writing of books*).

2   Keynes & Lapidge, 126; see also *GR* 1, 192–3 (ii. 123. 1). William of Malmesbury says of Alfred that 'no Englishman ... could translate with greater elegance' (... *nullus Anglorum fuerit ... in iterpretando elegantior*): *GR* 1, 192–3 (ii. 123. 1). Earlier he mentions that Asser expounded to Alfred 'with greater clarity the meaning of Boethius's books *On Consolation*, which the king himself turned into English' (*Hic sensum librorum Boetii De consolatione planioribus uerbis enodauit, quos rex ipse in Anglicam linguam uertit: GR* 1, 190–1 (ii. 122. 4), with note *GR* 2, 100).

3   *GR* 1, 192–4 (ii. 123. 1–3), with notes *GR* 2, 103–5.

4   Only the first fifty psalms were translated. William of Malmesbury relates that Alfred was engaged in translating the Psalter towards the end of his life, completing just the first part of it (*uix prima parte explicata uiuendi finem fecit*): *GR* 1, 192–3 (ii. 123. 2), with note *GR* 2, 104.

5   Keynes & Lapidge, 36; Wormald, 'Alfred', under *The reading and writing of books*.

6   Asser, 85 (98. 1–2); Keen, 'Dorset', 223, 233 with map (no. 77) showing the situation of the abbey in relation to the suggested burghal precinct.

7   RCHME *Dorset* 4 *North*, 56b, 75b.

offered a vulnerable community of women greater security and seems a more likely setting, when one compares it with the island monastery of Athelney safe within sight of Alfred's fortifications,[1] or the early minster at Wareham within a *castellum*, as previously noted.[2] The *burh* was certainly in existence before King Alfred founded the nunnery there, establishing his daughter as head of a community, which included, in Asser's words, 'many other noble nuns' (*aliæ multæ nobiles moniales*). It is not known who these other nuns were, but it is likely that they represented the families of the West Saxon nobility, perhaps the daughters, mothers and widows of the circle of thegns comprising Alfred's extended family and court. Their number, therefore, is likely to have been limited (Asser's *multæ* may be an exaggeration), perhaps the traditional number of twelve or thirteen to match the size of the nunnery supposedly founded at Wilton by Alfred around the same time. The length of Æthelgifu's rule as abbess is unknown, though it

1   For the origin of the name Athelney (*Æthelingæg*, so Asser, 44 [55.2], 79 [92.8]), 'the island of the *æpelingas*, or princes', see Stevenson's remarks in Asser, 259 n. 4.

2   See *supra* p. 2 nn. 3–4. The ancient borough of Wareham, rectangular in shape and bounded on its north by the River Piddle (or Trent) and on its south by the River Frome, was fortified by massive earthworks constructed by King Alfred still enclosing the town on its west, north and east sides (RCHME *Dorset 2 South-East*, pt. 2, 322–4; Keynes & Lapidge, 245 n. 87). These presumably comprised the *castellum* mentioned by Asser (37 [49. 8–10]), who describes the site as 'very secure ... except on the west, where it is joined by the mainland' (... *tutissimo ... nisi ab occidentale parte tantummodo, ubi contigua terra*; see also Keynes & Lapidge, 82, with n. 87). This evident strategic weakness would have been exploited by the Viking army, which occupied the town in 876 (*ASE* E, F 876; Asser, 36–7 [49. 1–5]; Keynes & Lapidge, 82–3, with n. 87), though it departed shortly after in accordance with the terms of a treaty made with Alfred, who persuaded it to leave, apparently paying it money to do so after exacting hostages and oaths (Asser, 36–7 [49. 10–17]; Keynes & Lapidge, 82–3, with nn. 88–9). Wareham, whose defences may not have been completed in 876, however, was one of the *burhs* named in the Burghal Hidage, where it is assessed at 1600 hides (Keynes & Lapidge, 193). While it should be noted that Asser's description of the borough may have been written from the standpoint of his own age, and that his use of the word *castellum* does not necessarily prove the existence of fortifications in 876, it is likely that these were established by the time the *Vita Alfredi* appeared in 893 (Keynes & Lapidge, 245 n. 87; RCHME *Dorset 2 South-East*, pt. 2, 322a).

may have been short on account of ill health that, according to later Shaftesbury tradition recorded in the abbey's spurious foundation charter, was the cause of her taking the veil.[1] In this case she may have predeceased Alfred, who died in 899, and in whose will she is mentioned (as his middle (*pære medemestan*) daughter,[2] but not abbess) as beneficiary of the royal estates at Kingsclere and Candover in Hampshire,[3] though the abbey apparently never acquired these,[4] perhaps because the bequest was never effected on account of her untimely death.[5]

Sources for the pre-Conquest history of Shaftesbury Abbey are sparse and include copies of Anglo-Saxon charters preserved in its early fifteenth-century cartulary.[6] Here occur references to Æthelgifu (**1**) and four later religious women (**2-5**) with known or possible connections with Shaftesbury, perhaps as vowesses[7] or lay associates rather than consecrated nuns living under a strict rule. Notable among these is Ælfgifu (**3**), a royal consort, who retired to Shaftesbury, where she died and was venerated as a saint with a cult apparently still active after the Conquest, though associated mainly with the abbey. Æthelgifu, Ælfgifu and Eadgifu (**5**), another royal consort, are also named in sources outside the charters, while the abbesses Herelufu (**6**), or Herleva, 'Æthelfreda' (**7**), and Leveva (**8**), or Leofgifu, are known only from these sources, the last being mentioned in Domesday Book.

---

1 Meyer 1981, 341–2; Keynes & Lapidge, 256 n. 146; Kelly, xiii–xiv, 28–9 no. 7; Keynes 1999, 41; Foot 2000 1, 12, and 2, 165–6; Yorke 2003, 76.

2 Birch, 74–80, at 78; Keynes & Lapidge, 175, 177, with n. 59.

3 Keynes & Lapidge, 177, with nn. 60 and 61; Keynes 1999, 41.

4 Keynes 1999, 30–1.

5 Ibid., 41.

6 *Lbl* Harley MS 61 (described by Davis *et al.*, 178, no. 885 ('...Intended apparently as a register of rights and privileges given and conceded rather than of title deeds'); *Monasticon* 2, 474b–476b; Hutchins 1868, 22–4; Kelly (with charters from 670 x 676 to 1019 only); Stacy (with charters from 1089 to 1216 only).

7 A useful, though dated account of this category of religious women from early times, often widows, is by André 1892.

Post-Conquest

The nunnery's status as an elite royal and aristocratic foundation was to diminish somewhat after the Conquest, though patronage continued to be maintained by the Norman and Angevin kings and their successors, who supported and protected the wealth and privileges enjoyed by this richly endowed house until its dissolution in the sixteenth century. No longer the preserve of the Anglo-Saxon ruling dynasty, its exclusive social identity was gradually to diversify in accordance with the requirements and expectations of a different age. The earliest most significant change appears to have been in the appointment of abbess. If Leveva (or Leofgifu), presumably the last of the English abbesses, was still alive in 1074, then she may have been deposed in favour of a Norman choice, Eulalia (9), or Eularia,[1] though there is no evidence that she was. She may well have been dead by this time, which is likely to have simplified the transition to the new regime. Eulalia was in office at least until 1106, but she had certainly passed away by 1113 around a decade before her successor Emma (27) appears in 1121/2.

In addition to the rebuilding of the abbey church and the enlargement of the monastery, the late eleventh and early twelfth centuries saw an increase in the number of nuns entering the convent from more diverse, though still affluent social backgrounds, corresponding with an augmentation of the abbey estates granted in dower on entry,[2] which served to enhance the foundation's growing influence and prosperity. This number rose steadily, apparently reaching unmanageable proportions by the early thirteenth century, when an inhibition was issued by Pope Honorius III in 1218 ordering the convent to limit its size to a maximum of one hundred nuns in view of its incapacity 'to support more or to give alms to the poor'.[3] Donations to the abbey of land, urban property and spiritualities from the late eleventh century had accompanied a number of mainly anonymous but evidently well-to-do young women, whose families had encouraged or obliged them to take the veil, no doubt in more than a few instances irrespective of their personal wishes and sense of

1   The abrupt appearance of this non-English name is notable.

2   Cooke 1990.

3   *CPL 1198–1304*, 51; *VCH Dorset* 2, 77a. For other thirteenth-century instances of such concerns, see Thompson, 186–7.

vocation. Included among these patrons were the great local families of de Burgh and Berkeley, but other names indicate that the rising knightly and mercantile classes of this period were also starting to make provision for their daughters in this way. Entry to this privileged nunnery was now becoming as much the adoption of a natural profession for socially advantaged young women (perhaps less likely to be married for financial or other reasons) as a genuine religious calling. Throughout the six and a half centuries of its existence Shaftesbury Abbey remained largely the spiritual preserve of what today would be designated the upper and middle classes of society, relaxing over time its original *raison d'être* as an exclusive foundation for royal and noble women. By the late Middle Ages the number of nuns representative of the aristocracy had significantly declined for familial, legal and personal reasons characteristic of the age,[1] when they became steadily outnumbered by those from the gentry and yeomanry, as their names indicate.[2] There were opportunities, too, for certain women of lesser means to enter the religious life by royal and episcopal dispensation. The king by prerogative could present a nun to the abbey during its voidance or at the time of his coronation. Thus, Agnes Turbervill (**69**) was nominated in 1345 following the death of Abbess Denise la Blunde (**65**) that year, while Margaret Tracy (**74**) in 1377 (1 Richard II), Idony Wodehill (**88**) in 1413 (1 Henry V), Joan Ashecombe (**94**) in 1430 (8 Henry VI), and Elizabeth Bryther (**178**) in 1483 (1 Richard III) were coronation appointments. Similarly, the bishop of Salisbury exercised his customary right on elevation to his see to place a young woman, or damsel (*domicella*), of suitable character as inmate of the house under the tutelage of one of the nuns responsible for her spiritual welfare and monastic instruction.[3] Catherine Brombelegh (**85**) and Eleanor Eliot (**205**) were thus provided for in 1408 and 1497 respectively, the former being assigned to Dame Agnes Poney (**86**) and the latter to Dame

1   An important general study of the reasons for this decline, though not including Shaftesbury, is by Harris, especially 106–13 (pt. III).

2   Representative of the local gentry, in particular, were the abbesses Cecily Fovent (1398–1423), **84**, Margaret Stourton (1423–97), **93**, Margery Twyneo (1497–1505), **180**, Elizabeth Shelford (1505–28), **206**, and Elizabeth Zouche (1528–39), **226**. Margaret St John (1460–92), **164**, was of the aristocracy and one of the last of her class in the convent.

3   *Monasticon* 2, 473a.

Agnes Asshe (**181**) for their care and supervision. Less privileged entrants, where fortunate enough to be received into the nunnery without patronage or endowment, may have served their vocations as lay sisters (*conversæ*) rather than professed regulars in the customary manner, though little seems to be known about these at Shaftesbury.

ST ANSELM AND THE NUNS OF SHAFTESBURY

Together with her nuns, the first Norman abbess Eulalia (**9**) was the recipient of three letters from St Anselm as archbishop of Canterbury,[1] the last of which was written after August 1106, following his return from second exile. St Anselm took a particular interest in the nuns of Shaftesbury and Wilton,[2] thanking them for their thoughts and prayers during his absence, and exhorting them to prayer, obedience (in particular to their abbess and bishop), harmony, and sanctity of thought, word and deed, actions conducive to the spiritual life. Their community (*congregatio*) should be a temple of God through prayer, discipline and strict observance, being earnestly mindful of even the smallest lapses of conduct and purpose, which would hinder their strivings for perfection. No sin should be considered too insignificant, particularly one committed through disobedience, which alone drove man from Paradise,[3] and which prevents the attainment of salvation,

---

1   *Anselmi opera* 4, 67–8 (*Ep*. 183, dated 1094, for which see Southern 1990, 228 n.1, 265); 5, 274–5 (*Ep*. 337, dated –September 1104) and 347–8 (*Ep*. 403, dated +August 1106). For the significance of Anselm's letters as sources for his life and thought, see Southern 1990, 146–7, 395–6, 485 *et passim*.

2   Southern 1963, 186; Elkins, 12, with n. 28, citing *Epistolæ Anselmi* nos. 183, 185 (*Anselmi opera* 4, 67–8, 70–1); Vaughn, 162, 165, 167–8. The Wilton Abbey letters, written about 1094, are nos. 168, 169 (*Anselmi opera* 4, 43–6, 46–50, for which, see Southern 1963, 185–93), ?184, 185 (*Anselmi opera* 4, 68–9, 69–70).

3   *Congregatio vestra templum dei debet esse, et »templum dei sanctum est.« Si ergo sancte vivitis, sicut spero, templum dei estis. Sancte autem vivitis, si ordinem et propositum vestrum diligenter custoditis. Diligenter vero hoc facitis, si minima non contemnitis. Vestrum enim propositum semper debet niti ad profectum, et toto corde horrere defectum … Qui autem decidit, non proficit. Proinde si vultis proficere et horretis deficere: nolite modica despicere … ita verum est quia qui modica non despicit, paulatim proficit. Nolite putare aliquod peccatum esse parvum, quamvis aliud alio sit maius. Nihil enim quod fit per inobœdientiam – quæ sola eiecit*

for 'he who gradually falls away profits not, but loses, and he who loses sinks rather than rises'.[1]

The rebuilding of the abbey church in the contemporary Romanesque style in the local greensand and Tisbury stone during the late eleventh century is believed to have been initiated by Eulalia, whose new edifice was dedicated by St Anselm to the Assumption of the Blessed Virgin on 14 April [1107? x 21 April 1109].[2] As well as enhancing the grandeur and prestige of the monastery, the new church would have provided a more imposing setting for the shrines of St Edward the Martyr and St Ælfgifu (**3**) with a view to promoting their cults and attracting pilgrims.[3] Significantly, the

hominem de paradiso – parvum dici debet (Anselmi opera 5, 347–8, Ep. 403, lines 15–26; see also Vaughn, 56, 162, 165, 168).

1 *Qui enim paulatim decidit, non proficit sed deficit; et qui deficit, non ascendit sed descendit* (*Anselmi opera* 4, 67–8 (*Ep.* 183), at 68, lines 17–18). Although Anselm is speaking generally here, his use of *qui* rather than *quæ* when he specifically has nuns in mind is notable. This repeats a gender bias typical of his time occurring earlier (lines 9–10) in the same letter, *Quippe quamdiu homo vivit: aut ascendit in cælum bene vivendo, aut descendit in infernum male vivendo.*

2 The dedication of Shaftesbury Abbey church on 14 April ('Dedicacio ecclesie monasterii schestonie / celebrata a beato Anselmo cantuariensis archie*piscopo* i*n* honore Assu*mpcionis* / gl*oriose* uirginis marie') was entered in red in the calendar of the Winchester, or St Swithun's Psalter (*Lbl* Cotton Nero MS C. iv, fols. 40r–45v, at 41v) in or after 1257 (probably +May 1258: see **44**), when it was acquired by Shaftesbury Abbey (Wormald 1973, 108, 112). Other thirteenth-century calendar additions, apparently in the same hand, include four feasts of St Edward king and martyr in red (13 February, *translatio*; 18 February, *adventus*; 18 March, *passio*; 20 June, *festivitas*). The dedication appears also in the calendar of the Shelford *horæ* (*Cfm* MS 2-1957, fol. 4v: Wormald 1973, 108). For the Winchester Psalter, which has been dated 1121/29 x 1161, see also Ker, *MLGB*, 177; Kauffmann 1975, 105–6, no. 78, with Plates 105–6; Haney 1980, 40–4; Haney 1986; Bell 1995, 165–6, no. 4. The church, together with the rest of the monastery, was razed to the ground in the mid-sixteenth century. What remains of it is described in detail in RCHME *Dorset 4 North*, 57b–61b, with a recent archaeological survey establishing the extent of the west end of the nave by Cox & Jones *et al.* Carved stone fragments of the pre- and post-Conquest periods are preserved in Shaftesbury Abbey museum (RCHME *Dorset 4 North*, 61, with Plates 3 and 59). The abbey site is now a scheduled historical monument (ibid., Plate 60).

3 The cult of St Edward the Martyr (*festum* 18 March) became wide-

Passio of St Edward attributed to Goscelin of Canterbury (see **7**) probably dates from the early years of Eulalia's rule,[1] when it may have been commissioned by her for this very purpose. Larger than the contemporary cathedral at Old Sarum consecrated by Bishop Osmund in 1092,[2] the abbey church, fittingly described by the Dorset historian John Hutchins (1698–1773) as 'the glory and the ornament of the town',[3] would have been one of the most imposing ecclesiastical buildings in the south-west during this period visible from afar on its hilltop setting. Its destruction in the sixteenth century is a significant and deplorable loss to the early architectural history of the region. A good idea of how it may have looked in the early twelfth century after its Norman rebuilding, however, may be gained from Laura Sydenham's conjectural but archaeologically plausible model of it, together with cloisters and chapter house, on display in Shaftesbury Abbey museum.[4]

The unusual dedication of the abbey church with its focus on a particularly important Marian *festum* merits comment. To summarize briefly, originating in the East the doctrine of the corporal assumption of the Blessed Virgin into heavenly glory began to be formulated in the West during the later sixth century, with its feast on 15 August being universally observed by the end of the eighth.[5] It was a natural

spread in the West of England and beyond during the Middle Ages largely through the dissemination of the secular Sarum rite (which commemorated both the *festum* and the *festivitas* [or second *translatio*] on 20 June) from the early thirteenth century. Of Shaftesbury origin, it was also observed by other Benedictine houses, including Winchcombe (Glos), Hyde and Romsey (Hants), and Leominster (Herefs): Luxford, 135, with n. 138.

1   See **7** '**Æthelfreda**'.

2   Keen 1999, 8; Thurlby, 1a. The cathedral was begun by Bishop Herman on the removal of the see from Sherborne to Old Sarum in 1075 and finally completed by Bishop Osmund in 1092 (RCHME *Salisbury*, 15–24 (2 *The Cathedral at Old Sarum*), at 15a).

3   Hutchins 1868, 32; Chandler, 41.

4   Illustration in Chandler, 43. An engraving of the double-towered west end and central tower features on the obverse of the conventual seal, ibid.

5   For a summary of the doctrine of the Assumption in the East and the West, see *ODCC*, 118–19 (art. 'Assumption of the BVM'). Concise and

consequence of the belief in the perfect sinlessness of Mary implicit in the title 'Theotokos' (Θεοτόκος, *Deipara*) upheld by the councils of Ephesus (431) and Chalcedon (451), and subsequently developed by St John of Damascus (*c.*675/676-749),[1] whence evolved the later Western belief that she was free from the taint of Original Sin from the moment of her conception by conjugal union. Established in the East by the seventh century, the feast of the Conception of the Blessed Virgin (*Conceptio beate Marie*) on 8 December[2] was known in southern Italy and Ireland by the ninth, and in England by the eleventh, when it became a peculiarly monastic observance of limited extent.[3] Appropriately, the feast of the Nativity of Mary (*Nativitas beate Marie*) occurs exactly nine months later on 8 September. Originating in England at the New Minster, Winchester, the *Conceptio* was adopted also at Worcester and Canterbury on liturgical calendar and other evidence. Unlike the feast of the Assumption, it was never widespread even in monastic circles and was suppressed at Canterbury after the Conquest, together with a number of other, usually obscure early English cults as the result of the calendar reforms initiated by Archbishop Lanfranc.[4] Theologically too significant to disappear

lucid introductions to Mariology in general may be found in O'Carroll, while St Anselm's Mariology is discussed by Bruder.

1   Janaro, 50: St John of Damascus was 'arguably, the first theologian to draw together the whole rich tradition of the Christian East regarding the "All-Holy" Theotokos and express it in terms that we can clearly recognize today as corresponding fully to the doctrine of the Immaculate Conception'.

2   *DTC* 7, pt. 1 (1922), cols. 845–1218 (X. Le Bachelet, art. 'Immaculée Conception'); *ODCC,* 826–7 (art. 'Immaculate Conception of the BVM'). The Orthodox Church celebrates this feast on 9 December as the Conception by Agia (Saint) Anne of the Most Holy Theotokos.

3   Of the twenty-seven early (pre-1100) calendars found in Rushforth 2008, three only include the *Conceptio* (nos. 14 (Wormald 1934, no. 9), Winchester, New Minster (Ælfwine's Prayer Book), 1023 x 1031; 21 (Wormald 1934, no. 17), Worcester (Wulfstan's Portiforium), *c.*1065; 23 (Wormald 1934, no. 12), Winchester, New Minster, *c.*1062) in contrast with the *Assumptio* entered in most of them.

4   For differing views regarding the extent of these reforms, see Gasquet & Bishop, 27 ff. (pt. III *The Calendar*, 3. 'The changes at Canterbury under Lanfranc'); Heslop, 53–85; and Pfaff 1998, 95–108. Heslop proposes a more realistic middle ground between Gasquet & Bishop, who argued

altogether, however, its subsequent revival initially as a Benedictine feast during the first half of the twelfth century,[1] and eventually as an English provincial observance,[2] corresponded with the later development of the doctrine of the Immaculate Conception, to which St Anselm famously, if tentatively, contributed,[3] although

for a radical 'Lanfrancian purge' of the Canterbury calendar, with the suppression of all or most of the Anglo-Saxon cults, and Pfaff, who is of the view that such a far-reaching liturgical reform barely took place at all ('[Lanfranc's calendar reforms represent] a composite of interest in major national and local Anglo-Saxon saints (the minor ones being removed) and the general sacramentary usage of the Norman abbey of Bec. All the evidence suggests that the Normans wished to shorten and to simplify what they found on their arrival' [Heslop, 67]).

1   The feast was first established at Bury St Edmunds between 1121 and 1148 by Abbot Anselm, who was the nephew of Archbishop Anselm (Bishop, 243–7; Janaro, 50, 54). The feast was also adopted at Westminster, Reading, St Albans, Gloucester, Winchcombe, and Worcester (Bishop, 247). The *Conceptio* is entered in red majuscules, denoting a high rank, in the calendar (fols. 3r–8v, at 8v [December]) of *Lbl* Lansdowne MS 383, the twelfth-century Shaftesbury Psalter (see *infra* p. 54 n. 2), with the *Assumptio* in green and blue majuscules, with octave in green, on fol. 6v [August].

2   The Provincial Council of Canterbury convened at St Paul's, London, in 1328 attributes the institution of the *Conceptio* to St Anselm, who is said to have supplemented the more ancient feasts (*antiquiora solennia*) of the Blessed Virgin with it (Wilkins, *Concilia* 2, 552b; Bishop, 238; Southern 1990, 436), though he did not actually prescribe its observance in England, even in his own church of Canterbury (Bishop, 245, 249). The feast had been celebrated in the Sarum rite from the thirteenth century (Legg, xxxii, 318–20), indicating that it would have been known throughout the Province of Canterbury long before 1328, when it finally became obligatory.

3   Southern 1990, 10. Inspired by St Anselm, this doctrine was later developed by his disciple Eadmer (d. *c*.1130), whose considerably influential *Tractatus de conceptione S. Mariæ* (*PL* 159, 301–18), originally attributed to St Anselm, was one of the earliest systematic treatises on the Immaculate Conception (Southern 1990, 432–6). This, 'Eadmer's greatest *Meditation* ... advocated a doctrine towards which Anselm pointed, but from which he had drawn back ... Eadmer here followed Anselm in method, and went beyond him in doctrine; in going along the same road, he reached a destination of which Anselm disapproved ... in writing about the Immaculate Conception, he was engaged on a more momentous adventure than he knew. He thought he was defending a local devotion; he was actually at the beginning of an international event.

paradoxically it is denied in *Cur deus homo*.[1] In his *De conceptu virginali et de originali peccato* written, on Eadmer's information, in 1099-1100,[2] he established two principles fundamental for its formulation by the later Scholastic theologians, in particular St Thomas Aquinas and Duns Scotus. The first emphasized the absolute purity of Mary, of which 'no greater could be imagined apart from God',[3] while the second reconsidered the nature of Original Sin and its transmission. This departed from the traditional Augustinian doctrine that regarded it as an inherited taint descending from one generation to another through concupiscence as a result of mankind's seminal presence in Adam.[4] By redefining Original Sin as 'the privation of the righteousness that every man ought to possess',[5] St Anselm separated it from concupiscence, arguing that a rational human nature deprived of its original virtue through Adam's guilt was henceforth the fateful burden of his descendants.[6] Thus, we are conceived in Original Sin because our corrupt human nature inherited from our parents remains Adam's fallen nature without Christ's salvation.[7] Underlying St Anselm's theology of Original Sin, and indeed all sin, is the redemption of mankind through the necessary death of God Incarnate as articulated especially in *Cur deus homo*.[8] His emphasis

There was a greater future in store for his treatise and for the cause which it advocated, than he could have foreseen' (ibid., at 432, 434).

1   O'Carroll, 33b; Janaro, 51, with n. 10; Reynolds, 352.

2   Southern 1972, 122 (xliiii), with n. 1, and *idem* 1990, 411. The *De conceptu virginali et de originali peccato* is edited by Schmitt, *Anselmi opera* 2, 137–73. Anselm's *Meditatio redemptionis humanæ* (*Anselmi opera* 3, 84–91), his last and longest meditation, also dates from this period (Southern 1972, 122 (xliiii), with n. 1).

3   *De conceptu originali*, 18, cited by O'Carroll, 33b; Janaro, 52, with n. 13; Reynolds, 352.

4   Janaro, 53 n. 17; Reynolds, 352.

5   Janaro, 52; Reynolds, 352.

6   *De conceptu originali*, 3, cited by Janaro, 52, with n. 14; Reynolds, 352.

7   Janaro, 53, with n. 18.

8   Ibid., 48, with n. 1. *Cur deus homo* (*Anselmi opera* 2, 42–96) was completed in Italy in 1098 (Southern 1972, 107 (xxx), with n. 2, and *idem* 1990, 279). A lucid analysis of *Cur deus homo* is by Southern 1990, 197–227, especially 205 ff.

on Mary's incomparable purity and his innovative interpretation of Original Sin and its transmission enabled later Western theologians to acknowledge her preservation by God from its corruption, although she had been conceived by carnal intercourse whence it was held to descend. Mary's freedom from Original Sin was eventually to evolve into the dogma of the Immaculate Conception promulgated by Pius IX on 8 December 1854.

St Anselm's Mariology is thus important for understanding what may have been his intention in dedicating Shaftesbury Abbey church to the Assumption of the Blessed Virgin. As Mary was received into celestial glory at the end of her earthly existence through her perfect sinlessness, so should the nuns aspire to this ideal through holiness, obedience and harmony in their own lives. Had they not already been earnestly reminded by St Anselm that their community was a temple of God, a sisterhood of sanctity, and that their aim was to attain perfection through keeping their rule and purpose, abhorring anything that might make them fall short of this? Humanly impossible to achieve but nevertheless presented for their contemplation and *exemplar vitæ*, the incomparable purity of the Blessed Virgin and its heavenly reward would remain the ideal for these imperfect daughters of Adam in their daily strivings for spiritual fulfilment, an ideal implicit in the carefully chosen dedication of their own church as a constant focus for their devotions and earthly endeavours.

A new and specially dedicated abbey church was one of a number of developments at this period associated with the new order, which would also have included the introduction of Anglo-Norman as the principal language of the cloister,[1] though English, which eventually gained ascendancy by the fifteenth century,[2] would have been spoken as well.[3] The inclusion of Eulalia in the obituary rolls of Abbess Matilda of Caen, 1113, and Abbot Vitalis of Savigny, 1122, is probably a mark of the high esteem in which she was held.[4] Indeed, her long and apparently productive rule, renowned in particular for its association with St Anselm and the rebuilding of the conventual

1   Bell 1995, 57, 78.

2   Power, 246–7; Bell 1995, 57–8.

3   Bell 1995, 57. English would have been used when communicating with abbey servants, for example.

4   See *infra* p. 53, n. 2.

church with the regeneration of its historic royal cults, would long be remembered as a golden age in the abbey's history. Like Herelufu (**6**) over a century earlier, who the sparse evidence suggests may have been involved in the monastic reforms of her time, Eulalia may well rank as one of the great abbesses of Shaftesbury, the extent of whose achievements must remain for the present largely conjectural.

THE ABBESSES

EMERGING FROM THE SHADOWS

The Anglo-Saxon and first of the post-Conquest abbesses have been mentioned briefly and are discussed more fully in the Appendix to this work. Among the latter there is no evidence for Eustachia, who followed Eulalia (1074-1106/7? x -1113?), **9**, according to some sources, though her existence is doubtful. The last two twelfth-century abbesses were Cecily (*c.*1135/6?-*c.*1158?), **29**, and Mary (*c.*1158? x *c.*1170?-1216), **30**, whose rules fell within the late Norman and early Plantagenet periods. The appointment of the sub-prioress Joan (1216-?23), **31**, who succeeded Mary as abbess, marks a new phase in the succession of heads of house in that their dates of appointment and demise can henceforth be traced regularly through the series of state, or official records as they begin to develop from the beginning of the thirteenth century. Particulars of abbesses and prioresses, and others holding monastic office, as well as ordinary nuns (those not holding monastic office), now begin to be recorded mainly in the Patent and Close Rolls (particularly the former), the sequence of royal chancery registers continuing throughout the Middle Ages and beyond.[1] The requirements and provisions of royal patronage, originating in pre-Conquest times, are readily apparent from these sources. Supplementing the Patent and Close Rolls are episcopal *acta* and registers, and papal registers. The earliest surviving register for the diocese of Salisbury is that of Simon of Ghent (1297-1315), though there is evidence for the registers of most of his predecessors from Walter de la Wyle (1263-71),[2] and even those from the periods

---

1   The Patent Rolls from 1216 (1 Henry III) up to 1572 (14 Elizabeth I), for example, have been calendared. Those for the reign of Henry VIII (1509–47) are included in *L & P Henry VIII.*

2   *EEA Salisbury* 36 (*1229–62*), Introduction, cxxxv. See also Cheney, 148,

of Robert de Bingham (1229-46) and Richard Poore (1217-28),[1]
who moved the see from Old Sarum to its present location in 1219.
Frequently, the registers and the earlier *acta* record the dates when
an abbess was confirmed and blessed by the bishop or his official,
information also found occasionally in the Patent Rolls.

Nuns named in papal registers include recipients of indults,
such as Joan Durneford (**83**), Agnes Poney (or Powne, **86**), Margaret
Stourton (**93**), and Margaret St John (**164**). The last was granted
dispensation in 1453 on account of her young age (said to be around
twenty-two at the time) otherwise preventing her election as abbess
eight years or so previous to her actual appointment in 1460. Other
sources include wills, which merit fuller exploration than has been
possible here. While it was canonically prohibited for nuns, or indeed
any religious, to make wills themselves (as notoriously in the case
of Abbess Joan Formage, **72**), it was permissible subject to certain
restrictions for them to be beneficiaries, as with Mabel Giffard (**54**),
Elizabeth de Favenham (**62**), Lucy Fitzherberde (**75**), Katherine
Slo (**87**), and Anastasia Stourton (**100**). Other names may no doubt
come to light as or when more wills are discovered.

A GROUP OF FEUDAL DAMES

As tenants-in-chief of the Crown the abbesses of Shaftesbury were
required by feudal custom to provide knight-service (*servitium
debitum*) for the king. This onerous burden fell on both Agnes de
Ferrers (1247-58), **41**, and her successor Juliana de Bauceyn (1258-
79), **44**, in 1257 and 1277, when both were nearing the ends of their
lives. Such an obligation arose because the abbesses of Shaftesbury,
like those of Wilton, the Nunnaminster (Winchester) and Barking
had the same feudal status as secular barons, which could require their
attending parliaments in addition to retaining armed knights holding
lands in fee in return for serving the king.[2] In practice, however, the
former of these duties was rescinded on grounds of gender in the

with nn. 6–7.

1   *EEA Salisbury* 36 (*1229–62*), Introduction, cxxxv.

2   *Monasticon* 2, 472b. The list of Shaftesbury knights' fees recorded in the
    abbey's principal cartulary (*Lbl* Harley MS 61 [see *supra* p. 13 n. 6], fol.
    22r-v) are examined, with details of their descent from Domesday Book
    (1086) to 1242, by Williams, 214–41.

predominantly male dominated society of the time. The alternative to the latter from the late twelfth century was increasingly commutation, which involved payment of a fine to the Exchequer in the form of a fixed lump sum usually far exceeding the normal scutage assessment.[1]

AT THE KING'S WILL: THEIR MANNER OF APPOINTMENT

By the second decade of the thirteenth century, and undoubtedly earlier, a formal process of electing an abbess by the prioress and nuns in chapter appears to have been regularized, and an established procedure was in place to select a replacement head of house subject to the royal assent (*assensus regius*).[2] With few changes, such as the increasing use of English rather than Latin for conducting parts of the process by the mid-fifteenth century,[3] this appears to have continued until the Dissolution. In preparation for an election the entire convent attended early morning mass of the Holy Spirit at the high altar of the abbey church followed by the ringing of the convent bell according to custom,[4] after which all assembled in the chapter house at the appointed time of chapter (0900 hours) to listen to a sermon by one of the abbey chaplains. After the singing of *Veni creator spiritus* a roll call was made to ensure that the entire convent was present, apart from those exempt by infirmity or sickness, as in the case of Dame Alice Chaundose (**102**), who, confined to the infirmary, was represented by proxy at the election of Edith Bonham (**96**) as abbess in 1441 The prioress as president of the chapter then read the customary monition for all laity and others, including

---

1   Poole, 16–17.

2   A detailed, late fifteenth-century record of an election is found in *Reg. Blyth*, 97–101, no. 365. See also *Reg. Aiscough*, second series, fols. 10v–12r. An amusing account of the election of an abbess of Elstow (Bedfordshire, Ben.) in 1529 and its aftermath, giving an idea of the personal differences and tensions that sometimes arose on these occasions, is related by Power, 46–51. For the election and appointment of abbesses in general, see Oestereich, 'Abbess'.

3   *Reg. Blyth*, 99.

4   Ibid., 98. The original register (Wright's edition (*Reg. Blyth*) is a calendar) reads: ... *post pulsationem cuiusdam campane prout moris est* ... (*CHIhc* D1/2/13, *The Register of John Blyth, Bishop of Salisbury, 1493–9*, fol. 95v); cf. also *Reg. Aiscough*, second series, fol. 12r.

excommunicants, not permitted to participate in the election to leave the chapter house. Only authorized officials (mainly canon lawyers appointed by the bishop, or his vicegerent) consisting of a director, a notary public and witnesses, together with a scribe for recording business, were allowed to remain. Once the the royal licence to elect had been proclaimed by the director, and the canonical statute *Quia propter* regulating the election expounded,[1] the next stage in the process was then conducted by the prioress and three nuns appointed as scrutineers (*scrutatrices, conscrutatrices*), who withdrew in private to a quiet corner of the chapter house accompanied only by the notary public and witnesses to disclose their own votes to one another. Immediately afterwards scrutiny (balloting) was taken of the rest of the convent, beginning with the sub-prioress. The votes were then counted, and the overall result, representing the choice of the greater part of the chapter (*major et sanior pars capituli*),[2] announced by one of the scrutineers. After the assent of the elect had been given to the two proctors (*procuratrices*) appointed by the prioress and convent (it was usual for her to retire to some secluded part of the monastery for reflection and deliberation previous to this), her formal acceptance of office was made before the notary public and witnesses. Accompanied by the singing of *Te deum laudamus* and the joyous pealing of bells, the new abbess was then accompanied by the younger nuns exultantly to the high altar of the conventual church, where she was presented to the assembled multitude of clergy and people, usually with a customary display of unwillingness on her part.

The endorsement of chapter elections by the Crown through returnable chancery writs appears to have been a post-Conquest practice, which developed as part of the growing royal bureaucracy

1   An exposition of *Quia propter*, recited first in Latin, was made *in vulgari* (in English) by this time (*Reg. Aiscough*, second series, fol. 11r). Decreed by the Fourth Lateran Council in 1215 (André 1844, 1, cols. 1126–30, at 1126), its precepts, intended originally for papal and episcopal elections, were subsequently applicable to all higher ecclesiastical appointments (ibid., cols. 1126–30), including those in nunneries, and appear to have been scrupulously observed at Shaftesbury no doubt because of the presence of canon lawyers directing the proceedings. The preamble of the statute continued *Quia propter diversas electionum formas quas quidam invenire conantur, et multa impedimenta proveniunt, et magna pericula imminent ecclesiis viduatis, statuimus ut cum electio fuerit celebranda ...* (ibid., 1126).

2   Ibid.

as it had become established by the late twelfth century, gradually
superseding an apparently less formal system of Crown nomination
dating from Anglo-Saxon times. Such a procedure seems to have been
well in place by the time Joan (**31**) was appointed abbess in 1216, and
was to continue until the election of Elizabeth Zouche (**226**), the last
abbess, in 1528. Letters patent of the prioress and convent in chapter,
who were responsible to the Crown for the abbey during its voidance,[1]
announced the death, deposition or resignation of an abbess to the
king. These were delivered usually by two, sometimes three or even four
nuns appointed as proctors of the prioress and convent, who received
by return through them the royal licence (*licencia regia*, or *litteras de
licencia eligendi abbatissam*) to elect *communiter et concorditer*.[2] The names
of these nuns begin to appear in the Patent Rolls from around the
mid-thirteenth century, though their duties were sometimes assumed
by abbey chaplains or officials acting as proctors, as previous to the
elections of Agnes Longespée (**38**) and Margaret de Leukenore (**71**)
in 1243 and 1350.[3] Nun proctors (*procuratrices*) informing the king
of the convent's choice of head as well as performing other duties[4]
were also appointed, as in the elections of Edith Bonham (**96**) and
Margaret St John (**164**) in 1441 and 1460.[5] On receiving news of the
death or changed circumstances of an abbess, a custodian, usually
the escheator, was appointed by the Crown to administer the abbey
and its temporalities during the royal pleasure, and to answer for
its issues at the Exchequer. At the same time, a writ of *De intendendo*
was issued to the abbey tenants informing them of their obligations

1   *Monasticon* 2, 473a.

2   Chapter 64 (*De ordinando abbate*) of the Holy Rule prescribes the qualities
    expected of a head of house elected from among its own members (*RB*,
    280–4).

3   *CPR 1232–47*, 329, and *1348–50*, 548.

4   An example of these duties was the representation of the aged and
    infirm Alice Chaundose (**102**) in chapter by Isabel Beynton (Beyngton*e*),
    128, who was appointed proctor at the election of Edith Bonham (**96**) in
    1441.

5   *Reg. Aiscough*, second series, fol. 12r (*Procuratorium ad eligendum* appointing
    Isabel Beyngton*e*, or B*e*ynton, and Maria Florey (**133**) as proctors, 14
    November 1441); *Reg. Beauchamp* 1, second series, fol. 35r (appointing
    Isabel Beynton, Joan Bulwardyn*e* (**129**) and Christine Pokeswell (**144**),
    29 March 1460).

to the custodian during the voidance. Following the grant of *congé
d'élire*, or royal licence to elect, a nun of appropriate qualities, usually
from within the community, was chosen as abbess. On one occasion,
however, the appointment in 1243 of Agnes Longespée, formerly
a nun of Wherwell in Hampshire, represents a significant break
with this tradition and appears to have been occasioned by a lack
of suitable Shaftesbury candidates during a disputed election. After
being informed of the election by the appointed convent proctor(s)
the bishop of Salisbury issued a mandate to the archdeacon of Dorset
to proclaim it publicly before confirmation. Once granted, the royal
assent was signified by writ to the bishop in his capacity as diocesan
and abbey visitor. Within two or three weeks the bishop, or his official
or vicegerent, confirmed and blessed the new abbess, who then
received her ring and crosier after making her solemn profession
of canonical obedience and subjection. Consecration was normally
required to take place in Salisbury Cathedral with the consent of
the dean and chapter from the thirteenth century, but abbesses with
the right connections were not above bending the rules to suit their
own convenience, as with Juliana de Bauceyn (**44**), Joan de Bridport
(**51**) and Mabel Giffard (**54**).[1] Finally, a mandate was issued by the
bishop to the archdeacon to induct and install the new abbess, after
which the monastery's temporalities were restored by the Crown by
further writ of *De intendendo* issued to the abbey custodian with the
resumption of normality. Circumstances and conduct permitting, an
abbess maintained her position for life as mother and spiritual *tutrix*
of her community, gently (one would hope) but firmly imposing her
will on her nuns, officials, servants, and tenants alike, and generally
ensuring the smooth and efficient running of the convent and its
extensive estates, with their various feudal and other obligations.
The longest serving abbesses were Eulalia (1074-1106/7? x -1113?),
9, Mary (*c.*1158? x *c.*1170?-1216), **30**, Joan Formage (1362-94), **72**,
and Margaret St John (1460-92), **164**, each in office for over thirty
years, in Eulalia's and Mary's cases possibly longer. By contrast, Joan

1   See *infra* pp. 62 n. 6, 65 n. 1, 65 n. 7. The requirement for elected
     abbots and abbesses to be consecrated in the cathedral first appears in
     the diocesan synodal statutes of Bishop Robert Bingham, 1238 x 1244
     (*Councils & Synods* 2, pt. 1 (*1205–65*), 384 [47]), an obligation later
     confirmed by the constitutions of Bishop Roger Martival, 1319 (*Statutes
     & Customs*, 205 XXIV). It was customary for the newly consecrated to
     present the cathedral with a choral cope (ibid.).

de Bridport (1290-91), **51**, ruled for a little over one and a half years, perhaps on account of ill health, with Agnes Longespée (1243-6), **38**, and the elegantly named Egelina de Counteville (1395-8), **81**, serving for just over two and a half, and three years respectively, suggesting that both may have been elderly on appointment.

The long rule of Joan Formage (**72**) coincided with a decline in the abbey's fortunes during the fourteenth century. The impoverishment of its estates in the half century previous to her appointment by increasingly adverse economic conditions, ruined harvests, famine, murrain, and especially the Black Death bringing labour shortages and rising wages led to the prioress and convent being awarded unqualified custody of the abbey estates in 1364 during its voidance in the event of Joan's death or deposition.[1] This privilege, which included immunity from royal officials, was confirmed by royal charter of *Inspeximus*, or confirmation, granted eighteen years later.[2] An apparently infirm woman, Joan received dispensation from the bishop in 1368 to vacate the abbey for a year and reside on her estates for health and recreation.[3] She appears to have been anxious to consolidate and strengthen the abbey's position in the light of both her failing health and the uncertain times in which she lived. Her successful petitioning of the Crown for ratification by *Inspeximus* of no fewer than nine previous charters in 1371 is a measure of these concerns.[4] The abbey's precarious situation during this period no doubt led to the request to crenellate its church and belfry, the royal licence for which was granted in 1367.[5] Enhanced fortifications were obviously deemed necessary even at this period. During the rule of one of Joan's predecessors earlier in the century, Denise la Blunde (1329-45), **65**, abbey property at Broughton Gifford in Wiltshire

1   *CPR 1364–7*, 21. A similar concession was made in 1397, when Egelina de Counteville (**81**) was abbess (*CPR 1396–9*, 152). A good general summary of the economic and social conditions in England during this period of agrarian change is by McKisack, 312–48 (Ch. XI, *Rural Society*).

2   On 20 October 1382 (*CPR 1381–5*, 177).

3   *Reg. Wyville* 2, fol. 230r; *VCH Dorset* 2, 78a; Chandler, 61–2.

4   *CPR 1370–4*, 72–4.

5   *CPR 1367–70*, 10. The massive and much repaired buttressed stone wall (originally crenellated?) bounding Gold Hill on its west (RCHME *Dorset 4 North*, 69b–70a, with Plate 64), probably forming part of the Abbey boundary, appears to date from the same period.

and at Shaftesbury itself suffered from the depredations of gangs of armed ruffians, against whom the Crown was petitioned by the abbess to take action by commissions of oyer and terminer (assize courts of enquiry) in 1338 and 1341.[1] Joan is remembered in particular for causing controversy in her day, when, blithely disregarding her standing as a religious subject to the rules of poverty and obedience, she made an illicit will in 1393 bequeathing monastery furniture, valuables and money to her friends, relatives, and nuns both of her own house and other Wessex foundations.[2] This was annulled by the bishop shortly after her death the following year, with sequestration of abbey property, including Joan's effects, both on the grounds of its illegality and its being obviously prejudicial to the house's material and spiritual interests.[3]

The prioress would present an obvious choice for abbess on account of experience, unless age, infirmity or other impediment prevented her from taking office. Five abbesses, Joan de Bridport (1290-91), **51**, Alice de Lavington (1302-15), **58**, Joan Duket (1345-50), **70**, Joan Formage (1362-94),[4] **72**, and Edith Bonham (1441-60), **96**, had been prioresses, while two, Joan (1216-23), **31**, and Margaret Aucher (1315-29), **61**, were previously sub-prioresses. Amice Russell (1223-42), **32**, was an exception as being formerly sacristan. Not every prioress, however, could expect to be promoted when the time of election for abbess came up, as in the case of Lucy Fitzherberde (**75**), who was bluntly pronounced by the Crown to be an unsuitable candidate in 1394. Maria Florey (**133**), who as a fully professed nun attended the election of Edith Bonham in 1441,[5] was prioress in

1   *CPR 1338–40*, 74; *CPR 1340–3*, 308.

2   The will occupies fol. 217r-v of Bishop John Waltham's register, 1388–95 (*CHIhc* D1/2/5; *Reg. Waltham*, 31–2 no. 121). An illustration of 217r may be seen in Chandler, 63. Contemporary nuns of Romsey also broke the law and made wills (Power, 337, with n. 6), and there were no doubt others. The making of wills by religious was forbidden by the Council of Oxford in 1222 (Wilkins, *Concilia* 1, 593), though the practice obviously continued.

3   *VCH Dorset* 2, 78a; Chandler, 62–3, 67–8.

4   Joan was formerly prioress of Shaftesbury (*CPR 1361–4*, 232), though this is not noted by the editors of *HRH* 2, 606, and 3, 689, where she is simply styled nun.

5   *Reg. Aiscough*, second series, fol. 10v.

1460,[1] when she was passed over in favour of Margaret St John (**164**) as abbess, whose election was manipulated by blatant family string pulling at papal level. Thomesine Kemer, or Kymer (**147**), who was at the elections of Edith Bonham as tacitly professed,[2] and Margaret St John as apparently fully professed,[3] and who first occurs as prioress in 1497,[4] may have been considered too old to be abbess in 1505, when Elizabeth Shelford (**206**) was elected.[5] Other prioresses who never became abbesses were Agnes (**12**) and her possible successor Aubrey (**13**), Katherine Slo (**87**), Margaret Selgrave (**92**) attending the election of Margaret Stourton (**93**) as abbess in 1423, and Katherine Hall (**199**) present as an ordinary nun at the election of Elizabeth Shelford in 1505,[6] and later succeeding Thomesine Kemer as prioress. Katherine was also at the election of Elizabeth Zouche the last abbess in 1528, and was discharged from office with a state pension (significantly modest in comparison with Elizabeth's) at the suppression of the monastery in 1539. In some instances, ordinary nuns holding no known monastic office were elected by popular choice in preference to the prioress and sub-prioress, perhaps reflecting the conventual politics and prejudices that would have played their part in the choice of head. Representing this category are Agnes Longespée (1243-6), **38**, Agnes de Ferrers (1247-58), **41**, Juliana de Bauceyn (1258-79), **44**, Laurentia de Muscegros (1279-90), **48**, Mabel Giffard (1291-1302), **54**, Denise la Blunde (1329-45), **65**, Margaret de Leukenore (1350-62), **71**, Egelina de Counteville (1395-8), **81**, Cecily Fovent (1398-1423), **84**, Margaret Stourton (1423-41), **93**, Margaret St John (1460-92), **164**, Alice Gibbes (1492-

---

1   *Reg. Beauchamp* 1, second series, fol. 34r.

2   *Reg. Aiscough*, second series, fol. 10v.

3   *Reg. Beauchamp* 1, second series, fol. 34r. For the meaning of tacit (implied) and express (made with the customary ceremonies) profession, see Vermeersch, 'Profession', 452a; Salih, 107 ff. (Ch. 4, *Containing Virginity: the veil and the wall*), at 135. Tacit profession, which allowed nuns freely to wear the habit of the professed, but without at this stage taking formal vows, was finally abolished by Pius IX in 1858 (Vermeersch, 'Profession', 452a).

4   *Reg. Blyth*, 97–100 no. 365.

5   *Reg. Audley*, fols. 126v–127r.

6   Ibid., fol. 126v.

6), **179**, Margery (or Margaret) Twyneo (1497-1505), **180**, Elizabeth Shelford (1505-28), **206**, and Elizabeth Zouche (1528-39), **226**. Agnes Longespée was not formerly of the Shaftesbury chapter, though apparently of sufficient standing to be nominated as its head. Good birth and the right family, political and ecclesiastical connections might also help a candidate for election, as notoriously in the case of Margaret St John (**164**), though they could not always guarantee promotion. In the earliest days of the foundation it was taken for granted that Æthelgifu (**1**) as the king's daughter would rightfully take her place as abbess as an accepted part of the pre-Conquest social and religious hierarchy, though it is also likely (in principle, at least) that she would have had to display the necessary qualities required by the *Rule* of St Benedict for this demanding office first. In post-Conquest times aristocratic, or well connected abbesses included Cecily, Mary, Juliana de Bauceyn, Joan de Bridport, Mabel Giffard, Margaret de Leukenore, and Elizabeth Zouche, in addition to Agnes Longespée and Margaret St John, as noted.

Elections of abbesses, subject to the requirements and provisions of royal patronage, were generally upheld without intervention by the Crown, though there are instances where exception was taken to the chapter's choice. Inhibiting circumstances, as in the election of Agnes de Ferrers (**41**), might mean that the royal assent was postponed (here for three and a half years) until matters were resolved to the king's satisfaction. Normally, however, the interval between election and the royal assent was generally between a week and a month. In two instances, Juliana de Bauceyn (**44**) and Elizabeth Shelford (**206**), the Crown's approval was forthcoming within a week, while Margaret de Leukenore (**71**) was notified of it after just a few days, probably through the influence of a presumed family member serving the queen as a senior official in the royal household. Prolonged voidance of the abbey following the death of an abbess was profitable to the Crown, which could appropriate its temporalities during the interim. This may be the reason why Margaret Aucher (**61**) and Elizabeth Zouche (**226**) each had to wait well over two months for the king's decision. The exceptionally long voidances caused by disputed elections after the deaths of Amice Russell (**32**), Agnes Longespée (**38**) and Joan Formage (**72**) in 1242, 1246 and 1394 would have been especially lucrative.

Impediments to election might include undesirable family

connections, unsuitability of conduct or character, illegitimacy, and age. Royal assent to the election of Agnes de Ferrers (**41**), first in 1243 and again in 1246, was deferred because of her alleged blood relationship with William Marsh (de Marisco) the traitor, who had been behind an assassination attempt on Henry III in 1238. Marsh was still at large in 1242, operating as a pirate from Lundy Island in the Bristol Channel before his capture and execution for treason later that year. Agnes renounced her initial election in favour of Constance Saunzaver (**37**), whose appointment by compromission of the bishop's commissaries was subsequently quashed by them to Agnes's long term advantage. Elected for the second time in October 1246, Agnes finally received the royal assent in January 1247 and was eventually blessed as abbess in early March, bringing to an end the long voidance following the death of Agnes Longespée (**38**) in May the previous year.

Conduct unbecoming a religious was taken nearly as seriously. The unapproved election of the prioress Lucy Fitzherberde (**75**) as abbess took place shortly after the death of Joan Formage (**72**) on 19 August 1394. At the king's intervention one of the nuns, Egelina de Counteville (**81**), was appointed by the bishop over Lucy, who was alleged to have been causing faction both within and outside the convent to further her candidature. Dame Egelina was duly installed as abbess in late April or early May 1395 with the royal assent, when the abbey returned to normal after eight months of unrest. Illegitimacy and age might also prevent an elected candidate from assuming office, though in two instances papal dispensations were forthcoming. Edith Bonham (**96**) received one for an alleged *defectum natalium*,[1] or bastardy, while the significantly underage Margaret St John (**164**) was permitted early election to the abbey's offices in the event of vacancy, including that of abbess, through the influence of her mother, Margaret Beauchamp, duchess of Somerset, who joined with her in audaciously petitioning the papacy.

THEIR SISTERS IN CHRIST

Apart from heads of house, the names of others holding monastic office as well as ordinary nuns also occur in the royal chancery records and bishops' registers, as noted, the latter, in particular, containing lists of convent members attending elections of abbesses

---

1   Hutchins 1868, 28a; see also Power, 45.

from around the mid-fifteenth century. Thus, there were fifty-seven sisters present at the election of Edith Bonham (**96**) on 16 November 1441, comprising forty-three expressly (*expresse*) and fourteen tacitly (*tacite*) professed. Full profession of the latter was received by the bishop on 1 July the following year.[1] Similar lists are also found at the elections of Margaret St John (**164**) on 26 March 1460, Margery Twyneo (**180**) on 11 February 1497, and Elizabeth Shelford (**206**) on 25 June 1505, which record respectively fifty-three, thirty-six (including eleven tacitly professed), and fifty (including twenty-two tacitly professed) nuns. These figures indicate a notable reduction of the chapter from the mid-fourteenth century due to the abbey's changing economic circumstances, contrasting with an earlier period, when numbers were substantially higher. In 1326 the bishop of Salisbury, despite attempting four years previously to reinforce a century-old papal prohibition limiting the convent's size to one hundred,[2] surprisingly raised this maximum to one hundred and twenty on the abbess's apparently unquestioned assurance that the monastery's income could sustain such a number.[3] If maintained, as it may well have been for the next decade or two, this level is likely to have stretched the foundation's means to their capacity at a time of their increasing diminution. The steady reduction of this unrealistically high figure to a more manageable one from the mid-fourteenth century was undoubtedly in response to concerns about the abbey's dwindling resources resulting from the Black Death during this troubled period. The royal concession of 1364 allowing the abbey relief on its estates,[4] normally appropriated by the Crown during its voidance, was intended to alleviate this situation. Political no less than economic circumstances are also likely to have affected the convent, and the significantly reduced size of the chapter at the election of Margery Twyneo in 1497 may have been due in some way to the dynastic unrest of the era preceding 1485, when national

1   *Reg. Aiscough*, second series, fol. 97v.

2   *Reg. Martival* 2, pt. 2, 409–10. Martival's warning to the abbess and prioress heavy handedly threatened excommunication, if the prohibition (issued by Honorius III in 1218, see *supra* p. 14 n. 3) and other monitions were ignored. See also *VCH Dorset* 2, 77a.

3   *Reg. Martival* 2, pt. 2, 574–6; see also ibid., 576–8, and *VCH Dorset* 2, 77a.

4   See *supra* p. 29 n. 1.

stability began to be restored with the accession of Henry VII that year.
By the early sixteenth century numbers had returned more or less to
normal, with a revived chapter of fifty nuns recorded at the election
of Elizabeth Shelford in 1505, a figure that was to increase to fifty
six in the three and a half decades preceding the dissolution of the
convent during the rule of its last abbess Elizabeth Zouche (**226**) in
1539.[1] This included two sisters from Cannington Priory (**238**, **262**),
who had earlier transferred to Shaftesbury after the suppression of
their Somerset house in 1536.[2]

The election lists in the later bishops' registers indicate that
it was common for members of apparently the same family to take
the veil according to custom, sometimes at or around the same time,
sometimes over generations. Thus, allowing for variant medieval
name forms, are noted Amice Russell (**32**) and Clemence Russell
(**50**); Idony Wodehill (**88**) and Agnes Wodehele (**132**); Margaret
Stourton (**93**), Mary Stourton (**95**) and Anastasia Stourton (**100**);
Joan Ashecombe (**94**) and Alice Aisshecombe (**116**); Edith Bonham
(**96**) and Philippa Bonham (**172**); Margery Spertegrane (**113**) and
Martha Spartygrane (**166**); Anastasia Bradeleigh (**115**), Constance
Bradeleighe (**141**) and Eleanor Bradeleygh (**145**); Elizabeth Becham
(**119**) and Isabel Beauchamp (**168**); Elizabeth Panys (**120**) and Isabel
Panys (**169**); Agnes Shelford (**125**) and Elizabeth Shelford (**206**);
Isabel Beynton (**128**) and Joan Beyntham (**177**); Joan Bulwardyne
(**129**) and Joyce Bulwarden (**185**); Maria Florey (**133**) and Katherine
Florey (**174**); Margaret Godewyn (**139**) and Elizabeth Goodwyne
(**204**); Ellen Rempston (**142**) and Edith Rempston (**146**); Thomasine
Kemer (**147**), Parnel Kemer (**158**) and Edith Kemer (**230**); Ellen
Poynes (**153**) and Elizabeth Poynes (**156**); Christine Pytney (**160**)
and Alice Pytney (**173**); Margaret St John (**164**) and Margery St John

1   Bettey 1989, 180–1 (Appendix XI), 182–3 (Appendix XII), at 183.

2   Less well endowed houses, such as Cannington, with an annual income
    not exceeding £200 were suppressed under The Suppression of Religious
    Houses Act 1535/6 (27 Henry VIII, c. 28), also known as The Act for the
    Dissolution of the Lesser Monasteries. The heads of such foundations
    were granted pensions for life, with other members having the choice
    of transferring to a larger house (one of the 'great and honourable
    monasteries of religion', as they are described in the preamble to the
    Act), as here, or obtaining a dispensation permitting them to leave
    the religious life altogether. Those under twenty-four years of age were
    dismissed without compensation or choice (Cooke 1996, 293).

(**187**); Agnes Ashe (**181**) and Margaret Aysshe (**256**); Maria Payn (**183**), Margaret Payn (**197**), Ursula Payne (**207**), and Alice Payne (**228**); Katherine Hall (**199**) and Agnes Halle (**209**).

DISSOLUTION

FROM THE CLOISTER INTO THE WORLD

What happened to the Shaftesbury nuns after the dissolution of their abbey in 1539? Most, presumably, returned to their families, or were afforded shelter by friends or well wishers, while those without relatives or connections may simply have disappeared into oblivion supported only by their pensions in their uncertain, even perilous passage into the world. There are no indications that any left to pursue their vocations in religious houses on the Continent. Marriage, which was permitted after 1549,[1] may also have been a possibility for some, especially the younger nuns on meagre pensions, though this was prohibited during the Marian Reaction after 1553.[2] Many were still alive in Mary's reign, perhaps hoping for a renewal of their old way of life in another convent. Any expectations of returning to their former Shaftesbury home had been cruelly dashed by the demolition of the monastery by the opportunist Sir Thomas Arundell, who purchased it from the Crown shortly after its suppression.[3] Plundered for its stone, lead, tiles, glass, timber, and fittings salvaged for building materials,[4] much of which was used around the town of Shaftesbury, its destruction was well nigh complete by the mid-sixteenth century, when a sketch of the remains of the abbey church and part of the precinct in a contemporary estate survey shows the startling extent of its ruination.[5] Only one of the

1   Cooke 1996, 300; Chandler, 98.

2   Cooke 1996, 300 n. 50.

3   Bettey 1992, 8; Chandler, 99.

4   Fragments of abbey stone and ornamentation may still be seen in buildings around the town in Shaftesbury, with a large and partly identified collection stored and selectively displayed in the Abbey museum.

5   Straton 2 (comprising the third roll), 492. This *supervisus generalis*, dated 1566–7 (9 Elizabeth I), includes a survey (1547–8 [2 Edward

two sturdy western towers of the church, together with part of the Romanesque north arcading of the roofless west nave and a section of the shattered south wall with its rubble survived, a poignant reminder of the foundation's former grandeur. Even this poor remnant had been levelled to the ground by 1573-4,[1] by which time the site had been in the possession of the earls of Pembroke for over two decades.[2] Any hopes of monastic revival finally disappeared with the death of Mary in 1558 and the accession of Elizabeth I, whose long and eventful reign had momentous consequences for the future of Catholicism in England, when the Old Religion and its adherents were finally outlawed. Two of the nuns (**233, 243**) still alive in the mid-sixteenth century were living in rented premises close to the site of their old abode.[3] There may well have been others residing with or near them

VI], renewed 1552-3) of the Shaftesbury lands and property formerly belonging to Sir Thomas Arundell and acquired by the earl of Pembroke in 1553 after the former's attainder and execution in 1552 (Straton 2, 487–501), a customary (of the *Barton juxta villam Shastonie*) with manorial extent (1545 [37 Henry VIII]), ibid., 501–9, and a rental and extent (*rentale et extenta*) made in 1573–4 (16 Elizabeth I), ibid., 510–33, 516. RCHME *Dorset* 4 *North*, Plate 58, incorrectly dates the survey c.1553 (actually 1547–8). The sketch, which stands at the beginning of the survey, is on membrane xxxviij of the third roll of the *supervisus generalis* (*CHIhc* 2057/S3/3). Shown in the background is Holy Trinity church (one of six medieval parish churches in the town and borough, if one includes St Rumbold's *juxta Shaston*') and part of the nuns' burial ground subsequently appropriated by Holy Trinity. Demolished and completely rebuilt in 1841–2, and declared redundant by the diocese of Salisbury in 1977, Holy Trinity now serves as a day centre with offices and workshops.

1   The Shaftesbury property rental and extent made for the earl of Pembroke in 1573–4 (see *supra* p. 36 n. 5) records *Totum Scitum nuper Monasterii de Shasburye ubi edificia jam prostrata sunt & omnia solum & fundamenta ab antiquo eidem pertinentia vocata lez Parke, continens per estimacionem iiij acras*, together with the abbey garden and hopyard, and a number of the buildings still surviving at this time (one of which, called 'lez Sextrye', was used as a stable with a loft for storing hay), a house and other accommodation, and a courtyard, or curtilage (Straton 2, 516; Hopton, 9b, 13b). The 'Sextrye', or 'Sextry', was formerly the abbey sacristy, with the sacristan living in the house provided (Hopton, 8 (Fig. 5), 9b).

2   William Herbert, the first earl, who acquired the site in 1553 (see *supra* pp. 36–7 n. 5), died in 1570.

3   Straton 2, 492, 516; Hopton, 13b.

in the manner of a few known other instances,[1] perhaps nostalgically and secretly trying to recreate some sort of communal religious life *sans habit* in a society increasingly unsympathetic to it. For them, as for generations since, these 'bare ruin'd choirs'[2] would long serve as a grim spectacle of the mutability of fortune, of the inexorable march of time and dissolution consigning all human endeavour to the vault of history. Today, Shaftesbury Abbey is a levelled ruin in a tranquil garden setting, a sanctuary of peace in a troubled and uncertain world. Desecrated, broken and forlorn, its spirit yet lives on, a silent witness to 'a higher reality, an inspiration felt by us all'.[3]

APPENDIX

SHAFTESBURY ABBESSES AND KNOWN NUNS FROM THE ABBEY'S FOUNDATION TO ITS DISSOLUTION[4]

The following numbered, chronological list of abbesses and identifiable Shaftesbury nuns, with biographical details where available, is compiled from official (state and ecclesiastical) and other sources. It cannot claim to be exhaustive, since most of the nuns associated with the abbey from its origins in the late ninth century to the first half of the fifteenth, around five hundred and fifty years,

1   Chandler, 98; Cooke 1996, 300, with n. 52. 'For a former nun who had little in the way of financial resources, familial support, or even the necessary emotional hardiness to cope with the changes in her life, this would be a way of enabling her to live as a single woman in an atmosphere similar to the one she had been used to' (Cooke 1996, 300–1).

2   Shakespeare, *Sonnet* 73, v. 4.

3   Bellenger, 129. Dom Aidan Bellenger OSB was later abbot of Downside, Stratton-on the-Fosse, Somerset.

4   Included are pre-Conquest religious women or vowesses (**2–5**) associated, or presumed to be associated with Shaftesbury rather than nuns living under a strict rule. Abbesses are indicated by bold type, with two (**37, 75**), elected but never appointed, in square brackets. Ordinary nuns having uncertain connections with Shaftesbury are also in square brackets. Alternative personal name forms occurring in the various sources are in round brackets.

must remain anonymous through sparseness or lack of documentary evidence. While the complement of the abbey from Anglo-Saxon to early Plantagenet times is indeterminate, the thirteenth-century papal and later episcopal inhibitions limiting its capacity to one hundred nuns is an indication that its numbers had apparently been exceeding this limit and causing concern probably long before this time.[1] This situation was to continue into the following century, when adverse economic and other circumstances made it increasingly necessary for the convent to downsize, as discussed.

1 Æthelgifu (Æðelgifu, Æthelgeofu, Agelyue, Ayeleua),[2] **c.888-c.895? x -899?** Third-born surviving child and second eldest, or middle daughter of Alfred the Great and Ealhswith (Ealhspið) his consort, and first abbess, conventionally described by Asser as *devotam Deo virginem*. The suggestion that she would 'have been born some time in the early 870s'[3] would have made her very young on appointment, perhaps no more than seventeen or eighteen, or even sixteen. The length of her rule is uncertain, but if she died in the mid or late 890s,[4] it would have been around ten years. Her successor is unknown, and after Æthelgifu there are considerable gaps in the sequence of pre-Conquest abbesses, which are not readily explained for a foundation of Shaftesbury's significance. The next one indisputably to be named abbess (Herelufu, **6**) appears around eight decades later, and the length of her rule is similarly uncertain.

2 Wynflæd (Wynnflæd, Wenflede, Winfled),[5] occ. 942 and 966.

1 See *supra* p. 14 n. 3.

2 PASE (Æthelgifu 4); Asser, 58 (c.75), 85 (c.98), both as *Æthelgeofu*; *GR* 1 (ii. 122. 3), with note *GR* 2, 100; John of Worcester, *Chronicle* 2, 328–9 ([(ix) 909 *sub anno* 887]), following Asser; *HRH* 1, 219; *VCH Dorset* 2, 73a; Meyer 1981, 341–2; Keynes & Lapidge, 36, 90, 105, 177, 256, 325; Murphy, 43–4; Kelly, no. 7, and pp. xiii, xiv n. 6, 29; Vernarde, 17, 20–1; Abels, 230; Keynes 1999, 40–1; Foot 2000 1, 12, 70, 160, and 2, 165–6; Chandler, 14, 17–18, 21; Yorke 2003, 76, 81–3, 111, 158.

3 Keynes 1999, 41.

4 Ibid.

5 PASE (Wynnflæd 1–4); *VCH Dorset* 2, 73b; Meyer 1981, 354; Kelly, nos. 13, 26, and pp. xiv, xv n. 11, xvi n. 17, xxvi–xxvii, 26–7, 56–8, 68, 71, 104, 110, 126; Keynes 1999, 43–6; Foot 2000 1, 1–3, 33, 112, 126, 136–40, 145, 182, and 2, 172–3; Chandler, 18, 21; Yorke 2003, 82–3, 86, 171.

Styled *cuidam religiose sancte conuersacionis monialis femine* (as Wenflede)
in a charter of Eadmund I (king of the English, reigned 939-46), 942,
restoring and confirming to her seven hides (*mansæ*) at Cheselbourne
and Winterborne Tomson (Dorset).[1] This Wynflæd is probably to be
identified with the Winfled, whose grant or bequest to Shaftesbury of
ten hides (*cassati*) of land at Piddletrenthide in Dorset was confirmed
by King Edgar in a charter of 966 naming her as his maternal
grandmother (*aua mea*).[2] It is uncertain, however, whether *monialis*
in the first of these charters is intended to indicate a consecrated
and cloistered nun, and therefore the equivalent of *mynecenu*, since
Wynflæd may have taken her vows in widowhood, living a chaste and
religious life clothed and veiled as a nun, but not under a strict rule.
A woman (often, though not necessarily a widow) who professed
thus, choosing at the same time to remain in the world with her own
property, servants and acquaintances, was regarded as a *nunne*. If any
'rule' was observed, it may have been a selectively adapted version
of the disciplined *regula* of the cloister suitable for such a vocation,
though this can be no more than conjecture. It would be tempting
to imagine some such spiritual guide as the *Ancrene Riwle* (or *Ancrene
Wisse*) of a later age,[3] but this comparison is inappropriate, since
the *Riwle* was originally intended for a small group of young women
recluses (though subsequently revised for larger numbers), and the
nunne, often of maturer years, would not have been of this category,
though she may have chosen to live a solitary life. Whether there was
a specific rule for non-claustrated religious women at this period is

---

1   Kelly, no. 13.

2   Ibid., no. 26.

3   The 'Rule' or 'Guide for Anchoresses', originally written in a West
     Midlands English dialect possibly by an Augustinian canon of Wigmore
     Abbey in Herefordshire for local anchoresses between 1215 and 1221
     (Dobson), was also translated into Latin and Anglo-Norman. *Ccc* MS 402
     ('Ancrene Wisse', available online with bibliography, https://parker.
     stanford.edu/parker/catalog/zh635rv2202), one of its earliest English
     versions and the one edited by Tolkien (*The English Text of the Ancrene
     Riwle*, 1962), is now considered to date between 1224 and 1235. A
     new edition is by Millett 2005–6 (with translation, Millet 2009), who,
     countering Dobson, 14–16, controversially argues for Dominican rather
     than Augustinian authorship of the first writing of the work. See also
     Millett 1992. An earlier translation is by Salu 1955.

difficult to determine, since little is known about their way of life.[1] There is also the possibility that Wynflæd, who seems to have been a widow,[2] was a lay associate of Shaftesbury, perhaps in the manner of her daughter Ælfgifu (3), in view of her relationship with the convent as benefactress. The Wynflæd, whose will bequeathing land, personal possessions and money to various beneficiaries, including Shaftesbury and Wilton, mentions her nun's clothing (*hyre nunscrude*),[3] may not be the same person despite attempts to make this identification.[4]

3 Ælfgifu (Ælfgife, Ælfgiuu, Ælgytha, Alfgife, Alfgiue, Algife, Algiue, Algyva, Elfgyuu, Elgiue, Elgiva) *sancta*,[5] d. 18 May 944. First wife of Eadmund I, mother of Eadwig (king of England, reigned 955-9) and Edgar (king of England, reigned 959-8 July 975), and thus grandmother of kings Edward the Martyr *sanctus* (king of England, reigned +8 July (?) 975-18 March 978)[6] and Æthelred II 'Unræd'

1   Foot 2000 1, 108.

2   Kelly, 56.

3   A transcript, with translation, of the will (Sawyer 1539) dated *c*.950, which survives as an eleventh-century single-leaf copy (*Lbl* Cotton Charter viii. 38), is online (http://www.esawyer.org.uk/org.uk/charter/1539. html). See also *ASW,* 10–15 (no. 3), and Owen, 199, 203, for Wynflæd's *nunscrude*, which includes her best veil.

4   Owen, 197 n. 1; Keynes 1999, 44–5; Yorke 2003, 100 n. 136. Whitelock (*ASW,* 109) went so far as to suggest that Wynnflæd was a 'lay abbess' of Shaftesbury, a view accepted without question by Meyer 1981, 350 n. 2, 354 n. 3. Arguments for identification, however, should note that Wynflæd's daughter, a principal beneficiary in the will, is named Æthelflæd (Æðelflæde), not Ælfgifu (see **3**).

5   PASE (Ælfgifu 3); Æthelweard, 54 (iv. 6); Liebermann, 17 C [36]), *sancta Ælfgifu,* with *sancte Eadweard cyninge,* Birch, 93; Meyer 1977, 48; Keynes 1996, fol. 38v; *ASC* D 955 (*Sancte Ælfgife*); *GP* 1, 293–5 (ii. 86. 1–3), with notes *GP* 2, 130–1; *GR* 1, 253–5 (ii. 154. 3–155), with notes *GR* 2, 137; *ODS,* 169a; Rollason, 65, 92; Ridyard, 170, 175n. 138, 243; Smith, 4, 6; Kelly, no. 28, and pp. xiii–xiv, xxvii, 56, 104, 110–11, 126; Keynes 1999, 45–7; Foot 2000 1, 136, 165, and 2, 166, 169; Blair, 503–4; Chandler, 18; Yorke 2003, 77, 82–3, 109, 115–16, 122, 171, 175.

6   *GP* 1, 276–7 (78.7), 295–7 (ii. 86. 4–7, 87. 1), 610–11 (256.1), with notes *GP* 2, 132–3; *GR* 1, 262–9 (ii. 161–3), with notes *GR* 2, 141–5. For Edward's cult, the politics behind it and its development, see Ridyard, 3–4, 41, 44–50, 154–75, 188, 194–5, 235, 246 *et passim*; *EKM,* xx–xxv (VIII); Fell 1978; Yorke 1999, 99–116.

(king of England, reigned +18 March 978-Autumn 1013 and February 1014-April 1016),[1] and Edith of Wilton *sancta* (d. 16 September 984).[2] As a royal benefactress of Shaftesbury Abbey,[3] Ælfgifu had a close but unspecified relationship with the nunnery, where she retired apparently as an invalided vowess or lay associate rather than a consecrated nun, and where she was buried and subsequently sanctified on account of healing miracles occurring at her tomb, according to a fragment of a now lost metrical *Vita* of her, perhaps composed for the nuns of Shaftesbury by William of Malmesbury.[4] Her choice of Shaftesbury may have been influenced by her mother Wynflæd (**2**) and perhaps also by Eadgifu (**5**) her mother-in-law, both of whom may have taken religious vows there. Her cult (*festum* 18 May,[5] with *inventio* 18 August commemorating the discovery of her body in 974,[6] and probable *translatio* 10 July[7]), which originated at Shaftesbury, was also observed at Winchester (New Minster), Sherborne, Worcester, Canterbury (St Augustine's and perhaps also

1 William of Malmesbury's significantly negative portrayal of Æthelred (*GR* 1, 268–77, 300–5, with notes *GR* 2, 145–9, 160–2) contrasts strikingly with his sympathetic treatment of his half-brother, King Edward the Martyr (*GR* 1, 262–9 (ii. 161–3), with notes *GR* 2, 141–5). It is worth noting that Æthelred's obit was observed at Shaftesbury on 22 April, according to one Shaftesbury calendar, that of the Shelford *horæ* (*Cfm* MS 2-1957, fol. 4v: Wormald & Giles, 516–21, at 18).

2 *GP* 1, 296–301 (ii. 87. 2–10), with notes *GP* 2, 134–6; *GR* 1, 260–1 (ii. 159. 2), 402–4 (ii. 218), with notes *GR* 2, 205; Birch, 93; Ridyard, 37–44, 140–75 (especially 140–54), 235, 238 *et passim*; Keynes 1996, fol. 38v; Blair, 528.

3 Kelly, no. 28.

4 *GP* 1, 294–5 (ii. 86. 3), with note *GP* 2, 131; Æthelweard, 54 (iv.6), *In eodem uero anno* [944] *obiit et regina Elfgyuu, Eadmundi regis coniux, postque sanctificatur. In cuius mausoleo, cooperante deo, usque ad præsens innumerosa equidem miracula fiunt in cœnobio, quod uulgo Sceftesbyrig nuncupatur*, Smith, 4, 13.

5 *AA.SS. Maii* IV (1866), 185–6. The *festum*, ranked highly as *duplex*, was observed at Shaftesbury (*Cfm* MS 2-1957 (the Shelford *horæ*), fols. 3r–8v, at 5r): Wormald & Giles, at 518.

6 *CM* 1 (*The Creation to A.D. 1066*), 446–7, 466 (*sub anno* 974). This rare feast is entered in the calendar (as *Eluiue regine* without rank) of the Shelford *horæ*, fol. 6v: Wormald & Giles, 518.

7 Rushforth 2008, no. 27; Wormald 1934, no. 7.

Christ Church), and probably Evesham on the evidence of late pre-Conquest calendars[1] and litanies of the saints.[2] Relics of St Ælfgifu and St Edward the Martyr had been acquired by the minster church of Exeter by the early eleventh century.[3] Beyond England there appears to have been a limited Scandinavian cult to judge by a thirteenth-century Winchester-influenced Danish martyrology.[4] During her life Ælfgifu was renowned for her compassion and generosity to the poor and desperate as well as for her prophetic powers.[5] It is likely that her cult was promoted for dynastic purposes in support of the royal

1   Rushforth 2008: Ælfgifu *regina* (nos. 9 [Wormald 1934, no. 5], Canterbury, St Augustine's (Bosworth Psalter), *s*.x/xi (as Ælfgifa, omitting *regina*); 12 [Wormald 1934, no. 15], ?Peterborough/?Canterbury (Missal of Robert of Jumièges), ?1014 x ?1023; 14 [Wormald 1934, no. 9], Winchester, New Minster (Ælfwine's Prayer Book), 1023 x 1031; 15 [Wormald 1934, no. 10], Winchester, New Minster, 1025 x ?[erasure]; 19 [Wormald 1934, no. 14], Sherborne, *c.*1061 (as Ælfgiua); 20 [Wormald 1934, no. 18], Worcester, *s.* xi *med.* (? x 1062), as Ælgifa; 22 [Wormald 1934, no. 16], ?Evesham/?Worcester, 1064 x 1070 (as Ælfgyua); 23 [Wormald 1934, no. 12], Winchester, New Minster, *c.*1062 (as Ælfgifa); 24 [Wormald 1934, no. 11], Winchester, New Minster, *c.*1073 (as Ælfgyfa); 27 [Wormald 1934, no. 7], Salisbury (Old Sarum), *s.*xi *ex*, as Ælfgfe in majuscules under 10 July).

2   Lapidge, 127 (VIII [Winchester (New Minster?), 1060s, probably for use at Sherborne]. i. 89), Ælfgiua, between Eadburga and Eadgiða; 145 (XII [Winchester, New Minster, *s.*xi²]. 163), Ælfgifa, between Wærburh and Mærwenna followed by Æþelflæda; 169 (XVI [?Winchester/?Nunnaminster, perhaps Shaftesbury, 1035 x 1040]. ii. 339), Ælfgyf, immediately before Eadburh, both names being added to lower margin of MS; 185 (XXI [Winchester, New Minster, *s.*xi (second quarter)]. 11ᵉ), Ælfgifuu, as last of the Virgins, immediately after Eadburh; 207 (XXIV [?Winchester, but also attributed to Ramsey, late *s.*x]. 197), Aldef, between Eugenia and Scolastica; 252 (XXXVI [?Canterbury/?Glastonbury, *s.*xi (second quarter)]. 101), Ælfgifu, between Æðeldryþa and Sexburh; 298 (XLV [Bury St Edmunds, *s.*xi (second quarter)]. 10?), Ælfgyfu, after Eadburh and Æþelburh, and before Toua).

3   Foot 2011, 201.

4   Toy, 27.

5   *GP* 1, 292–5 (ii. 86. 1–3), with note *GP* 2, 131; *GR* 1, 253–5 (ii. 154. 3–155), with notes *GR* 2, 137; Smith, 4, 12–13.

lineage through her descendants.[1] This family association may have been behind the translation of the presumed relics of her murdered grandson Edward the Martyr to Shaftesbury from Wareham in 979 by the ealdorman Ælfhere of Mercia.[2] As the resting-place of two royal saints Shaftesbury's status as an important *locus sanctus* favoured by the West Saxon ruling house was now assured. The confirmation of twenty hides (*mansæ*) at Tisbury (Wilts) to the nunnery in 984,[3] and the grant of the monastic cell (*cœnobium*) of Bradford-on-Avon (Wilts) with its lands in 1001[4] by King Æthelred II may represent acts of penance. Æthelred may at least have been aware of rumoured regicidal plots against his half-brother Edward despite his young age at the time, even if he was not personally involved in them. In one of two versions of the origin of Shaftesbury Abbey Ælfgifu is said by William of Malmesbury to have been its founder,[5] contradicting what he relates elsewhere about King Alfred and his daughter Æthelgifu, with whom Ælfgifu has probably been confused, since William names both Elfgiua.[6]

1   'The cult of the royal saints ... enhanced the prestige of the ancient West Saxon dynasty, which by the end of the tenth century was the oldest royal line still enthroned in western Europe. No fewer than thirteen royal women of the tenth and eleventh centuries can be found in the West Saxon genealogy who were venerated as popular saints' (Meyer 1981, 333, with n. 3).

2   For the translation to Shaftesbury, see Ridyard, 46–7, 155–6, 159–60, 170–1; and for the cult, ibid., 154–75, 238–9, 249; 171–5 ('The hagiography of Wilton and Shaftesbury: a response to Conquest?').

3   Kelly, no. 28.

4   Kelly, no. 29. The *cœnobium*, believed to have been founded by St Aldhelm before 705 (Haslam, 'Wiltshire', 90), is said by William of Malmesbury to have 'fallen into nothing' (*in nichilum defecere*) by his time, 'with only an empty name remaining' (*restatque tantum nomen inane*): *GP* 1, 522–3 (v. 198. 20). The early church, dedicated to St Laurence, one of the very few surviving from its time, is described by Taylor, 141–71.

5   *GP* 1, 292–3 (ii. 86. 1), with note *GP* 2, 130. John of Worcester, following William, similarly attributes the foundation of the nunnery to Ælfgifu (*Chronicle* 2, 314–15 ([ii] 902 *sub anno* 888), apparently also confusing her with Æthelgifu (ibid., 328–9 ([(ix) 909 *sub anno* 887]), where Asser is his source).

6   *Sceftoniense etiam monasterium sanctimonialibus compleuit, ubi et abbatissam filiam suam Elfgiuam instituit. GR* 1 (ii. 122. 3), with note *GR* 2, 100.

4 Ælfthryth (Alfþriþ),[1] occ. 948. Described as a religious woman (*cuidam religiose femine*) in a charter of King Eadred, 948, granting her eight hides (*mansas agelluli*) in the Isle of Purbeck (Dorset) in return for sixty mancuses (*mancusas*) of the purest gold,[2] an estate which later formed part of Shaftesbury's Domesday manor of Kingston assessed at sixteen hides. If Ælfthryth was associated with the Shaftesbury minster, it was probably as a vowess, or perhaps a lay associate rather than a consecrated nun. There are no indications that she lived under the strict rule of the cloister or that she was ever abbess.

5 Eadgifu [of Kent] (Adgiua, Edgifa, Edgiva, Ediva),[3] occ. 953; d. in or after 966. Third wife of King Edward the Elder, mother of Eadmund I and Eadred (king of the English, reigned 946-55), and Eadburh (Eadburg, Eadburga) of Winchester *sancta* (d. 951 x 953),[4] and thus mother-in-law of Ælfgifu (3). Included (as *coniunx Eadpeardi regis*) among the *nomina feminarum illustrium* in the 'Liber vitæ' of the New Minster and Hyde Abbey,[5] Winchester, next after

1   PASE (Ælfthryth 6); *HRH* 1, 219 (tentatively) and *VCH Dorset* 2, 79a (without foundation) include in their lists of abbesses; Kelly, no. 16, and pp. xxvii, 68; Foot 2000 1, 182, and 2, 171; Yorke 2003, 76, 158; Chandler, 18.

2   A *mancusa*, or *mancus*, was an early medieval gold coin, or, in this instance, a weight of gold of 4.25g equivalent to 30 gold pennies (Grierson & Blackburn, 327), which was the value of an ox in England at this time (Abels, 256). Sixty mancuses, representing here 255g of high grade gold, was thus a very considerable sum, indicating that Ælfthryth was a woman of substance.

3   PASE (Eadgifu 4); *GR* 1, 200-1 (ii. 126. 3), 400-1 (ii. 217. 1); Birch, 57; Meyer 1977, 38-45; Keynes 1996, 94b, fol. 26r; Kelly, nos. 13 (Eadgifu appears as second witness to charter of confirmation of King Eadmund to Wynflæd (2), 942: *Ego Adgiue ... regis mater ...*), 17, and pp. xiii, xxvii, and 71-2; Keynes 1999, 46; Foot 2000 1, 141, 165 with n. 72, 181-2, and 2, 171; Foot 2011, 43-4, 51, 56-8, 102, 112; Yorke 2003, 76-7, 83-5, 104 n. 247, 136 n. 102, 160, 171; Chandler, 18.

4   See *supra* pp. 5-6 n. 6.

5   Included in *Lbl* Stowe MS 944, fols. 1-61 (Gneuss & Lapidge, 403-4, no. 500), the greater part of which was written at the New Minster by a monk called Ælfsige (PASE, Ælfsige 85) in 1031. The *feminæ illustres* commemorated were women in confraternity with the New Minster, 'who were its fervent supporters, or who had commended themselves to the community's prayers by their almsgiving' (Keynes 1996, 94b, fol. 26r-v).

Ealhswith (as *coniunx Ælfredi regis*), who heads the list. A powerful royal matriarch, the dowager Eadgifu had the distinction of outliving her husband, her two sons and her daughter Eadburh (for her other daughter, see below), surviving to witness charters of her grandson King Edgar, most of them being grants to religious houses, though she never retained the influence that she had held under her son Eadred.[1] William of Malmesbury notes that 'she was known to the whole British world for her praiseworthy religious principles',[2] and attributes King Eadred's preventing Bishop Æthelwold's leaving England for Gaul in self-imposed exile to her influence.[3] Eadgifu is styled *famuli Dei*,[4] in a charter of King Eadred granting her thirty hides (*mansionum*) at Felpham in Sussex, 953,[5] assessed at twenty-one hides in Domesday Book.[6] This may suggest that she had taken religious vows at Shaftesbury some time after her husband's death in 924 in view of the abbey's subsequent acquisition of this substantial royal estate,[7] though this can only be surmised. Equally, as a pious royal widow she would have had the option of retiring to her estates as a *nunne* to pursue a quasi-religious life with a few like-minded companions (*devotæ*). Wherever she retired as a widow, however, she was conspicuously active in her later life supporting the monastic reforms of Dunstan and Æthelwold, whether or not she was a vowess.[8] Eadgifu and her other daughter, also named Eadgifu,[9] may both have died and been buried at the Nunnaminster, Winchester,[10] where the

---

1   Meyer 1977, 43.

2   ... *omni religionis laude orbi Britannico nota* (*GP* 1, 262–3[ii. 75.37]); Meyer 1977, 41.

3   As a result, Æthelwold remained in England and was granted the defunct monastery of Abingdon by Eadred, which was refounded through Eadgifu's generosity (Meyer 1977, 41–2).

4   *Sic* for *famule Dei*.

5   Kelly, no. 17.

6   *GDB*, fol. 17v, cited by Kelly, 72.

7   Kelly, 71.

8   Meyer 1977, 38–42; Foot 2000 1, 182; Stafford, 'Eadgifu'.

9   Stafford, 'Eadgifu'; Foot 2011, 50–1. Little seems to be known about Eadgifu *filia*.

10 Foot 2000 1, 165, with n. 72. Stafford 2004, 'Eadgifu', concludes that

former may have retired, perhaps from Shaftesbury.

6 Herelufu (Herleva),[1] **occ. 966, d. 982.** Herelufu is named as a witness (as Herleva) to a probably spurious charter of Dunstan archbishop of Canterbury, Oscytel archbishop of York, and others confirming lands and privileges granted to Crowland Abbey (Lincs) by kings Eadred and Edgar, and protecting its rights, 10 June 966.[2] She was apparently highly regarded with a reputation extending beyond Shaftesbury, since, like Eadgifu (**5**), she is included among the *nomina feminarum illustrium* in the New Minster and Hyde Abbey 'Liber vitæ'[3] next after Mærwynn (Merewenna, Merwinna), first abbess of Romsey (*Mærpÿnn abbatissa Hrumesig cœnobio*),[4] while her obit, together with that of Wulfwynn (Wulfwin, Wulfwun, Wulfwyn), abbess of Wareham, is recorded in the Abingdon manuscript of the *Anglo-Saxon Chronicle.*[5]

Eadgifu [*mater*] 'probably died and was buried at Winchester'.

1 PASE (Herelufu 1); John of Worcester, *Chronicle* 2, 432–3 ([(ix) 1004 *sub anno* 982]); *HRH* 1, 219; *VCH Dorset* 2, 79a; Keynes 1999, 49; Foot 2000 2, 168; Yorke 2003, 171; Chandler, 18.

2 Searle, 162, 183–4 no 409; Sawyer 1294. Other witnesses include the abbesses Merewenna (Mærwynn, Merwenna, Merwinna) of Romsey and Wulfwynn (Wulfwin, Wulwina) of Wareham. If this charter is genuine, both Romsey and Wareham were evidently established by 966, perhaps as refoundations by King Edgar.

3 Birch, 58; Keynes 1996, 95a, fol. 26r.

4 For Romsey, see p. 5 r. 1. William of Malmesbury mentions Mærwynn and Æthelflæd (Ælfflæd, Elfleda, Ethelfleda) her possible successor but one (*VCH Hampshire* 2, 132a; *ODS*, 181a, art. 'Ethelfleda') in passing, but confesses that he was 'ignorant of their story ... reserving it for more careful treatment, if ever I learn it' (*Apud Rumesiam ... noui iacere duarum uirginum corpora, Merewinnæ et Elfledæ, quarum gesta nescio ... quam ad maiorem scribendi diligentiam reseruo, si forte cognouero*), *GP* 1, 277 (ii. 78. 7), with note *GP* 2, 119–120, including hagiographical references. Æthelflæd (*Æðelflæd, Ælfflæd, Elfleda*) is also among the 'Liber vitæ' *feminæ illustres*, but further down the list (Keynes 1996, 95a, fol. 26r).

5 *ASC* C 982 (*Þæs ylcan geares forðferdon twa abbodessan on Dorsætum, Herelufu on Sceaftesbyrig 7 Wulfwin on Werham*). See also PASE (Wulfwynn 4); Whitbread, 583–4; Yorke 2003, 61, 75, 85, 171, 196 n.15. Abbesses are rarely recorded in the *Anglo-Saxon Chronicle* in contrast with their prominence in the Ottonian families (Whitbread, 583). Wulfwynn may have been a kinswoman of the ealdorman Æthelweard (ibid., at 583–4), who had an evident interest in Wareham and Shaftesbury as places associated with the successive burials of King Edward the Martyr (*ASC*

It may be supposed that the religious life at Shaftesbury became more disciplined and structured during Herelufu's rule (*c.*966?-82), which coincided with the English monastic reforms of this period associated with saints Dunstan and Æthelwold,[1] applicable to nunneries no less than male houses. Following the Benedictine tradition of St Benedict of Aniane (*c.*750-821) and influenced by the extensive reforms at Fleury-sur-Loire and Ghent,[2] this revitalization found expression in the *Regularis Concordia* attributed to Æthelwold (though probably inspired by Dunstan)[3] and approved by the Council of Winchester in 973.[4] One of the main purposes of the *Concordia* was

E 979–980) following his death in 978, and whose *Chronicon*, a Latin translation of a lost and apparently significant version of the *Anglo-Saxon Chronicle* down to 975 (Wormald, 'Æthelweard'), was written for his distant relative Mathilde (described as his cousin, *consobrina* (Æthelweard, 1–2 (*Prologus*), 38–9 [iv. 2]), abbess of Essen from 973 to 1011, granddaughter of the emperor Otho I and great-great granddaughter of King Alfred (Æthelweard, xii–xiii, 1–2 (*Prologus*), 38–9 [iv. 2]; Whitbread, 580), the founder of Shaftesbury Abbey. The inclusion of Herelufu and Wulfwynn in the 982 annal of the *Anglo-Saxon Chronicle* may, therefore, have been indirectly inspired by Mathilde (Whitbread, 583) as one of the most important Ottonian abbesses of Essen renowned especially for her monastic building, patronage of the arts and influential political associations (Freise, 374–5), though it may be that Herelufu and Wulfwynn were also significant in their own way, perhaps as reformers of their own convents, thus meriting mention for posterity.

1   For the origin and development of these reforms, see Farmer, 10–19; Cubitt, 77–94; Knowles 2004, 31–56 (Ch. 3, 'The monastic revival under Dunstan and King Edgar: the *Regularis Concordia*').

2   Fleury had been reformed in 930 by Odo of Cluny, and Ghent *c.*937 by Gerard of Brogne, who initiated the reform in Lower Lotharingia (*Regularis Concordia*, Introduction, xlvii; Symons 1975, 45–6). Influencing both, however, was Benedict of Aniane, 'who had left his mark on the whole of western monasticism, and [whose] ideas underlay, in a general way, all the Continental reforms of more than a century later' (*Regularis Concordia*, Introduction, xlvii; see also Symons 1975, 45–6).

3   *Regularis Concordia*, Introduction, li–lii; Symons 1975, 43; Knowles 2004, 31–56. The circumstances of this revival are examined by Bullough, 20–36.

4   Æthelwold (for whose life and career, see Yorke 1988 and *idem*, 'Æthelwold') was bishop of Winchester from 963 to 984. Symons originally assigned the Council of Winchester to 970 (*Regularis Concordia*, Introduction, xxiv), later arguing for the now more generally accepted

the regularization of divine service (the *opus Dei*), with its synthesis of English and Continental practices.[1] Among its provisions were customs to be observed throughout the liturgical year, with daily reception of the Eucharist and a *horarium* to include psalms and intercessions for the king, queen and benefactors as patrons of the monastic life at all the offices except Prime,[2] an apparently peculiarly English custom probably followed by Shaftesbury and other Wessex foundations subject to reform. It is likely that the abbey had always been governed by the precepts of the *Rule* of St Benedict from its foundation,[3] though just how rigorously is uncertain. The tenth century reform was an idealistic attempt to regularize the lives of cloistered religious under royal patronage.[4] bringing English monasteries into closer alignment with their Continental counterparts. Shaftesbury was among the principal Wessex nunneries under the special protection of Queen Ælfthryth[5] restored by the end of the tenth century, which also included the Nunnaminster (Winchester), Romsey, Wherwell, Wilton, Wareham, Horton, Berkeley, and Reading.[6] As part of this revival Anglo-Saxon translations of the *Concordia* and of the Holy Rule itself were produced with nuns in mind by way of encouraging,

date of 973 (Symons 1975, 37–43, especially 40–2).

1   *Concordia* customs that may reasonably be assigned to Continental reformed monasticism are discussed by Symons 1975, 48–59.

2   *Regularis Concordia*, 5, 12–14, 16, 20, 21, 22–23 (*Proœmium*, c.8, and Chapter 1, 16, 18–20, 24–5, 27); Symons 1975, 44. There were two different psalms for each occasion, with three collects. Other psalms and prayers were said for the king and queen after the principal mass and the morrow (or early) mass reserved for the king (*Regularis Concordia*, 16: *Eadem uero matutinalis missa pro rege uel quacumque imminente necessitate celebretur*; see also ibid., 14 n. 3).

3   The Holy Rule is cited frequently in the *Concordia* as the basis of reform (*Regularis Concordia*, xvi, xxx–xxxi, xxxiii–xlii, xlv n.1, 2–3, 5–8, 11, 14–15, 17–18, 22 *et passim*). 'Like other customaries of its class, *Regularis Concordia* is based on the Rule of St Benedict; unlike them, it was drawn up in response to a specific need at a Synodal Council convened by royal authority' (Symons 1975, 43).

4   See the provisions of the *Proœmium* to the *Concordia* (*Regularis Concordia*, 1–9).

5   *Regularis Concordia*, 2; Keynes 1999, 49.

6   *Regularis Concordia*, Introduction, xxiii.

or more probably imposing, stricter adherence to their precepts.[1]
Vernacular versions of both may have been introduced at Shaftesbury
by Herelufu, though to what extent she was active in reforming her
house, if at all, remains conjectural. Her commemoration in the New
Minster and Hyde Abbey 'Liber vitæ', and the *Anglo-Saxon Chronicle*, as
noted, may obliquely commemorate her otherwise unacknowledged
achievements here.

    **7 'Æthelfreda'[2] (for Æthelflæd?, Æthelthryth?), 'Alfrida', occ.
1001, 1009?**[3] A doubtful late (eleventh-century) hybrid name-form,
perhaps intended for Æthelflæd or Æthelthryth,[4] from the post-
Conquest *Passio* of King Edward the Martyr (attributed to Goscelin
of Canterbury and thus dated 1070 x 1080, probably shortly after
1075). Here, a certain Æthelfreda is named as abbess (... *uirginem
Æthelfredam quæ ceteris inibi* [Shaftesbury] *Deo famulantibus præest* ...)
present at the translation of the relics of King Edward the Martyr
from the north side of the high altar to the sanctuary of the abbey

1   *Regularis Concordia*, Introduction, xxiii, n. 2; Meyer 1981, 353; see also
Keynes 1999, 47. The translation of the Holy Rule is believed to be
the work of St Æthelwold. It is of interest to note here another English
version by a later bishop of Winchester, Richard Fox, or Foxe (d. 1528),
whose translation for the nuns of his diocese appeared in 1516–17 at
the request of the abbesses of Romsey, Wherwell and the Nunnaminster,
Winchester, and the prioress of Hartley Wintney (Cist.). Two copies
of this rare work (London: Richard Pynson, in-2°) survive: *Lbl* General
Reference Collection G.10245; *Obl* Arch. A. d. 15 (*ESTC* S110729; Bell,
1995, 168). Previous to the Reformation the Bodleian copy belonged
to Margaret Stanburne (Staynburn), prioress of Stamford (Lincs, Ben.)
from 1523 to 1529 (for whom, see *HRH* 3, 694; 'Houses of Benedictine
nuns: The priory of St Michael, Stamford', in R. M. Serjeantson and W. R.
D. Adkins (eds.), *VCH Northamptonshire* 2 (London: Constable & Co. Ltd,
1906), 98–101, at 100–1).

2   *EKM*, 12; *VCH Dorset* 2, 79a, *Alfrida*, following Hutchins 1868, 27, and,
ultimately, Brompton, *Chronicon* 10 *sub anno* 1001; Keynes 1999, 52, with
n. 125; Foot 2000 2, 168, with n. 3. See also *EKM*, xii.

3   The other date, 1009, given by *VCH Dorset* 2, 79a, after Hutchins 1868,
27, is difficult to substantiate (cf. Foot 2000 2, 168 n. 3).

4   I am indebted to Dr Simon Keynes of Trinity College, Cambridge, for
his observation on this name: 'Æthelfreda ... not a credible name, of
course, though presumably Æthelflæd' (personal communication with
the author). Æthelthryth as a possibility has also been suggested (Keynes
1999, 69 n. 2).

church on 20 June 1001 by St Wulfsige (Wulfsin, Wulsin),[1] bishop of
Sherborne (993-1002), Elfsinus *præsul* and other assembled prelates.[2]
There is a certain vagueness about Elfsinus (*magnæ sanctitatis*) in the
Passio, who has been identified with the abbot Ælfsige of the New
Minster, Winchester (938-1007) commemorated in the New Minster
and Hyde Abbey 'Liber vitæ'.[3] Significantly, Æthelfreda (or rather
the correct Old English form of her name) is not mentioned in King
Æthelred's charter of 1001 granting the *cœnobium* of Bradford-on-
Avon with lands to Shaftesbury Abbey,[4] the largest and most valuable
of its Domesday possessions. By contrast, Wulfsige (as Wlsige)
episcopus appears well up as ninth in the witness list,[5] with Ælfsige
(as Alfsige) *abbas* being represented by one of two of that name and
style, the other being the abbot of Ely (996 x 999-1012 x 1016), also
named in the 'Liber vitæ',[6] further down as twenty-fourth or twenty-
seventh.[7] The editors of the first volume of *Heads of Religious Houses*,[8]
overlooking or disregarding the *Passio*, omit Æthelfreda, but there
certainly appears to have been an abbess in 1001 according to early
Shaftesbury tradition, perhaps Æthelflæd or Æthelthryth, even if her
name was subsequently confused. The fifteenth-century Cistercian
chronicler John of Brompton calls her Alfrida, which seems to be the
only known reference to her apart from her occurrence in the *Passio*.[9]

8 Leveva (Leueua, Leofgifu?),[10] *fl.* -1066 x 1074? The Somerset
Domesday survey records possession by St Edward's Church

1   *EKM*, 12; Keynes 2005, 53–7; and Rushforth 2005 for variant forms of
     Wulfsige's name.

2   *EKM*, 12; Ridyard, 49–5c, 156, 171. See also *supra* p. 41 n. 6 for the cult
     of St Edward the Martyr.

3   *EKM*, 12; PASE (Ælfsige 81); Birch, 31; Keynes 1996, 90a, fol. 20v.

4   Kelly, 114–22 (no. 29).

5   Including Æthelred *rex*, who heads the list (ibid., at 116–17).

6   PASE (Ælfsige 82); Birch, 61; Keynes 1996, 96a, fol. 27r.

7   Kelly, 114–22 (no. 29), at 117.

8   *HRH* 1, 219.

9   See *supra* p. 50 nn. 2–3, and Foot 2000 2, 168, with n. 3.

10   PASE (Leofgifu 5); *HRH* 1, 219; Freeman 4 (1876) *The Reign of William
     the Conqueror*, 40 n. 3; *VCH Dorset* 2, 79a; Foot 2000 2, 168; Chandler, 18,
     44.

[Shaftesbury Abbey] of an estate of five hides at [Abbas] Combe (*Comba*) in that county,[1] which the Exeter Domesday Book mentions was held by Leveva the abbess (*Leueua abbatissa*) from King Edward in 1066,[2] perhaps to be identified, though this is not certain, with the Leveva *abbatissa* who held (*tenuit*) a church at Reading (*Reddinges*) with eight hides valued at £9 from King Edward in the Berkshire Domesday previous to this date.[3] An abbess of Reading, Leofrun,[4] is named in the New Minster and Hyde Abbey 'Liber Vitæ' next after Herelufu (**6**) indicating a women's religious community there by the early eleventh century, but it seems to have disappeared between the Conquest and 1086,[5] when the Domesday survey was made. It had long ceased to exist by 1121, when a new house (Reading Abbey, Clun.) was founded by Henry I, as recorded by William of Malmesbury.[6] The dissolved pre-Conquest minsters of Leominster (Herefs) and Cholsey (Berks, now Oxon) were transferred to Reading Abbey by charter of Henry I in 1125.[7] Leominster,[8] previously a nunnery, henceforth became a

1   *GDB* 1, fol. 91rb.

2   *EDB*, fol. 193rb.

3   *GDB* 1, fol. 60ra.

4   Birch, 58; Keynes 1996, 95a, fol. 26r; Foot 2000 1, 157, 170 n. 84, and 2, 146. The 'Liber Vitæ' dates from 1031 (Keynes 1996, 15a, 66a).

5   Foot 2000 2, 145–7. This community may, however, have disappeared as early as 1006 during the Viking depredations of this part of the Thames Valley, when Wallingford (Oxon) was burnt (*ASC* E 1006; *VCH Berkshire* 2 (1907), 62–73, at 62).

6   *GP* 1, 304–5 (ii. 89), with note *GP* 2, 138; *GR* 1, 746–7 (v. 413), with note *GR* 2, 377–8; John of Worcester, *Chronicle* 2, 539–41 ([(iiii) 1065 *sub anno* 1043]), whose source for Reading was William; *VCH Berkshire* 2, 62–73, at 62; Foot 2000 2, 146. William seems to imply that the new abbey was built on the site of the defunct nunnery (*GP* 1, 304–5 [ii. 89]). On topographical and uncertain archaeological evidence, however, the early minster (said to date from the ninth or tenth century) may have been on the site of the parish church of St Mary a little to the west of the medieval abbey (Astill, 'Berkshire', 58, 67, 70 with map (no. 27), 72).

7   *VCH Berkshire* 2, 62–73, at 62. Cholsey Abbey was founded by King Æthelred II *c*.994 to provide for the soul of his murdered half-brother, King Edward the Martyr (Yorke 2003, 173).

8   Foot 2000 2, 103–7.

dependency of Reading, receiving its first prior in 1139.[1] Leveva had died, or had been deposed by 1074, when she is presumed to have been succeeded by Eulalia (9), beginning a new era in the history of Shaftesbury Abbey.

9 Eulalia (Eularia),[2] **1074-1106/7? x -1113?** The first known Norman abbess of Shaftesbury during whose rule the convent church was rebuilt, Eulalia is also notable for having the name of an early fourth-century Spanish virgin-martyr, who had a considerable cult in pre-Conquest England. The *festum* of St Eulalia of Merida was on 10 December,[3] with her possible and less widely occurring *translatio* on 12 February.[4] Both feasts are included in a late eleventh-century

1   *HRH* 1, 93.

2   *AM* 2, 30 (*sub anno* 1074, as *Eulalia*); *Anselmi opera* 4, 67–8 (*Ep.* 183, dated 1094), 5, 274–5 (*Ep.* 337, dated –September 1104) and 347–8 (*Ep.* 403, dated +August 1106); Delisle 1866, 177–279 (XXXVI: *Rouleau funèbre de Mathilde, fille de Guillaume le Conquérant, abbesse de la Sainte-Trinité de Caen, 1113*), at 190 (no. 18, as *Eulalia*), and 281–344 (XXXVIII: *Rouleau mortuaire du bienheureux Vital, abbé de Savigni, 1122* [with facsimile version, Delisle 1909]), at 338 (no. 187, as *Eulalia*); *HRH* 1, 219, 295; *VCH Dorset* 2, 79a; RCHME *Dorset 4 North*, 58b; Ridyard, 172–3 n. 130; Foot 2000 2, 168; Chandler, 44, 47–8, 62, 66; Yorke 2003, 9; Stacy, xii, 34–6 no. 1, 37–40 no. 4. *VCH Dorset* 2, 79a, follows *Monasticon* 2, 473b, and its source Hutchins 1774 2, 412 (see also Hutchins 1868, 27a) in putting Eustachia *tempore incerto* after Eulalia, but she appears never to have existed and is therefore rightly omitted by the editors of *Heads of Religious Houses* (*HRH* 1, 219). Eustachia may be a misread duplication of Eulalia, since she occurs in no known primary source, and her occurrence must therefore be deemed mistaken.

3   *BHL* 2699–2703; see also *ODS*, 184b–185a. The feast occurs in seventeen of the twenty-seven calendars, mainly monastic, listed by Rushforth 2008: nos. 1, 4 [Wormald 1934, no. 1], 6 [Wormald 1934, no. 2], 7 [Wormald 1934, no. 4], 12 [Wormald 1934, no. 15], 13 [Wormald 1934, no. 6], 14 [Wormald 1934, no. 9], 15 [Wormald 1934, no. 10], 16 [Wormald 1934, no. 3], 17 [Wormald 1934, no. 20], 18 [Wormald 1934, no. 19], 19 [Wormald 1934, no. 14], 20 [Wormald 1934, no. 18], 21 [Wormald 1934, no. 17], 22 [Wormald 1934, no. 16], 25 [Wormald 1934, no. 8], 27 [Wormald 1934, no. 7].

4   Rushforth 2008, nos. 7 [Wormald 1934, no. 4], 9 [Wormald 1934, no. 5], 20 [Wormald 1934, no. 18], 27 [Wormald 1934, no. 7]. This may, however, represent the *festum* of St Eulalia of Barcelona noted by the Bollandists (*BHL* 2693–5), though the two saints may be one and the same (*ODS*, 185a). To compound the confusion other feasts of St Eulalia

Salisbury (Old Sarum) calendar,[1] though neither was observed in the Sarum rite as it subsequently evolved, indicating an apparent decline of her cult in England reflected also in their absence from the calendar of the Shaftesbury Psalter.[2]

Eulalia may be identified with the Shaftesbury nun of that name featuring in a twelfth-century account of a miracle of the Blessed Virgin, who admonishes her to recite the *Ave Maria* at the end of each of her daily psalms with less haste.[3] She also occurs, as abbess, in an apparently spurious charter of William II ('Rufus'), 1089 (... *Eularia abbatissa superstite* ...),[4] being named as former abbess in charters of Henry I, 1127? (... *Eularie abbatisse* ...),[5] and Stephen, 1136 (... *Eulalie abbatisse* ...).[6] Nothing is known of Eulalia's background, or of her Norman family and associations, apart from a relative (*cognatum*) named Thomas mentioned as a tenant of the monastery's alienated

occur on 11 February (Rushforth 2008, no. 16 [Wormald 1934, no. 3]); 26 March (ibid., no. 16 [Wormald 1934, no. 3]); 30 March (ibid., nos. 4 [Wormald 1934, no. 1], 20 [Wormald 1934, no. 18]); 31 March (ibid., no. 13 [Wormald 1934, no. 6]); and 12 December (ibid., no. 6 [Wormald 1934, no. 2]).

1   Rushforth 2008, no. 27 [Wormald 1934, no. 7].

2   *Lbl* Lansdowne MS 383, *s.* xii, second quarter (Ker, *MLGB*, 177; Kauffmann 1975, 82–4, no. 48, with plates 131–4; Bell 1995, 166, no. 5; Kauffmann 2001). The calendar occupies fols. 3r–8v of the manuscript. The absence of these two feasts contrasts with the inclusion of two of St Mary of Egypt (*BHL* 5415–21), fol. 4v, uncommon in later calendars (2 and 9 April, the latter in red majuscules perhaps representing a *translatio*, though the date would also coincide with the *festum* octave, in which case the prominence given to it is unusual).

3   The account, which begins *Fertur fuisse apud sanctum eduuardum sceftonie quedam sanctimonialis femina supra omnes que ibi habitabant sanctitate et religione famosissima*, occupies fols. 87r–v of *Ccc* MS 042, a twelfth-century (second quarter) *Vitæ sanctorum* from Dover Priory (Ben.), Kent. The entire manuscript may be viewed online, https://parker.stanford.edu/parker/catalog/kd968dg9386. *Lbl* Cotton Cleopatra MS C. x, fols. 101r–144v, is a twelfth-century collection of miracles of the Blessed Virgin, with the same story of Eulalia on fol. 136v (Ward & Herbert 2 (1893), 600–18, at 614).

4   *RRA-N* 1, 80 no. 309; Stacy, 34–6 no. 1.

5   *RRA-N* 2, 346–7 no. 155; Stacy, 37–40 no. 4.

6   *RRA-N* 3, 301 no. 818.

Wiltshire estates at Bradford-on-Avon, Atworth and Donhead, which, together with other property, the abbess Emma (1121/2? x 1127?-1135?), **27**, deraigned (*disrationavit*) before King Henry I at Eling in Hampshire.[1]

    10 Aileva (Æthelgifu, Elveva),[2] occ. *c.*1086 (+1089?), d. -1113? Together with Aubrey (Albereda) de Bosco Rohardi (**11**), Aileva was one of a number of otherwise anonymous girls or young women, who entered Shaftesbury Abbey as novices with dowries comprising land, urban property and spiritualities donated by their immediate families or relatives after the Conquest. Their sponsors were generally Norman barons and landowners principally from the south-west representing the new post-Conquest service nobility, a number of whom can be identified from Domesday Book as holding estates in 1086. Further afield, donors from Devon and East Anglia are recorded, while others from Winchester, Bristol and London (*quidam mercator de London*), members of a rising mercantile class, displayed a similar interest in this affluent nunnery as a permanent abode for their unmarried daughters. Most of the endowments were made by the father *cum filia sua*, though the names of most of the daughters are omitted. In two instances only are they mentioned (Aileva and Aubrey de Bosco Rohardi). Aileva, who may have become a nun after 1089, may be the Aileva *monacha* named in the post-Conquest endowments to Shaftesbury confirmed by Henry I in 1121/2? (*rectius c.*1127?).[3] If a further identification with Aileva (**19**) can be made, then she was evidently dead by 1113.

    11 Aubrey (Albereda) de Bosco Rohardi,[4] occ. *c.*1086 x -1113? (or 1121, perhaps *c.*1127 x 1130+). A relative (*cognata*) of Gundreda, who donated a church (*capella*) with its land and tithes at Broughton Gifford (Wilts) on Aubrey's becoming a nun of Shaftesbury. The toponym represents the village, now commune, of Bosc-le-Hard south of Dieppe (*département* Seine-Maritime, *arrondissement* Rouen).

---

1   *RRA-N* 2, 346–7 no. 155; 3, 301 no. 818. Late Latin *disrationare* (Old French *deraisnier*), a technical, but archaic legal term for defending or proving a claim at law.

2   Cooke 1990, 31, 32 (Table 1, no. 18), 43.

3   *RRA-N* 2, 346–7 no. 155, at 346 (… *cum quadam monacha Aileva nomine* …); Stacy, 37–40 (no. 4), at 37.

4   Cooke 1990, 31, 32 (Table 1, no. 16), 33; Stacy, 37–40 (no. 4), at 39–40.

Aubrey may have been related to the brothers William and Roger de Bosco Rohardi, Domesday tenants of Robert de Tosny. If Aubrey can be identified with the prioress Aubrey (**13**), then she was evidently dead by 1113.

12 Agnes,[1] prioress, d. -1113. Perhaps succeeded by Aubrey (**13**).

13 Aubrey (Albereda),[2] prioress, d. -1113.

14 Rotza,[3] d. -1113.

15 Adeliza,[4] d. -1113.

16 Cecilia,[5] d. -1113.

17 Susanna,[6] d. -1113.

18 Aluvena,[7] d. -1113.

19 Aileva (Æthelgifu, Elveva),[8] d. -1113. Perhaps to be identified with Aileva (**10**). Aileva and the small group of other English names here (**20**, **22-4**) contrast with the predominantly Norman names (**12-18**, **21**, **25-6**) mentioned in the Caen obituary roll,[9] and may represent some of the otherwise mainly anonymous girls or young women, who professed as nuns of Shaftesbury from *c.*1083. If Aileva was not among these and cannot be identified with Aileva (**10**), then she, together with Ediva (**20**), Eldeva (**22**), Edith (**23**), and Ediva (**24**), may have belonged to the late pre-Conquest English community at Shaftesbury now diminished by age.

1   Delisle 1866, 177–279 (XXXVI), at 190 (no. 18), and 281–344 (XXXVIII), at 338 (no. 187, as *Agnete priore*).

2   Delisle 1866, 177–279 (XXXVI), at 190 (no. 18, but not named as prioress), and 281–344 (XXXVIII), at 338 (no. 187, as *Albereda priore*).

3   Delisle 1866, 177–279 (XXXVI), at 190 (no. 18).

4   Ibid.

5   Ibid.

6   Ibid.

7   Ibid.

8   Ibid.

9   Only the abbess Eulalia (**9**), and the prioresses Agnes (**12**) and Albereda (**13**) are mentioned by name in the later (1122) Savigny obituary roll (Delisle 1866, 281–344 (XXXVIII) at 338, no. 187). The other nuns are remembered simply as *et ceteris sororibus defunctis*.

20 Ediva (Eadgifu),[1] d. -1113.

21 Savia,[2] d. -1113.

22 Eldeva (Ælfgifu?, Elgiva/Elfgiva?),[3] d. -1113.

23 Edith (Editha, Eadgitha, Eadgiða),[4] d. -1113.

24 Ediva (Eadgifu),[5] d. -1113.

25 Benigna,[6] d. -1113.

26 Adelaisa,[7] d. -1113.

27 Emma,[8] **1121/2? x 1127?- 1135/6?** Named as abbess and as former abbess in charters of Henry I (1121/2? *rectius c.*1127?), and Stephen (1136), suggesting that she had died by or during 1135.[9]

28 Juliana,[10] almoner (*elemosinaria de sancto Eduardo*), occ. 1130, when excused payment to the Exchequer of 4 shillings (*solidi*) Danegeld on two hides in Dorset. At the same time, the burgesses of Shaftesbury were excused payment of 40s aid (*de auxilio burgorum*) on account of their poverty (*pro paupertate eorum*).

29 Cecily (Cecilia),[11] **c.1135/6?-c.1158?** Third daughter of Robert fitz Hamon (d. 1107), lord of Gloucester and Glamorgan, who refounded Tewkesbury as an abbey at the instigation of his wife Sybil

---

1 Delisle 1866, 177–279 (XXXVI), at 190 (no. 18).

2 Ibid.

3 Ibid.

4 Ibid.

5 Ibid.

6 Ibid.

7 Ibid.

8 *HRH* 1, 219; *CRR 1201–1203*, 64; *VCH Dorset* 2, 74b, 79a; Stacy [xii] with n. 3.

9 *RRA-N* 2, 346–7 no. 155, 3, 301 no. 818; Stacy, 37–40 no. 4, at 37, 39.

10 Hunter, 16.

11 *Monasticon* 2, 473b; *HPH* 1, 219; *VCH Dorset* 2, 79a; Stacy [xii] with n. 3. The first three of these references precede Emma (**27**) by Cecily (**29**), giving her date of appointment as 1107, but Stacy's order is to be preferred.

in 1102.[1] Her sister Hawise was abbess of Wilton, 1160 x 1179,[2] while their elder sibling Mabel (Mabilia), countess of Gloucester, died in 1157.[3]

30 Mary,[4] *c.*1158? x *c.*1170?-1216. Occ. *c.*1170? x 18 November 1184,[5] 5 June 1194 x 5 September 1216 (by which time she was dead).[6] Daughter of Geoffrey V (Plantagenet), count of Anjou, and thus illegitimate half-sister of Henry II. The suggestion that Mary may be identified with the poet Marie de France,[7] *fl.* 1160-1215 (described by Legge as 'a thorny subject ... best left out of account'[8]), is not now generally accepted.

31 'J.' (Johanna, Joan),[9] **1216-1223?** Sub-prioress of Shaftesbury; el. abbess -29 November 1216;[10] conf. and bl. +29 November 1216;[11] d. -23 June 1223, when licence to elect without reason for the vacancy was granted.[12]

32 Amice Russell,[13] **1223-1242.** Sacristan of Shaftesbury; el. abbess +23 June 1223;[14] roy. ass. 3 July 1223;[15] conf. and bl. +3 July 1223; d. -11 September 1242, when licence to elect without reason for the

1   *Monasticon* 2, 53b, 60b; *VCH Gloucestershire* 2 (1907), 61.

2   *VCH Wiltshire* 3, 241a, 242a; *HRH* 1, 222, 297.

3   *AM* 1, 48; *HRH* 1, 222.

4   *HRH* 1, 219; *CRR 1196–1201*, 472; *VCH Dorset* 2, 74b, 79a; Bullock-Davies; Chandler, 65; Stacy [xii] with n. 5.

5   *EEA Salisbury* 18 (*1078–1217*), 102 no. 133.

6   Ibid., 199–200 no. 238. *HRH* 1, 219 gives her *floruit* as 1174 x 1188, and 'frequently to 1215 x 16'.

7   Proposed by Fox 1910 and *idem* 1911.

8   Legge, 49.

9   *HRH* 1, 219, and 2, 605; *CPL 1198–1304*, 49, 61–2; *CPR 1216–25*, 7, 12, 376; *VCH Dorset* 2, 77a note 78, 79a.

10 *CPR 1216–25*, 7.

11 Ibid., 12.

12 Ibid., 376.

13 *HRH* 2, 605; *CPL 1198–1304*, 49, 61–2; *CPR 1216–25*, 376; *CCR 1242–47*, 75, 77; *VCH Dorset* 2, 77a n. 78, 79a.

14 *CPR 1216–25*, 376.

15 Ibid.

vacancy was granted,[1] followed by another on 13 October that year apparently superseding the first one.[2] Amice is to be identified with the nun 'A.', sacristan, named in 1217-19, whose claim for election as abbess was initially declared void by the pope in favour of 'J.' (**31**).[3] The convent was without a prioress as late as November after Amice's death, when the royal assent was withheld until one was appointed. This was eventually granted in October the following year after Agnes Longespée (**38**) had been chosen as abbess from outside the convent, ignoring the intervening disputed elections of Agnes de Ferrers (**41**) and Constance Saunzaver (**37**) in July-September. Amice is named in a royal mandate of 10 January 1244 concerning the custody of her jewels directed to be delivered under seal to the warden of Tarrant Abbey (Dorset, Cist. nuns) for the use of that house.[4]

33 Maud (Matillis) de Baillol' (Balliol), occ. 6 October 1242. Maud resided (*moram fecit*) at Wherwell (Hants) by licence of the abbess (Amice Russell, **32**), now deceased, for reasons unspecified, but the convent of Shaftesbury is now directed by royal mandate to readmit her with sustenance and other necessities (*victualia et alia necessaria*) provided.[5]

34 Margery de London,[6] occ. 30 September 1243, with Mary de Hastinges (**35**), Clarice de Mere (**36**) and Agnes de Ferrers (**41**) as proctors of the prioress and convent, receiving and returning the royal licence to elect a new abbess following the death of Amice Russell.

35 Mary de Hastinges, occ. 30 September 1243.

36 Clarice (Claricia) de Mere, occ. 30 September 1243.

37 [**Constance Saunzaver**]. Nun of Shaftesbury; elected abbess,

---

1   *CPR 1232–47*, 324.

2   Ibid., 329–30.

3   *CPL 1198–1304*, 49, 61–2.

4   Ibid., 416. The Holy Rule regards private ownership of goods as a *vitium*, a vice or evil practice (*RB*, 230–1 c. 33, *Si quid debeant monachi proprium habere*). What it would have made of the possession of jewels, by a head of house at that, may be left to the imagination.

5   *CCR 1237–42*, 477.

6   *CPR 1232–47*, 396. The prioress had sought new licence to elect on 30 July 1243 (*HRH* 2, 605).

but never appointed.[1] Occ. 30 September 1243, when her election following the renunciation by Agnes de Ferrers (**41**) was quashed by the bishop's commissaries pending further licence to elect.[2]

38 Agnes Longespée (Longespee, Lungespe, Lungespee),[3] **1243-1246.** Nun of Wherwell (Hants);[4] el. abbess 11 September x 9 October 1243;[5] roy. ass. 9 October 1243;[6] conf. and bl. +9 October 1243; d. -14 May 1246, when licence to elect without reason for the vacancy was granted.[7] Agnes probably belonged to the family of the earls of Salisbury. If so, she may have been related to William Longespée II (d. 1250)[8] and his youngest brother Nicholas Longespée (d. 1297), treasurer of Salisbury Cathedral from 1274 to 1291, when he was elected bishop.[9]

39 Wimark (Wimarka) Cusin (Cosyn?),[10] occ. 14 May 1246, with Emma de Portibus (**40**) as proctors of the prioress and convent, receiving and returning the royal licence to elect a new abbess following the death of Agnes Longespée. The chaplain William Cosyn, who, with the consent of the abbess, Juliana de Bauceyn (**44**),

1   *HRH* 2, 605; *CPR 1232–47*, 396; *CCR 1242–7*, 28.

2   *CPR 1232–47*, 396.

3   *HRH* 2, 605; *CPR 1232–47*, 324, 329–30, 397, 416, 480; *VCH Dorset* 2, 79b.

4   For the abbey of Holy Cross and St Peter, Wherwell, a late tenth-century house traditionally founded by Ælfthryth (d. 17 November 1002) to expiate for her alleged complicity in the death of her stepson, King Edward the Martyr, see *GP* 1, 276–7 (ii. 78. 7), with notes *GP* 2, 119, and 296–7; *GR*, 1, 258–9 (ii. 157. 3) with note *GR* 2, 138, 266–7; *Monasticon* 2, 634–43; *VCH Hampshire* 2, 132–7; Meyer 1977, 57–61; Coldicott, 15–19; Foot 2000 1, 4, 6, 13, 92, 159, 161, 163–4 *et passim*, and especially 2, 215–19.

5   *CPR 1232–47*, 324, 397.

6   Ibid., 324, 397.

7   Ibid., 480.

8   *VCH Wiltshire* 3, 305a; Lloyd, 'Longespée'. William I, third earl of Salisbury, died in 1226 (Strickland, 'Longespée') and William III in 1257 (*VCH Wiltshire* 3, 308a).

9   *VCH Wiltshire* 3, 166a; *EEA Salisbury* 36 (*1229–62*), lx–lxii; Kemp, 'Longespée'.

10   *CPR 1232–47*, 480.

and convent established a chantry with two priests at St Anne's altar (*iuxta altare sancte Anne*) in the abbey church in 1273 to celebrate for his soul, those of his parents, all his benefactors, and all the faithful departed, as well as for the abbess and convent, may have been of the same family.[1]

40 Emma de Portibus (de la Porte), occ. 14 May 1246.

41 Agnes de Ferrers (de Ferrariis, Ferere, de la Ferere, Ferrere),[2] **1247-?1258.** Nun of Shaftesbury; el. abbess (1) +30 July 1243[3] (renounced on account of her alleged blood relationship with William Marsh (de Marisco, or Mariscis) the traitor in favour of Constance Saunzaver, whose election was quashed by the bishop's commissaries on 30 September pending further licence to elect, leaving the abbey void), (2) +17 October 1246;[5] roy. ass. 9 January 1247, with temps. restored 29 January 1247[6] (all suspicion regarding Agnes apparently having been lifted by this time[7]); conf. and bl. 4 March 1247;[8] d. -13 May 1258.[9] In 1257 Agnes, who may have belonged to the family of the earls of Derby,[10] was summoned to Chester by the king to fulfil obligation of knight-service in support of the campaign

1   *EEA Salisbury* 37 (*1263–97*), 362–5 (no. 287). Cosyn may have been one of the four secular chaplains (*capellani*) serving Shaftesbury Abbey known as prebendaries in the fourteenth century, whose offices originated in pre-Conquest times (ibid., at 365n.).

2   *HRH* 2, 605; *CCR 1242–7*, 28, 424; *CPR 1232–47*, 396, 484, 489, 495, 497; *CPR 1247–58*, 629; *Monasticon* 2, 473b; Hutchins 1868, 27; *VCH Dorset* 2, 79b; Powicke, 60–1; Wormald & Giles, 518.

3   *HRH* 2, 650 (under [**Constance Saunzaver**]).

4   *CPR 1232–47*, 396. An account of the Marsh, or de Marisco family and their association with Lundy Island is by Langham, 50 ff.

5   *CPR 1232–47*, 480.

6   Ibid., 495, 497.

7   *HRH* 2, 605.

8   From the calendar of *Cfm* MS 2-1957 (the Shelford *horæ*), fol. 4r, *Dies benedictionis agnetis de la ferere abbatisse* (Wormald & Giles, 518).

9   *CPR 1247–58*, 629. The abbey was void by this date, licence to elect without reason for the vacancy being granted on 18 May (ibid., 630).

10   Agnes may have been related to the fifth earl, William III de Ferrers (d. 1254), who was succeeded by his son Robert de Ferrers as sixth (Maddicott , 'Ferrers')

against Llywelyn ap Gruffudd, prince of Wales, which was performed by two knights and two serjeants-at-arms accounted as the equivalent of three of the seven knights assessed as due from the abbess after 1156.[1] The provision of four armed men by this time suggests that this was a cheaper option than paying the statutory Exchequer fine.

42 Eufemia,[2] occ. 18 May 1258, with Amice (**43**) as proctors of the prioress and convent, receiving and returning the royal licence to elect a new abbess following the death of Agnes de Ferrers.

43 Amice, occ. 18 May 1258.

44 Juliana de Bauceyn (Bauscan, Bauzan, Bauzeyn),[3] **1258-1279.** Nun of Shaftesbury; el. abbess +18 May 1258;[4] roy. ass. 23 May 1258, with temps. restored 30 May 1258;[5] conf. 29 May and bl. -4 June 1258;[6] d. 14 April 1279.[7] In 1277, twenty years after Agnes de Ferrers, Juliana also received the royal summons to provide knight-service for the Welsh wars. Entered in red in the calendar of the twelfth-century Winchester, or St Swithun's Psalter,[8] which was acquired by Shaftesbury

---

1   *VCH Dorset* 2, 75b. The *servitium debitum* was originally ten knights on which scutage was paid in 1156. The abbess refusing to acknowledge more than seven, a reduced obligation with concessions was eventually recognized by Henry III in 1233, when Amice Russell (**32**) was abbess (Williams, 215–16, with nn. 11–12).

2   *CPR 1247–58*, 630.

3   *HRH* 2, 605; *CPR 1247–58*, 630-1; *CPR 1272–81*, 307; *CPR 1266–72*, 38; *Monasticon* 2, 473b; Hutchins 1868, 27; *VCH Dorset* 2, 79b.

4   *CPR 1247–58*, 630.

5   Ibid., 630, 631.

6   *EEA Salisbury* 36 (*1229–62*), 256–7 (no. 198). The certificate confirming the election was granted by the bishop of Salisbury [Giles de Bridport] (*HRH* 2, 605). This was followed shortly after by Juliana's consecration at Bromehill Priory (Norfolk, Aug.), notwithstanding an earlier synodal constitution [see *supra* p. 28 n. 1] requiring an elected head of house in the diocese of Salisbury to receive benediction by the bishop nowhere else than in the cathedral (*SBca* Press I, Box 17, Shaftesbury/1: letters patent of J[uliana], abbess elect of Shaftesbury, to the dean and chapter acknowledging this constitution and promising to do nothing in its derogation despite her consecration outside the diocese, 4 June 1258).

7   *HRH* 2, 605.

8   *Lbl* Cotton Nero MS C. iv.

Abbey probably after May 1258, is the obit of Stephen Bauceyn,[1] or Bauzan, an esteemed knight of Henry III slain in an ambush near Carmarthen during a campaign against Llywelyn ap Gruffudd on 2 or 4 June 1257, and a probable relative of Juliana. Stephen, who came from a prominent Devonshire feudal family, is remembered also as a benefactor of Torre Abbey (Devonshire, Prem.).[2] Shaftesbury Abbey fell into debt during Juliana's rule, when its tenants were requested by the Crown in 1267 to grant aid to relieve losses occasioned by the recent barons' war against the king.[3] A special prayer for Juliana during her life and for her soul after death, together with remembrance at masses, was directed with her permission to be said daily in the chantry established by the chaplain William Cosyn in 1273.[4]

45 Denise (Dionysia) de Maundevile (Mandeville),[5] occ. 22 April 1279, with Margaret de Columbariis (**46**) and Maud de Gurnay (**47**) as proctors of the prioress and convent, receiving and returning the royal licence to elect a new abbess following the death of Juliana de Bauceyn.

46 Margaret de Columbariis (du Colombier?)[6] occ. 22 April 1279, 30 January 1290 (see **50**), and 5 October 1291 (see **52**).

47 Maud (Matilda) de Gurnay, occ. 22 April 1279.

48 Laurentia de Muscegros (Mucegros),[7] **1279-1290**. Nun of Shaftesbury; el. abbess +22 April 1279;[8] roy. ass. 8 May 1279, with

---

1 'Obitus Stephanus Bauceyn', entered under 4 June (*Lbl* Cotton Nero MS C. iv, fol. 42v; see also Wormald 1973, 108, 125). For Bauceyn, or Bauzan, see Ridgeway, 'Bauzan'.

2 Pole, 12, 137, 272, 312, 328, 347, 516, 457.

3 *CPR 1266–72*, 38.

4 See *supra* p. 61 n. 1. Prayers were intended in perpetuity for both the abbess and convent and not just Juliana, apparently (*EEA Salisbury* 37 (*1263–97*), 362–5 (no. 287), at 365 n.1).

5 *CPR 1272–81*, 307.

6 See also *CPR 1281–92*, 339, 447.

7 *HRH* 2, 605; *CPR 1272–81*, 307, 314, 318; *CPR 1281–92*, 338; *VCH Dorset* 2, 79b.

8 *CPR 1272–82*, 307. Laurentia's election as abbess was notified to the king by the convent on 30 April 1279 (ibid., 339; *EEA Salisbury* 37 (*1263–97*), 438–9 (no. 370), at 439n.).

temps. restored   5 July 1279;[1] conf. 14 June 1279;[2] d. -23 January 1290.[3]

49 Agnes de Dorset,[4] occ. June 1279, with Alice (Alicia) de Lavington (Lavinton'), **58**, as proctors of the prioress and convent, notifying the bishop of the election of Laurentia de Muscegros as abbess, which has formerly [on 8 May] received the royal assent.

50 Clemence (Clementia) Russell,[5] occ. 30 January 1290, with Margaret de Columbariis (**46**) as proctors of the prioress and convent, receiving and returning the royal licence to elect a new abbess following the death of Laurentia de Muscegros. Clemence may have been descended from the same family as Abbess Amice Russell (**32**), and was perhaps related to Alice Russell, one of two nuns abducted from Wilton Abbey probably before 14 November 1284.[6]

51 Joan (Johanna) de Bridport,[7] **1290-1291**. Prioress of Shaftesbury; el. abbess +30 January 1290;[8] roy. ass. 25 February 1290, with temps. restored 27 March 1290;[9] conf. 24 March 1290;[10] d. -4 October 1291.[11] Probably of the same family as Giles de Bridport, bishop of Salisbury (1256-92), Joan's rule as abbess was of short duration, perhaps as a result of illness.[12] Her request for benediction by the bishop elsewhere than in Salisbury Cathedral 'on account of

1   *CPR 1272–81*, 314, 318.

2   *EEA Salisbury* 37 (*1263–97*), 438–9 (no. 370); *HRH* 2, 605.

3   *HRH* 2, 605. The king was notified of Laurentia's death on 30 January 1290 (*CPR 1281–92*, 339).

4   *EEA Salisbury* 37 (*1263–97*), 438–9 (no. 370).

5   *CPR 1281–91*, 339.

6   *EEA Salisbury* 37 (*1263–97*), 472–4 (no. 397, with note).

7   *HRH* 2, 605; *CPR 1281–92*, 339, 347–8, 447; *VCH Dorset* 2, 79b.

8   *CPR 1281–92*, 339.

9   Ibid., 347–8.

10 The certificate confirming the election was granted by the bishop of Salisbury's *locum tenens* Master William de la Rivere (de Ripariis): *EEA Salisbury* 37 (*1263–97*), 493–4, no. 422, with note. The bishop, William de la Corner, was overseas at the time (*EEA Salisbury* 36 (*1229–62*), 62, lxxviii, n. 340; *CPR 1281–92*, 348).

11 *HRH* 2, 605.

12 *EEA Salisbury* 37 (*1263–97*), 493–4 (no. 422, with note).

circumstances, which in time might threaten her with danger' (*propter casus qui per tractum temporis sibi cum periculo possent im[m]inere*) was refused, though subsequently this took place at the abbey church with the consent of the dean and chapter of Salisbury.[1]

52 Sybil de Bruere,[2] occ. 5 October 1291, with Margaret de Columbariis (**46**) and Sarah de Meriet (**53**) as proctors of the prioress and convent, receiving and returning the royal licence to elect a new abbess following the death of Joan de Bridport.

53 Sarah (Sarra) de Meriet,[3] occ. 5 October 1291.

54 Mabel Giffard,[4] 1291-1302. Nun of Shaftesbury; el. abbess +5 October 1291;[5] roy. ass. 22 October 1291, with temps. restored 10 November 1291;[6] conf. +22 October 1291 and bl. 20 November;[7] d. 9 September 1302. Sister of Walter Giffard, archbishop of York (1266-79), and Godfrey Giffard, bishop of Worcester (1268-1302), of a family notorious for its nepotism. Mabel is named as a beneficiary in the latter's will, 1301, to receive twelve silver dishes (*xij. scutella argentes*), together with silver salt cellars, wine pitchers, and other choice plate

---

1   *EEA Salisbury* 37 (*1263–97*), 493–4 (no. 422, with note). The letter of consent was issued by the dean and chapter to the bishop on 17 July 1290 on Joan's assurance that the law and custom of the cathedral would not be infringed in any way, and that she would offer payment to cover her dues had her consecration taken place in the cathedral (*SBca* Press I, Box 17, Shaftesbury/2).

2   *CPR 1281–92*, 447.

3   Ibid.

4   *HRH* 2, 605; *CPR 1281–92*, 447–8, 450; *CPR 1301–7*, 48, 63; *VCH Dorset* 2, 79b; Chandler, 62, 64.

5   *CPR 1281–92*, 447.

6   Ibid., 448, 450.

7   Bishop Giffard of Worcester requested the dean and chapter of Salisbury on 17 November 1291 to accede to the royal wish to allow Mabel to be consecrated as abbess at Amesbury Priory (Font.) on the same day [20 November] that the king's daughter [Mary of Woodstock, the sixth or seventh named daughter of Edward I and Eleanor of Castile] was to be veiled as a nun there (*SBca* Press I, Box 17, Shaftesbury/3). Mary had entered the convent in 1285, when, aged just seven, she was dedicated to the religious life (*VCH Wiltshire* 3, 247a), though her subsequent career as a nun evidently left much to be desired (Power, 455; *VCH Wiltshire* 3 247a).

tableware for the use of her successors in perpetuity (*ita quod in vsus successorum suarum in illo monasterio, quamdiu durent, remaneant*).[1] The Master William Giffard, who was then chaplain of Shaftesbury Abbey (*chapelain del iglise seint Edward*), and who composed a version of the Apocalypse (Book of Revelation) with prologue and commentary in Anglo-Norman rhyming verse for the nuns shortly before 1300,[2] was probably related to Mabel. Supplemented by a poem on the Seven Deadly Sins (*Les set mortel pechez*), also in Anglo-Norman, this work may have been intended as a confessional manual, versified to enable memorization (*bien eit ke les mettra ben en memoire*). William also served as rector of Litton Cheney in Dorset from 1298 to 1302, the year of Mabel's death, when his association with the nunnery seems to have ended.

55 Christine (Christina) de Bampton,[3] occ. 20 September 1302, with Cecily de Basynges (**56**) as proctors of the prioress and convent, receiving and returning the royal licence to elect a new abbess following the death of Mabel Giffard.

56 Cecily de Basynges,[4] occ. 20 September 1302.

57 [Elizabeth de Hull*e*, d. *c*.1300? x *c*.1325?]. Perhaps a nun of Shaftesbury, commemorated in an obit apparently of this date under 31 October in the calendar (fols. 3r-8v, at 7v, 'o*bitus sororis* elizabet. de hull' no*nn*a') of the twelfth-century Shaftesbury Psalter.[5]

1   *Reg. Gainsborough*, 51–2.

2   Fox 1913; Rhys; Legge, 106–7; Pächt & Alexander, no. 703, with Plate LXXI; Bell 1995, 167b. This manuscript, *Ob* MS French e. 22 (https:// medieval.bodleian.ox.ac.uk/catalog/manuscript_4894 and http://www. bodley.ox.ac.uk/dept/scwmss/wmss/medieval/chklst/chkfr.htm), is now considered to be of the late fourteenth century, making it a copy of Giffard's late thirteenth-century original produced for the nuns of Shaftesbury (cf. Bell 1995, 168). Ker, *MLGB*, 177 rejects a Shaftesbury provenance, presumably for this reason.

3   *CPR 1301–7*, 63.

4   Ibid.

5   *Lbl* Lansdowne MS 383 (see *supra* p. 54 n. 2). The last word of the obit, abbreviated as *no*ᵃ (rectius *no*ᵉ), would represent *nonna* (rectius *nonne*), a term originally used for a lay sister (see **2** Wynflæd), since Elizabeth, styled *soror* rather than *domina*, may well have been one. By this time, however, the term may have relaxed its meaning and become the equivalent of *monialis*, or *monacha*, a consecrated nun in the usual sense, in which case *soror* in preference to *domina* would be unusual (see entry *nonna* in

Elizabeth may have been related to Robert de Hull, priest and proctor of Shaftesbury Abbey, who presented the election of Margaret Aucher (**61**) as abbess to the bishop of Salisbury on 24 December 1315.[1] This is the second of three female obits (the first and third (**90**, **91**) of the fifteenth century, being under 8 April and 7 November respectively[2]), perhaps also of Shaftesbury nuns, entered in this calendar, which appears to derive from a Shaftesbury exemplar. It is uncertain whether the Psalter was originally intended for Shaftesbury use, however, despite the calendar (at fol. 4r, 'Sancti Eadwardi regis et martyris' entered prominently in red majuscules under 18 March), litany (fols. 146v-148r, at 146v, Sancte Edguarde in majuscules immediately after St Stephen protomartyr,[3] and, at 148r, St Ælfgifu (as Eluiua) last among the virgins after St Edith),[4] and prayers to all the martyrs (fol. 173r, St Edward named in majuscules), or whether it was commissioned for a private owner not necessarily having a connection with the abbey. There are grounds, indeed, for supposing that it might have been. It has been argued that the Psalter was made for Adeliza (Adelicia, or Adela) of Louvain (d. 1151),[5] second queen

Latham).

1   *Reg. Martival* 1, 412. Margaret was elected mid-September 1315, but the royal assent was not granted until the beginning of December that year, leaving the abbey void for around two and a half months.

2   Kauffmann 2001, 272. These, together with two fifteenth-century obits for priests (*Dominus Ricardus Wrangylle canon et sacerdos*, 11 October, and *Ricardus canon et sacerdos* (in red), with *bone memorie* (also in red) written in the left-hand margin, 20 October), indicate continuous use of the Psalter throughout the later Middle Ages, though where and by whom remain unknown. The nuns' obits may relate to Shaftesbury, but that is far from certain, nor can it be assumed that these two priests were associated with the abbey, perhaps as chaplains. The name Wrangylle, or Wrangle, is of Lincolnshire origin, a toponym representing the village of that name. A Richard Wrangle is recorded as a chantry chaplain in the church of St Paul's, London, in 1412 (*CPR 1408–13*, 383, 385–6), and (as Wrangylle) in the church of All Hallows, Legbourne, Lincolnshire, in 1422 (*CCR 1422–9*, 4), though they cannot be assumed to be the same person.

3   See also Morgan, 84a–87a (no. LXXVI), at 84a.

4   Ibid., at 86a. Neither Ælfgifu's *festum* (18 May) nor *inventio* (18 August) appear in the calendar.

5   Kauffmann 2001, 271–2. For Adeliza, see Round, 'Adeliza'; Huneycutt, 'Adeliza'.

consort of Henry I, whose known or assumed associations included Wilton rather than Shaftesbury (her foundation and endowment of the leper hospital (*leprosarium*) of St Giles at nearby Fugglestone some years before Henry's death on 1 December 1135,[1] and her possible temporary retirement to Wilton Abbey shortly after this time previous to her remarriage to William d'Aubigny, who became first earl of Arundel[2]). This may account for notable Wilton elements in the calendar (St Edith, *festum* 16 September, with *translatio* 3 November, both in red majuscules, fols. 7r, 8r) and litany (St Edith (as Edgitha), a young princess, preceding her grandmother St Ælfgifu, formerly a king's consort, significant in a hierarchy of liturgical intercessions, fol. 148r, as noted). In the litany of *Cfm* MS 2-1957 (fols. 58r-62r, at 60v),[3] an early sixteenth-century book of hours belonging to Dame Elizabeth Shelford (**206**), abbess of Shaftesbury, 1505-28 (a manuscript with a definite Shaftesbury provenance), this order is reversed, with St Ælfgifu (as Eluiua) taking priority over St Edith (as Editha).[4] There is a possibility, therefore, that Lansdowne MS 383, if it was made for Adeliza, was intended for her use at Wilton despite its Shaftesbury calendar, litany and prayers,[5] the prominence given to St Edward in each being perhaps not remarkable in view of his high royal status and relationship (as half-brother) to St Edith.

58 Alice (Alicia) de Lavington (Lavynton, Lavyngton) *alias* de

---

1   Strickland, *Lives* 1, 173, 193; *VCH Wiltshire* 3, 362b; Brenner, 25. Strickland, *Lives* 1, 193, follows Hoare, *History of Modern Wiltshire* (1825) in stating that Adeliza resided at the hospital after Henry's death.

2   Anon., 'Adeliza' (under *Widowhood and remarriage*) states that Adeliza retired to Wilton Abbey on Henry's death, but gives no evidence for it. According to Round, 'Adeliza', 138a, she probably withdrew to Arundel Castle (Sussex), which she held in dower for life after Henry's death. Adeliza married d'Aubigny in 1137 or 1138 (White, 'Aubigny'), when the earldom was conferred by King Stephen, who also created him earl of Lincoln *c.*1141.

3   See also Morgan, 84b–87b (no. LXXVII), at 86b.

4   Ibid., 85b–86b.

5   Kauffmann 2001, 272, suggests that the Psalter may have been produced for Adeliza while at Arundel Castle under the direction of her chaplains. In any event, its provenance is uncertain, though it (or rather its calendar, litany and prayers) clearly derives from a Shaftesbury exemplar.

Winchester (Wyntonia),[1] **1302-1315**. Prioress of Shaftesbury; el. abbess +20 September 1302;[2] roy. ass. 12 October 1302, with temps. restored 9 November 1302;[3] conf. 8 November 1302[4] and bl. 2 December 1302;[5] d. -14 September 1315.[6] Alice may have been related to John de Lavynton, or Lavyntone, clerk, who was presented to the nearby church of Melbury Abbas by Edward II on 19 September 1315,[7] a short-lived appointment revoked by royal writ just over a month later.[8] Later in the century a Cecilia de Lavington occurs as abbess of Wherwell, 1375-1412,[9] and a Felise Lavington as abbess of Wilton, 1395-?1403,[10] both of whom may have been descended from the same family as Alice. Her toponym may represent one or the other of two Wiltshire villages, West and Market Lavington, between Devizes and Salisbury.

59 Christine (Cristina) Baryl,[11] occ. 19 October 1309, when named in the bishop's letter to the abbess following a recent visitation, forbidding her to allow the nuns to venture into the town of Shaftesbury without permission, 'lest scandal arise from their various excursions, and not without negligence on your part' (*ne scandala ex multiphario illarum egressu, non sine negligencia vestra suborta*). Christine especially is not to be let out (*omnem interdici egressum*) of the convent, where she is to be confined until further notice from the bishop. Her misdemeanour is not specified and can only be guessed.

60 Denise Blunt,[12] occ. 14 September 1315, with Joan Duket

---

1   *HRH* 2, 606; *CPR 1301–7*, 64, 70; *CPR 1313–17*, 349; *VCH Dorset* 2, 79b.

2   *CPR 1301–7*, 63.

3   Ibid., 64–70.

4   *Reg. Ghent* 2, 619.

5   Ibid.

6   *CPR 1313–17*, 349. The abbey was still void on 12 October 1315 (ibid., 360–1).

7   *Reg. Martival* 1, 2.

8   Ibid., 9.

9   *VCH Hampshire* 2, 137.

10   *VCH Wiltshire* 3, 241.

11   *Reg. Ghent* 1, 374–5; *VCH Dorset* 2, 78a; Chandler, 70.

12   *CPR 1313–17*, 349. Perhaps to be identified with Denise la Blunde (**65**),

(Dukett), **70**, as proctors of the prioress and convent, receiving and returning the royal licence to elect a new abbess following the death of Alice de Lavington. Joan later became prioress and was elected abbess in 1345.

61 Margaret Aucher (Auchier),[1] **1315-1329**. Sub-prioress of Shaftesbury; el. abbess +14 September 1315;[2] roy. ass. 2 December 1315, with temps. restored 1 February 1316;[3] conf. 8 January 1316[4] and bl. 8 February 1316;[5] d. -16 June 1329.[6] Margaret was niece (*nepta*) of Godfrey Giffard, bishop of Worcester (see **54**), in whose will, 1301, she is named as a beneficiary to receive 40 shillings (*solidi*).[7]

62 Elizabeth de Favenham, occ. [29 March] 1319, when named as a beneficiary in the will of Margery de Crioll of Corby Glen (Lincs) to receive a paternoster of coral and white pearls given to the testatrix by the countess of Pembroke.[8]

63 Alice Longecote,[9] occ. 26 June 1329, with Joan Moghtheres (**64**) as proctors of the prioress and convent, receiving and returning the royal licence to elect a new abbess following the death of Margaret Aucher.

64 Joan (Johanna) Moghtheres,[10] occ. 26 June 1329.

who became abbess in 1329.

1   *HRH* 2, 606; *CPR 1313–17*, 349, 371, 382; *CPR 1327–30*, 400; *VCH Dorset* 2, 79b.

2   *CPR 1313–17*, 349.

3   Ibid., 372, 382.

4   *Reg. Martival* 1, 413.

5   *Reg. Martival* 1, 413. The calendar of *Cfm* MS 2-1957 (the Shelford *horæ*), fol. 3v, also records the blessing on this date, *Dies benedictionis domine margarete auehyet'* (Wormald & Giles, 517). The blessing was conducted in Lincoln Cathedral by the bishop of Salisbury under licence (*Reg. Martival* 1, 413, and 2, 164).

6   *HRH* 2, 606.

7   *Reg. Gainsborough*, 52.

8   *ELW*, 5; Gill, 106; Luxford, 198. The countess of Pembroke mentioned here may be Beatrice de Clermont (d. 1320), who married Aymer de Valence, 2nd earl of Pembroke before 1295 (Phillips, 5–6).

9   *CPR 1327–30*, 400.

10 Ibid.

65 Denise (Dionisia, Dionysia) la Blunde (Blounde, Blount?, Blunt?),[1] **1329-1345.** Nun of Shaftesbury; el. abbess +26 June 1329;[2] roy. ass. 8 July 1329,[3] with temps. restored 19 July 1329;[4] conf. 15 July 1329[5] and bl. 23 July 1329;[6] d. -20 August 1345.[7] Joan le Blount, prioress of Aconbury (Herefs, Aug.),[8] occ. September 1363, may have been a relative.

66 Joan (Johanna) le Despenser (Despensere),[9] c.1317-84, occ. 25 November 1343. One of nine children of the ill-fated Hugh le Despenser the younger,[10] 1st Lord Despenser (d. 1326) and Eleanor de Clare (d. 1337), Joan was the second eldest sister of Hugh le Despenser, 2nd Baron le Despenser (1308–49), lord of Glamorgan. Two of her four sisters became Gilbertine nuns, Eleanor at Sempringham (Lincs) and Margaret at Watton (Yorks). The Juliana la Despenser (Despensere), for whom a corrody at Shaftesbury was requested by the Crown in July 1310,[11] may have been a relative.

67 Isabella Quarel,[12] occ. 25 August 1345, with Ellen Rous (**68**) as proctors of the prioress and convent, receiving and returning the royal licence to elect a new abbess following the death of Denise la Blunde.

1 *HRH* 2, 606; *CPR 1327–30*, 400, 404, 412; *CPR 1343–5*, 539; *VCH Dorset* 2, 79b.

2 *CPR 1327–30*, 400.

3 Ibid., 404, the election being previously presented to the king on 3 July (*HRH* 2, 606), but *Reg. Martival* 1, 398, dates the royal assent 23 July. The bishop was notified on 6 July (*Reg. Martival* 1, 398).

4 *CPR 1327–30*, 412.

5 *Reg. Martival* 1, 398.

6 Ibid.

7 *CCR 1343–6*, 599–600.

8 *HRH* 2, 537.

9 *CPR 1343–5*, 158 (royal licence permitting Hugh II to grant the abbess and convent 10 marks rent from his Wiltshire manor of 'Brodeton' [Broughton] during Joan's lifetime, perhaps as a contribution towards her maintenance); see also *VCH Dorset* 2, 75a.

10 McKisack, 58–65, 73–7, 83–7 *et passim*.

11 *CCR 1307–13*, 328.

12 *CPR 1343–5*, 539.

68 Ellen Rous,[1] occ. 25 August 1345.

69 Agnes Turbevill (Turberville),[2] occ. 26 August 1345 (19 Edward III), when nominated as a nun by royal prerogative during the voidance of the abbey following the death of Abbess Denise la Blunde.

70 Joan (Johanna) Duket (Dukett),[3] **1345-1350**. Prioress of Shaftesbury; el. abbess +25 August 1345;[4] roy. ass. +2 September 1345,[5] with temps. restored 28 September 1345;[6] conf. 24 September 1345;[7] d. -20 June 1350.[8] Occ. 1315 as an ordinary nun (see **60**).

71 Margaret de Leukenore (Lewknor),[9] **1350-1362**. Nun of Shaftesbury; el. abbess 1 July 1350;[10] roy. ass. 5 July 1350, with temps. restored 19 July 1350;[11] conf. 17 July 1350;[12] d. 29 June 1362.[13] Perhaps related to John de Leukenore, who was steward of the household of Queen Philippa, consort of Edward III,[14] and who appears also to have served as a royal justice.[15] A Roger Leukenore likewise occurs as

1   *CPR 1343–5*, 539.

2   *CCR 1343–6*, 604; Power, 189, 192 n. 5.

3   *HRH* 2, 606; *CPR 1313–17*, 349; *CPR 1343–5*, 539, 551; *CPR 1348–5*, 548; *VCH Dorset* 2, 79b.

4   *CPR 1343–5*, 539.

5   The election was presented to the king for the royal assent on 2 September (*HRH* 2, 606).

6   *CPR 1343–5*, 551.

7   *HRH* 2, 606.

8   *CPR 1349–54*, 190.

9   *HRH* 2, 606; *CPR 1348–50*, 548, 550; *CPR 1361–4*, 224; *VCH Dorset* 2, 79b.

10 The election was presented to the king for the royal assent on 1 July (*HRH* 2, 606).

11 *CPR 1348–50*, 548, 550.

12 *HRH* 2, 606.

13 Ibid.

14 *CPR 1348–50*, 93, 106, 203, 270, 272, 284.

15 Ibid., 586. The Leukenore family had an apparently long history of royal service. A Geoffrey de Leukenore was appointed as one of two custodians of the abbey during the voidance caused by the death of Abbess Agnes de

a justice.[1] The king was notified of the death of Abbess Joan Duket by Ralph de Codeford, proctor of the prioress and convent, receiving and returning the royal licence to elect her successor, 24 June 1350.[2]

72 Joan (Johanna) Formage (Firmage, Furmage),[3] 1362-1394. Prioress of Shaftesbury; el. abbess 5 x 11 July 1362;[4] roy. ass. 16 July 1362, with temps. restored 3 August 1362;[5] conf. 30 July 1362;[6] d. 13 August 1394.[7] Named as Furmage in a charter of *Inspeximus* to the abbess and convent confirming earlier royal endowments, 21 April 1371.[8] The William Formage, together with other abbey officials, witnessing letters patent of the abbess granting a yearly pension to a clerk, 25 March 1370, confirmed by royal charter of *Inspeximus* of 20 May 1376,[9] is likely to have been a relative. Her illicit will dated 4 May 1393,[10] whose beneficiaries included several Shaftesbury nuns (**76-81, 84, 93**), was annulled by the bishop on 2 September 1394 less than a month after Joan's death,[11] all of her effects having been sequestrated

Ferrers (**41**) in 1258 (*CPR 1247–58*, 629, 631).

1   *CPR 1348–50*, 585.

2   Ibid., 548.

3   *HRH* 2, 606, and 3, 689; *CPR 1361–4*, 224, 232, 241; *CPR 1391–6*, 565; *Reg. Wyville* 2, fol. 297v; *Reg. Waltham*, 31–3 nos. 120–2; *Monasticon* 2, 473a; *VCH Dorset* 2, 77b, 78a, 79b; Power, 338; Chandler, 61–4, 67–73.

4   Licence to elect was granted on 5 July (*CPR 1361–4*, 224), with the election presented to the king for the royal assent on 11 July (*HRH* 3, 689).

5   *CPR 1361–4*, 232, 241

6   *Reg. Wyville* 2, fol. 297v.

7   *CPR 1391–6*, 565.

8   *CPR 1370–4*, 72.

9   *CPR 1374–72*, 268

10 *Reg. Waltham*, 31–2 no. 121; *HRH* 2, 606.

11 *Reg. Waltham*, 30 no. 118. Joan had an evident penchant for convent asset stripping, paying the considerable sum of £53 6s 8d (around £35,313 in today's money) for the establishment of her obit (said to have been for forty years: Hutchins 1868, 27; Sydenham, 54), together with those of her family and friends, in Salisbury Cathedral in 1375 (*SBca* Press I, Box 17, Shaftesbury/128). Like her will, these may also have been annulled by the bishop, since none appears to be included in the medieval Sarum

on 31 August and put into custody.[1]

73 Agnes de la Ryver,[2] occ. 1374 and February 1407, d. -January 1410. Agnes is said to have entered Shaftesbury Abbey at the age of seven, professing nine years later in 1374, when she left shortly after, apparently to claim an inheritance. She subsequently became the wife of Richard Clyvedon (perhaps Richard Clyvedon, or Clevedon, of Somerset[3]), who maintained in 1392 that she had never formally professed as a nun. The Henry de la Ryver of Gloucestershire, 'chivaler', together with his son Thomas and grandson Maurice, named in a royal commission to the escheator, 24 November 1409,[4] may have been relatives.

74 Margaret Tracy,[5] occ. 20 July 1377 (1 Richard II), when nominated as a nun by royal prerogative following the king's coronation. Joan de Eketon (or Oketon) was similarly nominated as a nun of Wilton a week later.[6]

75 [**Lucy Fitzherberde**]. Prioress of Shaftesbury; elected abbess, but never appointed.[7] *Congé d'élire* for the new abbess following the death of Joan Formage was granted on 26 August 1394,[8] and Lucy was duly elected early September[9] by a majority vote of the chapter, but was opposed by the king, who deemed her unsuitable to rule one of the great houses of the country, as he was to inform the bishop.[10] In consequence, the abbey remained void until 12 April the following year, when Egelina de Counteville (**81**) was appointed by the bishop

obit calendar (Wordsworth, 342–50, especially 345).

1 *Reg. Waltham,* 31 no. 120, 32–3 no. 122.

2 *Reg. Mitford,* fol. 122r; *Reg. Hallum,* 200–1 nos. 1080–1; Logan, 16, 259; Chandler, 68.

3 *CPR 1391–6,* 93, 359, 674.

4 *CPR 1408–13,* 179.

5 *CCR 1377–81,* 13.

6 *CCR 1377–8,* 12–13.

7 *CPR 1391–6,* 511; *Reg. Waltham,* 196 no. A39 n. 2; *VCH Dorset* 2, 78b.

8 *CPR 1391–6,* 479; cf. *Reg. Waltham,* 30, no. 114.

9 *HRH* 3, 689.

10 *A-NL,* 167–8 no. 112; *HRH* 3, 689.

in pursuance of the royal letter of assent.[1] Although Lucy appealed to the apostolic see against this provision on the grounds of her election by the greater part of the convent, she had omitted to present it to the bishop for confirmation within the statutory time and was thereby disqualified.[2] Lucy was sister of Lady Alice West of Hinton Martel (Dorset), in whose will, 1395, she is named as a beneficiary to receive 40 marks [£26 13s 4d].[3] Another sibling, Thomasine Blount, a nun of Romsey, was also left 40 marks.[4]

76 Joan (Johanna) Ordere,[5] occ. 4 May 1393, when named as a beneficiary in the will of Abbess Joan Formage to receive 20 shillings (*vint sould'*). Perhaps not yet formally professed, since not styled *dame*.

77 Joan (Johanna) Cros,[6] occ. 4 May 1393, when named as a beneficiary in the will of Abbess Joan Formage to receive 20 shillings (*vint sould'*). Perhaps not yet formally professed, since not styled *dame*.

78 Maud Chynham,[7] occ. 4 May 1393, when named as a beneficiary in the will of Abbess Joan Formage to receive 10 shillings (*diz sould'*) and a cloak of grey furred black cloth (*un amis de noir drap furrez de gris*).

79 Jonette Anger,[8] occ. 4 May 1393, when named as a beneficiary in the will of Abbess Joan Formage to receive 20 shillings (*vint sould'*) and two feather quilts (*deux queltes de plume*). Perhaps not yet formally professed, since not styled *dame*.

80 Jonette Usschere (Ussher),[9] occ. 4 May 1393, when named as a beneficiary in the will of Abbess Joan Formage to receive 20 shillings (*vint sould'*) and a long chest (*une longue coffre*). Perhaps not yet formally professed, since not styled *dame*.

---

1   *A-NL*, 168–9 no. 113; *HRH* 3, 689.

2   *CPL 1362–1404*, 524–5; *HRH* 3, 689.

3   *EEW*, 6.

4   Ibid.

5   *Reg. Waltham*, 31 no. 121.

6   Ibid.

7   Ibid., 31–2 no. 121.

8   Ibid.

9   Ibid.

81 Egelina de Counteville (Countvylle, Countevile, Countevyle),[1] **1395-1398.** Nun of Shaftesbury; appointed abbess by the bishop after royal letter of assent 12 April 1395,[2] with temps. restored 17 May 1395;[3] d. 30 April 1398.[4] Various forms of the name include Countvylle in a royal grant of 28 May 1397 awarding free custody of the abbey during its voidance to the prioress and convent, apart from knights' fees and advowsons customarily due to the king.[5] This confirms a similar grant made to Abbess Joan Formage in 1364, with *Inspeximus,* 1382.[6] Egelina occurs earlier (as an ordinary nun) as a beneficiary in the will of Abbess Joan Formage, 4 May 1393, to receive 20 shillings (*vint sould'*) in addition to other money.[7]

82 Alice (Alicia) Wilton,[8] occ. January 1397. The bishop was requested by the pope to restore Alice to her previous position in the abbey forfeit on account of her unchastity (she had become pregnant by a married man). She was duly reinstated after penance and absolution, when the bishop approved her eligibility for all offices in the convent except that of abbess.

83 Joan Durneford,[9] occ. 6 February 1398, when named as a recipient of a papal indult licensing the confessor of her choice to grant her plenary remission at the hour of death on condition of penance. It is uncertain whether Katherine (Katerina) Durneford, perhaps a relative of Joan, named as a beneficiary in the will of Abbess Joan Formage, 4 May 1393,[10] to receive one mark (*une marc* [13s 4d]) was a nun.

1   *HRH* 3, 689; *CPR 1391–6,* 565, 568; *CPR 1396–9,* 138; *VCH Dorset* 2, 78b, 79b.

2   *A-NL,* 168–9 no. 113; *CPR 1391–6,* 565; *HRH* 3, 689.

3   *CPR 1391–6,* 568.

4   *HRH* 3, 689.

5   *CPR 1396–9,* 152.

6   *CPR 1364–7,* 21; *CPR 1381–5,* 177.

7   *Reg. Waltham,* 31–3 nos. 120–2, 196 A39.

8   *Reg. Mitford,* fol. 122r-v, recording the bull of Boniface IX in Alice's favour (7 January 1397) and the bishop's dispensation and absolution of the same year; *VCH Dorset* 2, 78a n. 93; Power, 470 n. 3.

9   *CPL 1396–1404,* 122.

10 *Reg. Waltham,* 31 no. 121.

84 Cecily (Cecilia) Fovent,[1] **1398-1423.** Nun of Shaftesbury; el. abbess 10 x 22 May 1398;[2] roy. ass. 31 May 1398, with temps. restored 23 June 1398;[3] conf. 13 June 1398;[4] d. 1 November 1423.[5] Cecily was the daughter of Robert Osegod *alias* Fovent of Fovant, Donhead St Mary (Wilts), and Edith his wife, who gave lands in Fovant and Shaftesbury for the endowment of a chantry in the conventual church dedicated to saints Katherine, Margaret and Faith.[6] Robert Fovent was member of parliament for Shaftesbury, 1390.[7] Cecily occurs earlier (as an ordinary nun) as a beneficiary in the will of Abbess Joan Formage, 4 May 1393, to receive 20 shillings (*vint sould*).[8]

85 Catherine Brombelegh,[9] occ. 14 September 1408. Daughter of John Brombelegh of Sherborne (Dorset) nominated as a nun by the bishop of Salisbury (Robert Hallum, 1407-17) in accordance with his customary right on appointment to his see, and assigned to the tutelage of Agnes Poney (**86**), 'who is to instruct her in the regular disciplines'.[10] Eleanor Cokkyng, damsel (*domicella*), was similarly nominated as a nun of Wilton in January the following year.[11]

86 Agnes Poney (Powne),[12] occ. 14 September 1408, and 12 March 1415, when named (as Powne) as a recipient of a papal indult

1   *HRH* 3, 689–90; *CPR 1396–9*, 338, 349, 387; *CPR 1422–9*, 141; *VCH Dorset* 2, 79b.

2   Licence to elect 10 May (*CPR 1396–99*, 338); petition for the royal assent 22 May (*HRH* 3, 689).

3   *CPR 1396–9*, 349, 387.

4   *HRH* 3, 689.

5   Ibid., 690.

6   Davis *et al.*, 178b, no. 886. The deeds of gift, 1396–1407, for the endowment are recorded in an abbey cartulary (*Lbl* Egerton MS 3135, fols. 109r–118r), which also includes a copy of the form of ordination of the chantry on 20 September 1415 by Cecily Fovent added in a contemporary hand on blank leaves at fols. 100v–103v.

7   *Reg. Waltham*, 176 no. 1127.

8   Ibid., 31 no. 121.

9   *Reg. Hallum*, 138 no. 941.

10   Ibid.

11   Ibid., no. 942.

12   Ibid., no. 941.

licensing the confessor of her choice to grant her plenary remission at the hour of death on condition of penance.[1]

87 Katherine Slo,[2] prioress, occ. 29 August 1411, when named as a beneficiary in the will of William Felawe called 'Congesbury', clerk, rector of Portishead (Somerset), to receive 13*s* 4*d* and other money, together with a bed of worsted with sheets in return for praying for the souls of the testator and others.

88 Idony (Idonia) Wodehill,[3] occ. 16 May 1413 (1 Henry V), when nominated as a nun by royal prerogative following the king's coronation on 9 April 1413. Described as 'of good life and honest conversation, fervently desiring to leave the world and serve God' (*bonæ vitæ et conversationis honestæ, ac in firmo proposito et desiderio mundum relinquendi, ac Deo ... servitura*). Idony was perhaps dead by 1441, since she is not named in the voting body at the election of Edith Bonham (**96**) as abbess that year.[4] Agnes Wodehele (Wodehyll), **132**, who was present at this election, may have been a relative.

89 [Lucy Fyherse (?), *c*.1420? x -1441?]. Perhaps a nun of Shaftesbury and probably a member of the Forsey family of Bridport in south-west Dorset.[5] She is named in a fifteenth-century rubbed and faded book-hand inscription, *Liber Sororis Lucie ffyherse* (?),[6] on the lower margin of fol. 18v of an illuminated Flemish Book of Hours of Sarum Use, possibly used at, though not made for Shaftesbury Abbey,[7] attributed to a follower of the Boucicaut Master of Paris (*fl*.

1   *CPL 1404–15*, 355.

2   *SMW (1383–1500)*, 47.

3   *Fœdera* 9, 11; *VCH Dorset* 2, 76b.

4   *Reg. Aiscough*, second series, fol. 10v.

5   Campbell-Kease, 21–4.

6   There appears to be another rubbed and illegible inscription (*H* (?)... [= *Hic est liber* (?) ...]) in a cursive hand beneath this.

7   The occurrence of feasts of St Edward the Martyr in the calendar (*festum* 18 March, *translatio* 20 June) cannot be taken as an indication that the book 'was destined for Shaftesbury' (*pace* Keen 1999, 10), since both were observed by the widely used Sarum rite. The masculine forms of the two special prayers to the Virgin, *Obsecro te* (fols. 75r–77v) and *O intemerata* (fols. 78r–80r) suggest that it was not specifically commissioned for Shaftesbury Abbey, though it may nevertheless have been acquired for use by Lucy, if she was a nun there.

1390–1430), c.1420.[1] If Lucy was a nun of Shaftesbury, she may have been dead by 1441, since she is not named in the voting body at the election of Edith Bonham (**96**) as abbess that year.[2] It may be that she had professed at another Dorset house, perhaps as a Cistercian at Tarrant Keyneston, though this is difficult to establish.

90 [Joan (Joanna, Johanna) de Leueryngton, d. c.1425? x c.1450?]. Perhaps a nun of Shaftesbury, commemorated in an obit ('D*omina.* Iohanna. de leue*r*yngton*e*') apparently of this date under 8 April in the calendar of the Shaftesbury Psalter.[3] Joan's toponym suggests that she may have originated from Leverington in Cambridgeshire.

91 [Agnes Cressy, d. c.1425? x c.1450?]. Perhaps a nun of Shaftesbury, commemorated in an obit ('D*omina* Agnes Cressy M*onialis*') apparently of this date under 7 November in the calendar of the Shaftesbury Psalter.[4]

92 Margaret Selgrave,[5] prioress, occ. 8 November 1423, when she and the convent received royal licence to elect a new abbess following the death of Cecily Fovent (**84**).

93 Margaret Stourton,[6] **1423-1441.** Nun of Shaftesbury; el. abbess 8 x 16 November 1423;[7] roy. ass. +16 November 1423, with

---

1   The manuscript was part of the Plettenberg Library at Schloss Nordkirchen near Münster (North Rhine Westphalia) purchased by the 9th duke of Arenberg in 1903 and later sold to Jacques Seligmann & Co. of New York (*Arenberg MSS*, no. 78; Lemaire, 102 no. 78). It was auctioned by Christie's of London on 3 June 1998 (Catalogue no. 18, 26–8, lot 5974) and is now *US-DAubl* Special Collections MS 9. I am greatly indebted to Dr Arvid Nelsen, Bridwell Library Special Collections curator at Southern Methodist University, Dallas, for kindly providing information about this manuscript, together with an image of the inscription on fol. 18v.

2   *Reg. Aiscough*, second series, fol. 10v.

3   *Lbl* Lansdowne MS 383, fol. 4v.

4   Ibid., fol. 8r.

5   *CPR 1422–9*, 141.

6   *HRH* 3, 690; *CPR 1422–9*, 141, 156, 162; *Reg. Chandler*, second series, fols. 39v–40r; *Reg. Aiscough*, second series, fol. 10v; *House of Stourton* 1, 65, 83, 91, 95–6, 129; *VCH Dorset* 2, 79b; Chandler, 64.

7   Licence to elect 8 November (*CPR 1422–9*, 141); petition for the royal assent 16 November (*HRH* 3, 690).

temps. restored   8 December 1423;[1] conf. and bl. 9-10 December
1423;[2] d. 25 October 1441,[3] or 4 November 1441.[4] Margaret was the
sister of John Stourton I (d.1438) of Preston Plucknett, who served
as member of parliament for Somerset from 1419 to 1421, and
intermittently from 1423 to 1435.[5] Her aunt Mary[6] (**95**) and sister
Anastasia (**100**),[7] or Anastatia, were also nuns of Shaftesbury. She is
named earlier (as an ordinary nun) as a beneficiary in the wills of
Abbess Joan Formage (**72**), 1393, and Robert Corff *alias* Remston,
canon of Wells Cathedral (Somerset) and rector of Corfe (Dorset),
1395, to receive 20 shillings (*vint sould*) and a breviary (*une brever
que dame Margarete ... achatera a sa volunte*),[8] and a pair of sheets.[9] In
1431 Margaret was granted a papal indult allowing her to choose her
own confessor with authority to grant absolution,[10] thus making her
independent of the bishop in this respect. Heraldic tiles unearthed
from the remains of the abbey church and chapter house during
the nineteenth century decorated in white clay inlay with the arms
of Stourton (*Sable a bend or between six fountains proper*) and other
notable local families[11] may be seen, together with other heraldic and

1   *CPR 1422–9*, 162.

2   *Reg. Chandler*, second series, fols. 39v–40r.

3   Ibid., fol. 10v.

4   *HRH* 3, 690.

5   *History of Parliament*, art. 'Stourton, John I (d.1438)'.

6   *House of Stourton* 1, 65, 91.

7   *Reg. Aiscough*, second series, fol. 10v; *Reg. Beauchamp* 1, second series, fol.
    34r; *House of Stourton* 1, 65, 83, 95.

8   *Reg. Waltham*, 31–2 no. 121 (... *achatera a sa volunte*, a strange statement,
    since the breviary was apparently bequeathed).

9   Ibid., 27 no. 108.

10 *CPL 1427–1447*, 212.

11 Illustrations in Hutchins 1868, 34; *House of Stourton* 1, 96; Emden, no.
    132. Other white clay inlay tiles from the abbey include those with the
    arms of Clare, earls of Gloucester, *c.*1220–*c.*1350 (*three chevronels* [Emden,
    no. 140]), Montacute, earls of Salisbury, 1339–1428 (*three fusils conjoined
    in fess* [ibid., no. 131]), and Bonham (*a chevron wavy between three crosses
    pattées* [ibid., no. 133]), influential local magnates and land holders.
    Edith Bonham (**96**) was abbess from 1441 to 1460. The Stourton and

patterned encaustics, displayed in Shaftesbury Abbey museum.

94 Joan (Johanna) Ashecombe (Aisshcombe, Aysshecoombe),[1] occ. 11 January 1430 (8 Henry VI),[2] when nominated as a nun by royal prerogative following Henry's coronation as king of England on 6 November 1429 (8 Henry VI);[3] 16 November 1441 (then tacitly professed);[4] 1 July 1442 (when fully professed);[5] 26 March 1460.[6]

95 Mary Stourton. Perhaps dead by 1441, since she is not named in the voting body at the election of Edith Bonham (**96**) as abbess that year.[7] Named as aunt of Margaret Stourton (**93**),[8] abbess, 1423-41.

96 Edith Bonham,[9] **1441-1460.** Prioress of Shaftesbury; el. abbess 16 November 1441;[10] roy. ass. 25 November 1441, with temps. restored 16 December 1441;[11] conf. 5 December 1441;[12] d. 17 March 1460.[13] The voting body at the election consisted of forty-three fully professed (*expresse professe*) nuns (**97-138**, plus Edith) and fourteen

Bonham tiles probably originated in 'the east end of the apsidal chapel in the north aisle of the presbytery', according to Emden (ibid., 27).

1   *VCH Dorset* 2, 76b–77a.

2   *Fœdera* 10, 438.

3   *VCH Dorset* 2, 76b erroneously gives the year of nomination as 1480. Henry was crowned king of France (disputedly as Henri II) in Paris on 16 December 1431.

4   *Reg. Aiscough*, second series, fol. 10v.

5   Ibid., fol. 97v. The interval between Joan's nomination and her profession, nearly thirteen years, is notable.

6   *Reg. Beauchamp* 1, second series, fol. 34r.

7   *Reg. Aiscough*, second series, fol. 10v.

8   *House of Stourton* 1, 65, 91.

9   *HRH* 3, 690; *CPR 1441–6*, 24, 27, 32; *CPR 1452–61*, 573; *VCH Dorset* 2, 77a, 79b.

10 *Reg. Aiscough*, second series, fols. 10v–12r.

11 *CPR 1441–6*, 27, 32.

12 *Reg. Aiscough*, second series, fol. 12r-v. The election was confirmed by the bishop's official, Master John Druell.

13 *HRH* 3, 690.

tacitly professed (*tacite professe*), **94**, **139-50**, **164**,[1] who made full profession on 1 July 1442.[2] Among the latter was Margaret St John (**164**), who was elected abbess in 1460.[3]

97 Joan (Johanna) Crouke, sub-prioress, occ. 16 November 1441.[4]

98 Joan (Johanna) Hanleigh*e* (Hanlegh), occ. 16 November 1441.[5]

99 Isabel (Isabella) Uppehauyn*e*, occ. 16 November 1441.[6]

100 Anastasia (Anastatia) Stourton (Stowrton),[7] occ. 16 November 1441,[8] 26 March 1460.[9] Sister of Abbess Margaret Stourton (**93**) and niece of Mary Stourton (**95**), also a nun of Shaftesbury. Named, though not apparently as a nun, in the will of her brother Sir John Stourton of Preston [Plucknett] and Brimpton (from 1448, 1st Baron Stourton), Somerset, who died in 1462.[10]

101 Alice (Alicia) Graunte (Graunt), occ. 16 November 1441,[11] 26 March 1460.[12]

102 Alice (Alicia) Chaundose, occ. 16 November 1441.[13] Confined to the infirmary[14] and unable to attend the election of Edith Bonham (**96**) as abbess through old age and infirmity (... *propter senectutem et aduersam valitudinem corporis notorie impedimenta*),[15] being

1   *Reg. Aiscough*, second series, fol. 10v; Hutchins 1868, 29b–30b.

2   *Reg. Aiscough*, second series, fol. 97v.

3   *Reg. Beauchamp* 1, second series, fol. 34v.

4   *Reg. Aiscough*, second series, fol. 10v.

5   Ibid., fols. 10v, 12r.

6   Ibid, fol. 10v.

7   *House of Stourton* 1, 83, 91, 95.

8   *Reg. Aiscough*, second series, fol. 10v.

9   *Reg. Beauchamp* 1, second series, fol. 34r.

10   *SMW (1383–1500)*, 144.

11   *Reg. Aiscough*, second series, fol. 10v.

12   *Reg. Beauchamp* 1, second series, fol. 34r.

13   *Reg. Aiscough*, second series, fol. 10v.

14   Ibid., fol. 12r.

15   Ibid.

represented by Isabel Beyntone (**128**) *ipsius procuratricem sufficienter ei legatorie constitutam.*[1] Isabel was one of two election proctors appointed by Alice and Joan Hanlegh (**98**) *commoniales* on 14 November,[2] the other being Maria Florey (**133**). She also served as proctor with Joan Bulwardyne (**129**) and Christine Pokeswell (**144**) at the election of Margaret St John (**164**) on 26 March 1460.[3]

103 Joan (Johanna) Edyngdone, occ. 16 November 1441.[4]

104 Joan (Johanna) Anger, occ. 16 November 1441.[5]

105 Christine (Cristina) Swyneffelde (Swynfelde), occ. 16 November 1441.[6]

106 Juliana Tychebourne, occ. 16 November 1441.[7]

107 Edith (Editha) Boore, occ. 16 November 1441.[8]

108 Amice (Amisia) Hardyng, occ. 16 November 1441.[9]

109 Agnes Pourestock, occ. 16 November 1441.[10]

110 Amice (Amisia) Clowes, occ. 16 November 1441.[11]

111 Isabel (Isabella) Clauerynge, occ. 16 November 1441.[12]

112 Anne (Anna) Wadesworth, occ. 16 November 1441.[13]

113 Margery (Margeria) Spertegrane (Spartygrane), occ. 16 November 1441.[14]

114 Isabel (Isabella) Leigh, occ. 16 November 1441.[15]

1   *Reg. Aiscough*, second series, fol. 11r.

2   Ibid., fol. 12r.

3   *Reg. Beauchamp* 1, second series, fol. 35v.

4   *Reg. Aiscough*, second series, fol. 10v.

5   Ibid.

6   Ibid.

7   Ibid.

8   Ibid.

9   Ibid.

10 Ibid.

11 Ibid.

12 Ibid.

13 Ibid.

14 Ibid.

15 Ibid.

115 Anastasia Bradeleigh*e* (Bradeley), occ. 16 November 1441,[1] 26 March 1460.[2]

116 Alice (Alicia) Aisshecombe, occ. 16 November 1441.[3]

117 Alice (Alicia) Pounde, occ. 16 November 1441.[4]

118 Alice (Alicia) Savage, occ. 16 November 1441,[5] 26 March 1460.[6] Perhaps related to Eleanor Savage (occ. February 1410), the eldest daughter of John Savage of Tollard Royal (Wilts), in whose will she is named as a beneficiary to receive '20 marks [£13 6s 8d] ... as her share of all his goods and chattels, that she may be settled in a suitable religious house where she may be supported and find food and necessities for her life'.[7] The local choices were Shaftesbury, Tarrant Keyneston (Cist.) and Wilton abbeys, and Amesbury priory (Font.), though it is not known which Eleanor entered, if at all.

119 Elizabeth Becham (Beauchamp?), occ. 16 November 1441.[8]

120 Elizabeth Panys, occ. 16 November 1441.[9]

121 Felice (Felicia) Chichestere, occ. 16 November 1441.[10]

122 Eleanor (Alianora) Goviz, occ. 16 November 1441.[11]

123 Anne (Anna) Culmer, occ. 16 November 1441.[12]

124 Agnes Wodeford (Wodeforde, Wooford, Woodford), occ.

---

1   *Reg. Aiscough*, second series, fol. 10v.

2   *Reg. Beauchamp* 1, second series, fol. 34r.

3   *Reg. Aiscough*, second series, fol. 10v.

4   *Reg. Aiscough*, second series, fol. 10v.

5   Ibid.

6   *Reg. Beauchamp* 1, second series, fol. 34r.

7   *Reg. Hallum*, 88 no. 698.

8   *Reg. Aiscough*, second series, fol. 10v.

9   Ibid.

10 Ibid.

11 Ibid.

12 Ibid.

16 November 1441,[1] 26 March 1460,[2] 4 and 11 February [1497].[3]

125 Agnes Shelford, occ. 16 November 1441,[4] 26 March 1460.[5]

126 Alice (Alicia) Amberleighe (Amberley), occ. 16 November 1441,[6] 26 March 1460.[7]

127 Isabel (Isabella) Westeleighe, occ. 16 November 1441.[8]

128 Isabel (Isabella) Beyntone (Beynton), occ. 16 November 1441,[9] 26 March 1460 Appointed proctor with Maria Florey (**133**) at the election of Edith Bonham (**96**) as abbess on 16 November 1441,[10] and with Joan Bulwardyne (**129**) and Christine Pokeswell (**144**) at the election of Margaret St John (**164**) on 26 March 1460.[11]

129 Joan (Johanna) Bulwardyne (Bulfordyne), occ. 16 November 1441 (as Bulfordyne),[12] 26 March 1460.[13] Appointed proctor with Isabel Beyntone (**128**) and Christine Pokeswell (**144**) at the election of Margaret St John (**164**) on 26 March 1460.[14]

130 Joan (Johanna) Mouresleyghe (Morsley), occ. 16 November 1441,[15] 26 March 1460.[16] A miscellaneous collection of devotional writings,[17] including works by Richard Rolle of Hampole, was owned by Joan on the evidence of two inscriptions therein (fols. 2r, 4v, *Iste*

1 *Reg. Aiscough*, second series, fol. 10v.

2 *Reg. Beauchamp* 1, second series, fol. 34r.

3 *Reg. Blyth*, 98–9 no. 365.

4 *Reg. Aiscough*, second series, fol. 10v.

5 *Reg. Beauchamp* 1, second series, fol. 34r.

6 *Reg. Aiscough*, second series, fol. 10v.

7 *Reg. Beauchamp* 1, second series, fol. 34r.

8 *Reg. Aiscough*, second series, fol. 10v.

9 Ibid.

10 Ibid., fol. 12r.

11 *Reg. Beauchamp* 1, second series, fol. 34r.

12 *Reg. Aiscough*, second series, fol. 10v.

13 *Reg. Beauchamp* 1, second series, fol. 34r.

14 Ibid., fol. 35r.

15 *Reg. Aiscough*, second series, fol. 10v.

16 *Reg. Beauchamp* 1, second series, fol. 34r.

17 *Cu* MS Ii. 6. 40, *s.* xv, first half (1400 x *c.*1440).

liber constat domine Johanne Mouresleygh).[1]

131 Christine (Cristina) Cosyn (Cosin), occ. 16 November 1441,[2] 26 March 1460.[3]

132 Agnes Wodehele (Wodehyll), occ. 16 November 1441,[4] 26 March 1460.[5]

133 Maria Florey (fflorey), occ. 16 November 1441,[6] 26 March 1460 (as prioress).[7] Appointed proctor with Isabel Beyntone (**128**) at the election of Edith Bonham (**96**) as abbess on 16 November 1441.[8]

134 Margaret (Margareta) Landaffe (Landaff), occ. 16 November 1441,[9] 26 March 1460.[10]

135 Margaret (Margareta) Brome, occ. 16 November 1441.[11]

136 Isabel (Isabella) Mousbury (Musbury), occ. 16 November 1441,[12] 26 March 1460.[13]

137 Alice (Alicia) Oke, occ. 16 November 1441,[14] 26 March 1460.[15]

138 Agnes Alberton, occ. 16 November 1441.[16]

139 Margaret (Margareta) Godewyn, occ. 16 November 1441

1   Bell 1995, 164 no. 2.

2   *Reg. Aiscough*, second series, fol. 10v.

3   *Reg. Beauchamp* 1, second series, fol. 34r.

4   *Reg. Aiscough*, second series, fol. 10v.

5   *Reg. Beauchamp* 1, second series, fol. 34r.

6   *Reg. Aiscough*, second series, fol. 10v.

7   *Reg. Beauchamp* 1, second series, fol. 34r.

8   *Reg. Aiscough*, second series, fol. 12r.

9   Ibid., fol. 10v.

10   *Reg. Beauchamp* 1, second series, fol. 34r.

11   *Reg. Aiscough*, second series, fol. 10v.

12   Ibid.

13   *Reg. Beauchamp* 1, second series, fol. 34r.

14   *Reg. Aiscough*, second series, fol. 10v.

15   *Reg. Beauchamp* 1, second series, fol. 34r.

16   *Reg. Aiscough*, second series, fol. 10v.

(then tacitly professed),[1] 1 July 1442 (when fully professed).[2]

140 Elizabeth Bekyngham, occ. 16 November 1441 (then tacitly professed),[3] 1 July 1442 (when fully professed),[4] 26 March 1460.[5] Followed by Joan Ashecombe (Aisshcombe, Aysshecoombe), **94**, in the 1441 election list of fourteen tacitly professed nuns (*moniales tacite professe*),[6] who formally professed in 1442,[7] when she also appears after Elizabeth.

141 Constance (Constancia) Bradeleighe (Bradley), occ. 16 November 1441 (then tacitly professed),[8] 1 July 1442 (when fully professed),[9] 26 March 1460.[10]

142 Ellen (Elena) Rempston, occ. 16 November 1441 (then tacitly professed),[11] 1 July 1442 (when fully professed).[12]

143 Joan (Johanna) Sampson, occ. 16 November 1441 (then tacitly professed),[13] 1 July 1442 (when fully professed),[14] 26 March 1460.[15]

144 Christine (Cristina) Pokeswell (Pokeswel), occ. 16 November 1441 (then tacitly professed),[16] 1 July 1442 (when fully

1   *Reg. Aiscough*, second series, fol. 10v.

2   Margaret is named as the first of fifteen *moniales tacite professe*, whose profession was received by the bishop on 1 July 1442 (ibid., fol. 97v, which also includes their oath of obedience).

3   Ibid., fol. 10v.

4   Ibid., fol. 97v.

5   *Reg. Beauchamp* 1, second series, fol. 34r.

6   *Reg. Aiscough*, second series, fol. 10v.

7   Ibid., fol. 97v.

8   Ibid., fol. 10v.

9   Ibid., fol. 97v.

10 *Reg. Beauchamp* 1, second series, fol. 34r.

11 *Reg. Aiscough*, second series, fol. 10v.

12 Ibid., fol. 97v.

13 Ibid., fol. 10v.

14 Ibid., fol. 97v.

15 *Reg. Beauchamp* 1, second series, fol. 34r.

16 *Reg. Aiscough*, second series, fol. 10v.

professed),[1] 26 March 1460,[2] 4 and 11 February [1497].[3] Appointed proctor with Isabel Beyntone (**128**) and Joan Bulwardyne (**129**) at the election of Margaret St John (**164**) on 26 March 1460,[4] and scrutineer (*scrutatrix*) of the chapter votes, together with Philippa Bonham (**172**) and Joyce (Jocosa, Jocia) Bulwarden (**185**) at the election of Margery Twyneo (**180**) as abbess on 11 February 1497.[5] Christine, Philippa and Joyce all voted for Margery as the successor of Alice Gibbes (**179**) previous to taking scrutiny of the votes of the prioress and nuns.[6]

145 Eleanor (Alianora, Alienora) Bradeleygh (Bradeleigh, Bradley), occ. 16 November 1441 (then tacitly professed),[7] 1 July 1442 (when fully professed),[8] 26 March 1460.[9]

146 Edith (Editha) Rempston (Ramston*e*), occ. 16 November 1441 (then tacitly professed),[10] 1 July 1442 (when fully professed),[11] 26 March 1460.[12]

147 Thomesine (Thomesia, Thomesina) Kemer (Kymer), occ. 16 November 1441 (as Thomesia Kemer, then tacitly professed),[13] 1 July 1442 (as Thomasia Kymer, when fully professed),[14] 26 March 1460 (as Thomasia Kymer),[15] 4 and 11 February [1497] (as Thomesina

1   *Reg. Aiscough*, second series, fol. 97v.

2   *Reg. Beauchamp* 1, second series, fol. 34r.

3   *Reg. Blyth*, 98–9 no. 365.

4   *Reg. Beauchamp* 1, second series, fol. 35r.

5   *Reg. Blyth*, 99 no. 365.

6   Ibid.

7   *Reg. Aiscough*, second series, fol. 10v.

8   Ibid., fol. 97v.

9   *Reg. Beauchamp* 1, second series, fol. 34r.

10 *Reg. Aiscough*, second series, fol. 10v.

11 Ibid., fol. 97v.

12 *Reg. Beauchamp* 1, second series, fol. 34r.

13 *Reg. Aiscough*, second series, fol. 10v.

14 Ibid., fol. 97v.

15 *Reg. Beauchamp* 1, second series, fol. 34r.

Kemer, prioress),[1] 25 June 1505 (as Thomesina Kymer, prioress).[2] Followed by Katherine Werlonde (**148**) in the 1441 election list of fourteen tacitly professed nuns (*moniales tacite professe*),[3] who formally professed in 1442,[4] when she also appears after Thomasia, as her name was spelt.

148 Katherine (Katerina) Werlonde (Warlond), occ. 16 November 1441 (then tacitly professed),[5] 1 July 1442 (when fully professed),[6] 26 March 1460.[7]

149 Katherine (Katerina) Aisshekewe (Aiscough, Ascough, Ayscogh), occ. 16 November 1441 (then tacitly professed),[8] 1 July 1442 (when fully professed),[9] 26 March 1460.[10] Followed by Margaret St John (**164**) in the 1441 election list of fourteen tacitly professed nuns (*moniales tacite professe*),[11] who formally professed in 1442,[12] when she also appears after Katherine. Perhaps related to William Aiscough, bishop of Salisbury, 1438-50.

150 Elizabeth Momperson (Mompesson, Mounpessone, Mumpson), occ. 16 November 1441 (then tacitly professed),[13] 1 July 1442 (when fully professed),[14] 26 March 1460,[15] 4 and 11 February

---

1   *Reg. Blyth*, 97–100 no. 365.

2   *Reg. Audley*, fol. 126v.

3   *Reg. Aiscough*, second series, fol. 10v.

4   Ibid., fol. 97v

5   *Reg. Aiscough*, second series, fol. 10v.

6   Ibid., fol. 97v.

7   *Reg. Beauchamp* 1, second series, fol. 34r.

8   *Reg. Aiscough*, second series, fol. 10v.

9   Ibid., fol. 97v.

10   *Reg. Beauchamp* 1, second series, fol. 34r.

11   *Reg. Aiscough*, second series, fol. 10v.

12   Ibid., fol. 97v.

13   Ibid., fol. 10v.

14   Ibid., fol. 97v.

15   *Reg. Beauchamp* 1, second series, fol. 34r.

[1497],[1] 25 June 1505.[2]

151 Elizabeth Humfray, occ. 1 July 1442 (when fully professed)[3] as additional to the 1441 election list of fourteen tacitly professed nuns (*moniales tacite professe*),[4] suggesting that she entered the convent between 16 November 1441 and 1 July 1442.[5]

152 Isabel (Isabella) Mawes, occ. 8 January 1453 (when fully professed).[6]

153 Ellen (Elena) Poynes (Pownys), occ. 8 January 1453 (when fully professed),[7] 26 March 1460.[8]

154 Joan (Johanna) Walbertone (Warberton), occ. 8 January 1453 (when fully professed),[9] 26 March 1460,[10] 4 and 11 February [1497],[11] 25 June 1505.[12]

155 Alice (Alicia) Abram (Abraham), occ. 8 January 1453 (when fully professed),[13] 26 March 1460.[14]

156 Elizabeth Poynes, occ. 8 January 1453 (when fully professed),[15] 26 March 1460.[16]

157 Margaret (Margareta) St George (Seintiorge, Seint Georg),

1   *Reg. Blyth,* 98–9 no. 365.

2   *Reg. Audley,* fol. 126v.

3   *Reg. Aiscough,* second series, fol. 97v.

4   Ibid., fol. 10v.

5   *Reg. Beauchamp* 1, second series, fol. 34r.

6   *Reg. Beauchamp* 1, second series, fol. 150r.

7   Ibid.

8   Ibid., fol. 34r.

9   Ibid., fol. 150r.

10 Ibid., fol. 34r.

11 *Reg. Blyth,* 98–9 no. 365.

12 *Reg. Audley,* fol. 126v.

13 *Reg. Beauchamp* 1, second series, fol. 150r.

14 Ibid., fol. 34r.

15 Ibid., fol. 150r.

16 Ibid., fol. 34r.

occ. 8 January 1453 (when fully professed),[1] 26 March 1460.[2]

158 Parnel (Perinoi,[3] Petronilla) Kameys (Kemer), occ. 8 January 1453 (when fully professed),[4] 26 March 1460.[5]

159 Margaret (Margareta) Combe, occ. 8 January 1453 (when fully professed),[6] 26 March 1460.[7]

160 Christine (Cristina) Pytteney (Pytney), occ. 8 January 1453 (when fully professed),[8] 26 March 1460.[9]

161 Alice (Alicia) Leversheg (Leversey), occ. 8 January 1453 (when fully professed),[10] 26 March 1460.[11]

162 Edith (Editha) Howchyn (Huchyne), occ. 8 January 1453 (when fully professed),[12] 26 March 1460.[13]

163 Katherine (Katharine, Katheryn, Katerina) Moleyns, occ. 8 January 1453 (when fully professed),[14] 26 March 1460.[15] Appointed prioress of Kington St Michael (Ben., Wilts) by the bishop as the convent's choice on 9 April 1492 on the resignation of Alice Lawrence (Laurens) earlier that year;[16] dead by (?) c.August 1506.[17] Adam Moleyns, dean of Salisbury, 1441-6 (from 1446 bishop of

1   *Reg. Beauchamp* 1, second series, fol. 150r.

2   Ibid., fol. 34r.

3   Perhaps for Périneau.

4   *Reg. Beauchamp* 1, second series, fol. 150r.

5   Ibid., fol. 34r.

6   Ibid., fol. 150r.

7   Ibid., fol. 34r.

8   Ibid., fol. 150r.

9   Ibid., fol. 34r.

10 Ibid., fol. 150r.

11 Ibid., fol. 34r.

12 Ibid., fol. 150r.

13 Ibid., fol. 34r.

14 Ibid., fol. 150r.

15 Ibid., fol. 34r.

16 *Reg. Langton*, 69 nos. 480–2; *HRH* 3, 690; *VCH Wiltshire* 3, 260b–261b; Chandler, 69.

17 *Reg. Audley*, fol. 132r.

Chichester), may have been a relative.[1]

164 Margaret St John (Seint John, Seynt John),[2] 1460-1492.
Nun of Shaftesbury (occ. 16 November 1441,[3] then tacitly professed;
1 July 1442,[4] when fully professed); el. abbess 26 March 1460;[5] roy.
ass. 12 April 1460, with temps. restored 1 May;[6] conf. 19 April (by
the bishop of Lincoln) and bl. 20 April 1460;[7] d. 1 June 1492.[8] The
youngest daughter of Sir Oliver St John of Bletsoe, Spelsbury and
Lydiard Tregoze (d. 1437), and Margaret Beauchamp, duchess of
Somerset (d. -3 June 1482), and aunt of Henry VII (reigned 1485-
1509), Margaret had aspired to election as abbess, prioress or other
dignity within the abbey as early as 1453, when, at her own petition
and that of her mother, she was granted papal dispensation *super
defectum ætatis* on account of her years.[9] Said to be around twenty-two
at the time,[10] she would therefore have been about eleven when she
fully professed in 1442, and almost thirty by 1460. The voting body at
her election consisted of fifty-three nuns, including Margaret, many
of whom (**94, 100-101, 115, 118, 124-6, 128-34, 136-7, 140-41, 143-
50**) had witnessed the election of Edith Bonham (**96**) nearly twenty
years earlier in 1441. A number of the others present (**153-63, 179**),
including Alice Gibbes (**179**), who became abbess in 1492, were fully
professed in 1453. The remainder (**165-77**), occurring for the first
time in 1460, were probably just tacitly professed. In March 1492,

1   *VCH Wiltshire* 3, 12, 208b.

2   *HRH* 3, 690; *CPR 1452–61*, 570, 573, 600; *House of Stourton* 1, 76n, 86n,
    91, 98, 119, 205, 240, 254, 275; *VCH Dorset* 2, 77a, 79b; Chandler, 67.

3   *Reg. Aiscough*, second series, fol. 10v.

4   Ibid., fol. 97v.

5   *Reg. Beauchamp* 1, second series, fols. 34r–35r.

6   *CPR 1452–61*, 570, 600.

7   *Reg. Beauchamp* 1, second series, fol. 35r–v. Certificate of confirmation of
    election by bishop of Salisbury 20 April 1460 (*HRH* 3, 690).

8   *Reg. Langton*, 121 no. 590.

9   *CPL 1447–55*, 245. The dispensation was granted by Pope Nicholas V.

10 The minimum age for election as head of a house was said to be twenty-
    one (Power, 45), but twenty-two was evidently considered still too young
    for such an important foundation as Shaftesbury at this period, hence the
    dispensation.

shortly before her death, Margaret endowed a perpetual chantry at the altar of the Lady Chapel in the abbey church with a chaplain to pray for the king and queen, and Margaret [Beaufort] countess of Richmond and Derby, the king's mother, in addition to herself, as well as for the souls of her parents.[1] She was related to the Stourton family through her maternal grandmother Edith (d. 1441), second wife of Sir John Beauchamp, third Baron Beauchamp of Bletsoe (d. c.1413).

165 Alice (Alicia) Hardyng, occ. 26 March 1460.[2] Perhaps to be identified with Amice (Amisia) Hardyng (**108**).

166 Martha Spartygrane, occ. 26 March 1460.[3]

167 Alice (Alicia) Aishtone, occ. 26 March 1460.[4]

168 Isabel (Isabella) Beauchamp, occ. 26 March 1460.[5]

169 Isabel (Isabella) Panys, occ. 26 March 1460.[6]

170 Margaret (Margareta) Brown, occ. 26 March 1460.[7] Perhaps to be identified with Margaret (Margareta) Brome (**135**).

171 Elizabeth Vinfrey, occ. 26 March 1460.[8] Perhaps to be identified with Elizabeth Humfray (**151**).

172 Philippa Bonham, occ. 26 March 1460,[9] 4 and 11 February [1497],[10] 25 June 1505.[11] Appointed scrutineer (*scrutatrix*) of the chapter votes, together with Christine Pokeswell (**144**) and Joyce

1   *CPR 1485–94*, 369. The number of perpetual chantries established in the abbey church by the late Middle Ages was at least thirteen (Hutchins 1868, 35a–36. Luxford, 132, with nn. 111–13, notes eight, omitting the additional ones mentioned by Hutchins), with two others established for parish use in the nearby church of St James (Hutchins 1868, 38b). For the Lady Margaret Beaufort, see Jones & Underwood, and *idem* 'Beaufort'.

2   *Reg. Beauchamp* 1, second series, fol. 34r.

3   Ibid.

4   Ibid.

5   Ibid.

6   Ibid.

7   Ibid.

8   Ibid.

9   Ibid.

10   *Reg. Blyth*, 98, 99–100 no. 365.

11   *Reg. Audley*, fol. 126v.

(Jocosa, Jocia) Bulwarden (**185**) at the election of Margery Twyneo (**180**) as abbess on 11 February 1497.[1]

173 Alice (Alicia) Pytney, occ. 26 March 1460.[2]

174 Katherine (Katerina) Florey (fflorey), occ. 26 March 1460.[3]

175 Agnes Prynce, occ. 26 March 1460,[4] 4 and 11 February [1497],[5] 25 June 1505.[6]

176 Isolde (Isota, Isolda) Grene, occ. 26 March 1460,[7] 4 and 11 February [1497].[8]

177 Joan (Johanna) Beyntham, occ. 26 March 1460.[9]

178 Elizabeth (Elisabeth) Bryther (Brethyr, Bruyther), occ. +6 July 1483 (1 Richard III), 4 and 11 February [1497] (by then fully professed),[10] 25 June 1505,[11] 22 March 1539.[12] Nominated as a nun by royal prerogative at the suit of one Edward Hardguylle following the king's coronation on 6 July 1483,[13] remaining at Shaftesbury Abbey for fifty-six years until 1539, when she was discharged with an annual pension of £6 13s 4d. Certainly one of the oldest members of the community and perhaps aged around eighty,[14] she appears to have

1   *Reg. Blyth*, 99 no. 365.

2   Ibid.

3   Ibid.

4   Ibid.

5   Ibid., 98–9 no. 365.

6   *Reg. Audley*, fol. 126v.

7   *Reg. Beauchamp* 1, second series, fol. 34r.

8   *Reg. Blyth*, 98–9 no. 365.

9   *Reg. Beauchamp* 1, second series, fol. 34r.

10 *Reg. Blyth*, 98, 100 no. 365.

11 *Reg. Audley*, fol. 126v.

12 *Monasticon* 2, 485b.

13 *Lbl* Harley MS 433, fol. 22b (letter of recommendation of Richard III for Elizabeth to become king's *mynchyne* [nun] at Shaftesbury (*Harleian Manuscripts* 1, 258b no. 83; *Monasticon* 2, 473a; *VCH Dorset* 2, 77a, citing Harley MS 433, fol. 22d (*rectius* 22b); Horrox & Hammond 1 (*Register of grants for the reigns of Edward V and Richard III*), 68–9).

14 Elizabeth appears near the head of the 1539 pension list, occurring

died by the beginning of Mary's reign (1553).

179 Alice (Alicia) Gibbes (Gibbis, Gibbys, Gybbes, Kybbys),[1] **1492-1496**. Nun of Shaftesbury; el. abbess +25 July 1492;[2] roy. ass. 24 August 1492,[3] with temps. restored 16 September 1492;[4] conf. 6 September 1492; d. 18 December 1496.[5] Fully professed 8 January 1453,[6] Alice appears in the list of nuns voting at the election of Margaret St John (**164**) as abbess on 26 March 1460.[7]

180 Margery (Margeria, or Margareta) Twyneo (Twinhoe, Twinyhoe, Twyneho, Twynyho),[8] **1497-1505**. Nun of Shaftesbury; el. abbess 11 February 1497;[9] roy. ass. 27 February 1497, with temps. restored 20 April 1497;[10] conf. and bl. 13 and 14 March 1497;[11] d.

after the abbess, prioress and sub-prioress (*Monasticon* 2, 485b).

1 *HRH* 3, 690; *CPR 1485–94*, 386, 405, 409; *Reg. Langton*, 121 no. 590; *Reg. Blyth*, 97 no. 365; *VCH Dorset* 2, 79b.

2 *CPR 1485–94*, 386.

3 Ibid., 409.

4 Ibid. 405. Temps. were petitioned on 6 September (*Reg. Langton*, 121, no. 590).

5 *Reg. Blyth*, 97 no. 365.

6 *Reg. Beauchamp* 1, second series, fol. 150r.

7 Ibid., fol. 34r.

8 *HRH* 3, 690; *CPR 1494–1509*, 77, 108, 418; *Reg. Blyth*, 97–101 no. 365; *Reg. Audley*, fol. 126v (records the year (1505) of Margery's death, but the spaces for the day and month are left blank); *VCH Dorset* 2, 77a, 79b; Chandler, 91, 94, 98.

9 *Reg. Blyth*, 97–101 no. 365. Arranged initially for 6 February, the election was prorogued for unspecified reasons to 9 February, and then again to 13 February, because the royal letters patent granting licence to elect on 15 January (*CPR 1494–1509*, 77) had been mislaid (*Reg. Blyth*, 98–9 no. 365). Finally, the election went ahead on 11 February, probably as the result of insistence by exasperated bishop's officials (*Reg. Blyth*, 99 n. 1).

10 *CPR 1494–1509*, 108–9; *Reg. Blyth*, 101 nos. 366, 367 with n. 2. The royal assent was actually dated 22 February, but was delivered on 27 February (*Reg. Blyth*, 101 no. 367 n. 2).

11 *Reg. Blyth*, 101 no. 367. The calendar of the Shelford *horæ* (*Cfm* MS 2-1957), fol. 3v, dates the blessing 13 February (as *Reg. Blyth*, 99 no. 365), with *Dies benedictionis domine me abbatisse* entered in red (Wormald & Giles, 517). The blessing was conducted by Augustine [Church], bishop

-18 June, 1505.[1] Belonging to a Somerset gentry family, Margery was aunt to George Twynyho of Keyford near Frome, whose will was dated 2 March 1524,[2] and who was buried before the high altar of the abbey church.[3] Her father had been member of parliament for Shaftesbury,[4] and her brother Christopher, who served as abbey seneschal, or steward,[5] was in holy orders, later becoming archdeacon of Berkshire from 1507 to 1509.[6] A surviving register of abbey deeds (*Kalendare munimentorum*) was begun by Alexander Cater (or Katour), lay sacristan of the abbey, for Margery in 1500 on Christopher's advice and completed in 1505, the year of her death.[7] The voting body at Margery's election on 11 February 1497 consisted of twenty-five fully professed nuns (**124, 144, 147, 150, 154, 172, 175-6, 178, 181-94, 206**, plus Margery), including Elizabeth Shelford (**206**) elected abbess in 1505, and eleven tacitly professed (**195-204, 226**),[8] including Elizabeth Zouche (**226**), the last abbess elected in 1528.

181 Agnes Asshe (Ayshe), occ. 4 and 11 February [1497],[9] 25

of Lydda in Holy Trinity church, Shaftesbury, just outside the abbey on its north side (*Reg. Blyth*, 101 no. 367).

1 *CPR 1494–1509*, 418.

2 *NQSD* 19 (1929), 197–201.

3 Ibid., 197.

4 Chandler, 91.

5 Luxford, 193, with n. 275.

6 Le Neve, *Salisbury*, 11.

7 *Lbl* Egerton MS 3098 (Davis *et al.*, 178b–179a, no. 887; Hutchins 1868, 86–8; Bell 1933; Luxford, 193, with n. 275). A fragment of Alexander Cater's freestone floorslab incised with his epitaph is displayed in Shaftesbury Abbey museum (Chandler, 75, with illustration; Luxford, 193). This register, which may have been intended for Christopher's use as abbey steward (Bell 1933, 21), remained in the possession of the Twinyhoe family until the early twentieth century, when it was acquired by the British Museum Department of Manuscripts (ibid., 19).

8 *Reg Blyth*, 97–8 no. 365; Hutchins 1868, 30.

9 *Reg. Blyth*, 98–100 no. 365.

March 1497,[1] 25 June 1505.[2]

182 Alice (Alicia) Purry (Pury, Pyry), occ. 4 and 11 February [1497],[3] 25 June 1505 [4]

183 Maria Payne, occ. 4 and 11 February [1497],[5] 25 June 1505.[6]

184 Agnes Laurence (Laurance), occ. 4 and 11 February [1497],[7] 25 June 1505.[8]

185 Joyce (Jocosa, Jocia) Bulwarden (Bulwardyn), occ. 4 and 11 February [1497].[9] 25 June 1505.[10] Appointed scrutineer (*scrutatrix*) of the chapter votes, together with Christine Pokeswell (**144**) and Philippa Bonham (**172**) at the election of Margery Twyneo (**180**) as abbess on 11 February 1497.[11]

186 Thomesine (Thomesina, Thomesyn) Hosy (Hoosey, Husy, Hussey), occ. 4 and 11 February [1497],[12] 25 June 1505,[13] 22 March 1539;[14] alive 1553.[15] Irrespective of her long service as a nun (over forty years), Thomesine received a significantly lower pension (£4) in 1539 than many of her *commoniales*, who had entered the convent later. There is no known reason for this, even though she was fully

1   *Reg. Blyth*, 37 no. 263. *Monasticon* 2, 473a, names Agnes as *tutrix* of Eleanor Eliot (**205**), but misdates (20 May for 25 March) the latter's appointment as a nun.

2   *Reg. Audley*, fol. 126v.

3   *Reg. Blyth*, 98, 100 no. 365.

4   *Reg. Audley*, fol. 126v.

5   *Reg. Blyth*, 98–9 no. 365.

6   *Reg. Audley*, fol. 126v.

7   *Reg. Blyth*, 98–9 no. 365.

8   *Reg. Audley*, fol. 126v.

9   *Reg. Blyth*, 98–100 no. 365.

10 *Reg. Audley*, fol. 126v.

11 *Reg. Blyth*, 99 no. 365.

12 Ibid., 98, 100 no. 365.

13 *Reg. Audley*, fol. 126v.

14 *Monasticon* 2, 486b.

15 Ibid., 474 n. q; Bettey 1989, 180–1 (Appendix I), at 181.

professed by 1497. Alice Hussey, a nun of Wilton pensioned around the same time as Thomesine, may have been a relative.[1]

187 Margery (Margeria, Margareta) St John (Saynt John), occ. 4 and 11 February [1497],[2] 25 June 1505 (as Margareta).[3] Probably related to Margaret St John (**164**), abbess 1460-92.

188 Emma Roderford (Rotherford), occ. 4 and 11 February [1497],[4] 25 June 1505.[5]

189 Anne (Anna) Deynton (Dentoy), occ. 4 and 11 February [1497],[6] 25 June 1505.[7]

190 Elizabeth (Elisabeth) Monmouth (Monmouthe), occ. 4 and 11 February [1497],[8] 25 June 1505,[9] 22 March 1539 (as sub-prioress).[10]

191 Alice (Alicia) Pevesy (Pewsy), occ. 4 and 11 February [1497],[11] 25 June 1505.[12]

192 Katherine (Katerina) Thornhylle (Thornuell), occ. 4 and 11 February [1497],[13] 25 June 1505.[14]

193 Joan (Johanna) Stokes, occ. 4 and 11 February [1497],[15] 25 June 1505.[16]

194 Joan (Johanna) Bulstrod*e* (Bulstrood*e*), occ. 4 and 11

---

1   *Monasticon* 2, 329b.

2   *Reg. Blyth*, 98, 100 no. 365.

3   *Reg. Audley*, fol. 126v.

4   *Reg. Blyth*, 98–9 no. 365.

5   *Reg. Audley*, fol. 126v.

6   *Reg. Blyth*, 98–9 no. 365.

7   *Reg. Audley*, fol. 126v.

8   *Reg. Blyth*, 98, 100 no. 365.

9   *Reg. Audley*, fol. 126v.

10   *Monasticon* 2, 485b.

11   *Reg. Blyth*, 98, 100 no. 365.

12   *Reg. Audley*, fol. 126v.

13   *Reg. Blyth*, 98, 100 no. 365.

14   *Reg. Audley*, fol. 126v.

15   *Reg. Blyth*, 98, 100 no. 365.

16   *Reg. Audley*, fol. 126v.

February [1497],[1] 25 June 1505.[2]

195 Margaret (Margareta) Hemmerford (Hymerford, Hymmerford), occ. 4 and 11 February [1497] (then tacitly professed),[3] 25 June 1505 (when fully professed),[4] 22 March 1539;[5] alive 1553.[6]

196 Eleanor (Alienora, Elianora) Pulter, occ. 4 and 11 February [1497] (then tacitly professed),[7] 25 June 1505 (when fully professed).[8]

197 Margaret (Margareta) Payn (Payne), occ. 4 and 11 February [1497] (then tacitly professed),[9] 25 June 1505 (when fully professed).[10]

198 Alice (Alicia) Abbot, occ. 4 and 11 February [1497] (then tacitly professed),[11] 25 June 1505 (when fully professed).[12]

199 Katherine (Katerina) Halle, occ. 4 and 11 February [1497] (then tacitly professed),[13] 25 June 1505 (when fully professed),[14] 22 March 1539 (as prioress).[15]

200 Joan (Johanna) Amys (Ames), occ. 4 and 11 February [1497] (then tacitly professed),[16] 25 June 1505 (when fully pro-

1   *Reg. Blyth*, 98, 100 no. 365.

2   *Reg. Audley*, fol. 126v.

3   *Reg. Blyth*, 98, 100 no. 365.

4   *Reg. Audley*, fol. 126v.

5   *Monasticon* 2, 486a.

6   Ibid., 474 n. q; Bettey 1989, 180–1 (Appendix I), at 180.

7   *Reg. Blyth*, 98, 100 no. 365.

8   *Reg. Audley*, fol. 126v.

9   *Reg. Blyth*, 98, 100 no. 365.

10   *Reg. Audley*, fol. 126v.

11   *Reg. Blyth*, 98, 100 no. 365.

12   *Reg. Audley*, fol. 126v.

13   *Reg. Blyth*, 98, 100 no. 365.

14   *Reg. Audley*, fol. 126v.

15   *Monasticon* 2, 485b.

16   *Reg. Blyth*, 98, 100 no. 365.

fessed),[1] 22 March 1539;[2] alive 1553.[3]

201 Philippa Catesby (Cattisby), occ. 4 and 11 February [1497] (then tacitly professed),[4] 25 June 1505 (when still tacitly professed),[5] 22 March 1539.[6] She presumably had fully professed by 1539 in view of her position, together with Margaret Coke (**202**) and Elizabeth Goodwyne (**204**), well up in the pension list, receiving an annual award of £6.

202 Margaret (Margareta) Coke (Cocks), occ. 4 and 11 February [1497] (then tacitly professed),[7] 25 June 1505 (when still tacitly professed),[8] 22 March 1539.[9]

203 Joan (Johanna) Maunshill (Maunshyll), occ. 4 and 11 February [1497] (then tacitly professed).[10]

204 Elizabeth Goodwyne (Godwyn, Goodewyne), occ. 4 and 11 February [1497] (then tacitly professed),[11] 25 June 1505 (when still tacitly professed),[12] 22 March 1539;[13] alive 1553.[14]

205 Eleanor (Alienora) Eliot, damsel (*domicella*), occ. 25 March 1497,[15] 25 June 1505 (when still tacitly professed).[16] Nominated as a nun by the bishop of Salisbury (John Blyth, 1493-9) in accordance with his customary right on appointment to his see, who assigns her

1   *Reg. Audley*, fol. 126v.

2   *Monasticon* 2, 486a.

3   Ibid., 474 n. q; Bettey 1989, 180–1 (Appendix I), at 180.

4   *Reg. Blyth*, 98, 100 no. 365.

5   *Reg. Audley*, fol. 126v.

6   *Monasticon* 2, 486a.

7   *Reg. Blyth*, 98, 100 no. 365.

8   *Reg. Audley*, fol. 126v.

9   *Monasticon* 2, 486a.

10 *Reg. Blyth*, 98, 100 no. 365.

11 Ibid., 98, 100 no. 365.

12 *Reg. Audley*, fol. 126v.

13 *Monasticon* 2, 486a.

14 Ibid., 474 n. q; Bettey 1989, 180–1 (Appendix I), at 180.

15 *Reg. Blyth*, 37 no. 263.

16 *Reg. Audley*, fol. 126v.

to the care of Dame Agnes Asshe (**181**) to be her instructress in the monastic life.

    206 Elizabeth (Elisabeth) Shelford,[1] **1505-1528**. Nun of Shaftesbury; occ. as fully professed 4 and 11 February [1497];[2] el. abbess 25 June 1505;[3] roy. ass. 1 July 1505, with temps. restored 11 July 1505;[4] conf. and bl. 12 July 1505;[5] d. -24 November 1528.[6] The daughter of John Shelford of Hereford and Gwen More his wife (d. 1504), named (*dame Elizabeth Shelforde / Abbes of the monastery of Shaftysbriry*) on the latter's memorial brass in the Brocas Chapel of the parish church of Bramley (Hants).[7] Elizabeth is remembered especially for the finely decorated book of hours (the Shelford *horæ*) made for her as abbess, now in the Fitzwilliam Museum, Cambridge.[8]

1   *HRH* 3, 690; *CPR 1494–1505*, 418–19, 431; *Reg. Audley*, fols. 126v–127r; *Monasticon* 2, 474a; *L & P Henry VIII* 4, pt. 2 (*1526–8*), 2153 no. 4968; *VCH Dorset* 2, 79b.

2   *Reg. Blyth*, 98, 100 no. 165.

3   *Reg. Audley*, fols. 126v–127r. The election is entered in the calendar of the Shelford *horæ* (*Cfm* MS 2-1957), fol. 5v, under this date, *Hac die domina elizabeth shelford electa in abbatissam anno domini m°cccc°v* [*sic*] … (Wormald & Giles, 518).

4   *CPR 1494–1505*, 419, 431.

5   The calendar of the Shelford *horæ*, fol. 6r, commemorates the blessing on 12 July, but confuses this date with the Translation of St Thomas the Martyr (*in die translacionis s. thome martiris*: Wormald & Giles, 518), which is actually 7 July.

6   *L & P Henry VIII* 4, pt. 2 (*1526–8*), 2153 no. 4968.

7   *NQSD* 10 (1907), 31–3 no. 28 (with illustration of the More memorial brass on the chapel floor). The brass includes Elizabeth's personal arms (*on a pale three roses impaling a chevron engrailed between three boars' heads erased at the neck*), which appear also, with her initials, on two roof bosses in the parish church of Tisbury in Wiltshire (*WANHM* 36 (1909–10), 599–614; Wormald & Giles, 516).

8   *Cfm* MS 2-1957 (Ker, *MLGB*, 177; Bell 1995, 163–4 no. 1; Luxford, 5, 44, 70, 83–4, with Plate 1). The manuscript contains Elizabeth's 'ES' monogram (fols. 11r, 34r, 105v) and her rebus, a scallop shell over water ('shell-ford'). After her death in 1528 the manuscript passed into the possession of a local parish priest, from whom it was purchased by another nun of Shaftesbury, Dame Alice Champnys, or Champeneys (**212**), whose ownership inscription appears on fol. 132v (Wormald & Giles, 520; Luxford, 5).

As abbess she appears as party to land purchased by the testator at Hindon (Wilts), 1522, in the will of John Chaper *alias* Nicolls of Fontmell, Dorset, 1526.[1] Dame Agnes Shelford (**125**), who appears to have died between 1460 and 1497, may have been related. The voting body at Elizabeth's election on 25 June 1505 consisted of twenty-eight fully professed nuns (**147, 150, 154, 172, 175, 178, 181-200, 226**, plus Elizabeth), including Elizabeth Zouche (**226**) elected abbess in 1528, a number of whom had witnessed the election of Margery (Margaret) Twyneo (**180**) in 1497, and twenty-two (**201-2, 204-5, 207-24**) tacitly professed.[2]

207 Ursula Payne (Pame), occ. 25 June 1505 (then tacitly professed),[3] 22 March 1539;[4] alive 1553.[5]

208 Alice (Alicia, Elise) Jakes, occ. 25 June 1505 (then tacitly professed),[6] 22 March 1539 (when described as 'sicke and lame').[7]

209 Agnes Halle, occ. 25 June 1505 (then tacitly professed).[8]

210 Joan (Johanna) Faringdon (Farrendon), occ. 25 June 1505 (then tacitly professed),[9] 22 March 1539 (when described as 'sicke and lame');[10] alive 1553.[11]

211 Alice (Alicia, or Avice) Brent (Brente), occ. 25 June 1505 (then tacitly professed),[12] 22 March 1539 (as Avice Brente).[13]

212 Alice (Alicia) Champeneys (Champnes, Champeney,

1   *SMW (1501–1530)*, 254.

2   *Reg. Audley*, fol. 126v; Hutchins 1868, 30b.

3   *Reg. Audley*, fol. 126v.

4   *Monasticon* 2, 486a.

5   Ibid., 474 n. q; Bettey 1989, 180–1 (Appendix I), at 180.

6   *Reg. Audley*, fol. 126v.

7   *Monasticon* 2, 486a.

8   *Reg. Audley*, fol. 126v.

9   Ibid.

10 *Monasticon* 2, 486a.

11 Ibid., 474 n. q; Bettey 1989, 180–1 (Appendix I), at 180. Joan was evidently more robust than her two infirm *commoniales* Alice Jakes (**208**) and Alice Payne (**228**), neither of whom apparently survived until 1553.

12 *Reg. Audley*, fol. 126v.

13 *Monasticon* 2, 486a

Champnys), occ. 25 June 1505 (then tacitly professed),[1] 22 March 1539;[2] alive 1553.[3] From an inscription on fol. 132v Alice owned the *horæ* once belonging to her late abbess, Dame Elizabeth Shelford (**206**), which she purchased for the not inconsiderable sum of 10*s* (around £220 in today's money) from Richard Marshall, rector of the parish church of St Rumbold (1506-35), Cann, just outside Shaftesbury ('Iste liber *pert*inet domine Alicie / Champnys Moniali Monesterij [*sic*] Shastonie / que*m* dicta Alicia emit p*ro* sumna [*sic*] / decem solidor*um* de domino Richardo / Marshall' Rectore ecclesie p*ar*ochial*is* sancti / Rumbaldi de Shastina predicta.').[4]

213 Grace (Gracia) Balga, occ. 25 June 1505 (then tacitly professed).[5]

214 Isabel (Isabella) Alford, occ. 25 June 1505 (then tacitly professed).[6]

215 Margaret (Margareta) Skyllyng, occ. 25 June 1505 (then tacitly professed).[7]

216 Brigid (Brigett) Frauntleroy (ffrauntleroy, Fanntelaroy), occ. 25 June 1505 (then tacitly professed),[8] 22 March 1539.[9]

217 Alice (Alicia) Walker, occ. 25 June 1505 (then tacitly professed).[10]

---

1 *Reg. Audley*, fol. 126v.

2 *Monasticon* 2, 486a.

3 Ibid., 474 n. q; Bettey 1989, 180.

4 Wormald & Giles, 516. Luxford, 5, 45–6. A prayer in the same hand as the ownership inscription is written on fol. 78r (Luxford, 46, with n. 106).

5 *Reg. Audley*, fol. 126v. Her apparently Spanish name may suggest that Grace was originally connected in some way with the circle of the future queen Catherine of Aragon, who stayed at Shaftesbury Abbey during her journey from Plymouth to London in 1501 to marry the future King Henry VIII's older brother Prince Arthur (Chandler, 91).

6 *Reg. Audley*, fol. 126v.

7 Ibid.

8 Ibid.

9 *Monasticon* 2, 486a.

10 *Reg. Audley*, fol. 126v.

218 Maria Merwyn, occ. 25 June 1505 (then tacitly professed).[1]

219 Joan (Johanna) Kelly (Kelley, Kellie), occ. 25 June 1505 (then tacitly professed),[2] 22 March 1539;[3] alive 1553.[4]

220 Katherine (Katerina, Katheryn) Gyles (Gelise), occ. 25 June 1505[5] (then tacitly professed), 22 March 1539;[6] alive 1553.[7]

221 Alice (Alicia) Baker, occ. 25 June 1505[8] (then tacitly professed), 22 March 1539.[9]

222 Elizabeth Cary (Care), occ. 25 June 1505[10] (then tacitly professed), 22 March 1539;[11] alive 1553.[12]

223 Anne (Anna) Croft, occ. 25 June 1505 (then tacitly professed).[13]

224 Joan (Johanna) Blanford, occ. 25 June 1505 (then tacitly professed).[14]

225 Bartholomia Raynold,[15] occ. *c.*1520 x *c.*1537? Entered Shaftesbury Abbey around 1520 at the age of ten, professing nine years later, apparently reluctantly, though she remained at the convent until about two years before its suppression, perhaps abandoning a

1   *Reg. Audley*, fol. 126v.

2   Ibid.

3   *Monasticon* 2, 486a.

4   Ibid., 474 n. q; Bettey 1989, 180–1 (Appendix I), at 180.

5   *Reg. Audley*, fol. 126v.

6   *Monasticon* 2, 486a.

7   Ibid., 474 n. q.

8   *Reg. Audley*, fol. 126v.

9   *Monasticon* 2, 486a.

10 *Reg. Audley*, fol. 126v.

11 *Monasticon* 2, 486a.

12 Ibid., 474 n. q. Elizabeth Care and Elizabeth Core are one and the same person (*pace* Bettey 1989, 180–1 (Appendix I), at 180). *Monasticon* 2, 486a, has only Elizabeth Care (for Cary).

13 *Reg. Audley*, fol. 126v.

14 Ibid.

15 *TAr* D/D/cd/4 (Bath & Wells diocese, Bishop's Consistory Court Deposition Book (1535–40), deposition dated 18 February 1540), cited by Chandler, 68–9.

regretted vocation and returning to her family home at Melcombe Regis, Weymouth (Dorset). Her absence from the 1539 pension list[1] indicates that she had certainly departed by this time.

226 Elizabeth (Elisabeth) Zouche (Souche, Zowch, Zowche, Zuche),[2] 1529-1539. Nun of Shaftesbury; occ. as tacitly professed 4 February [1497],[3] but fully professed by [25 June] 1505;[4] el. abbess +24 November 1528;[5] roy. ass. 13 February 1529,[6] with temps. restored 22 February 1529;[7] conf. and bl. -22 February 1529; resigned 23 March 1539, when the abbey, together with all its possessions in Dorset and elsewhere, was formally surrendered to the royal commissioner by the abbess and convent.[8] Her generous yearly pension of £133 6s 8d (around £56,181 in today's money) assigned 22 March 1539[9] was still being paid in 1553.[10] The prioress Katherine Hall (**199**) and the sub-prioress Elizabeth Monmouth (**190**) were granted £20 and £7 respectively,[11] emoluments significantly lower than that awarded to the abbess,[12] with the remaining fifty-three nuns (**178, 186, 195, 200-2, 204, 207-8, 210-12, 216, 219-22, 227-62**) receiving annual amounts

1   *Monasticon* 2, 485b–486.

2   *HRH* 3, 690; *Monasticon* 2, 474a, 485b–486; Hutchins 1868, 51; *VCH Dorset* 2, 78b–79; Bettey 1989, 115, 180; Bettey 1992, 3–11; Chandler, 92–5.

3   *Reg. Blyth*, 98 no. 365.

4   *Reg. Audley*, fol. 126v.

5   *L & P Henry VIII* 4, pt. 2 (*1526–8*), 2153 no. 4968.

6   Ibid. 4, pt. 3 (*1529–30*), 2329 no. 5290.

7   Ibid., 2338 no. 5316.

8   Ibid. 14, pt. 1 (*January–July 1539*), 230 no. 586.

9   Ibid.; *Monasticon* 2, 485b; *HRH* 3, 690; Bettey 1989, 180–1 (Appendix I), at 180. The same size pension was also awarded to Dorothy Barley, last abbess of Barking, Essex (now Greater London), Ben. (Cooke 1996, 289). The largest pension of all, £200, was received by Agnes Jordan, last abbess of Syon (Middlesex. Brig.), ibid.

10 *Monasticon* 2, 474 n. q; Bettey 1989, 180–1 (Appendix I), at 180.

11 *Monasticon* 2, 485b; Bettey 1989, 180–1 (Appendix I), at 180.

12 This inequity of payment was general and not just confined to Shaftesbury (Cooke 1996, 297–8).

ranging between £6 13*s* 4*d* and 66*s* 8*d*,[1] according to seniority and age. The abbess and thirty-seven nuns (**186, 195, 200, 204, 207, 210, 212, 219-20, 222, 227, 229, 231, 234, 236, 238-42, 244-55, 257-61**), around sixty-eight per cent of the former convent, continued to receive their pensions into Queen Mary's reign.[2] Margaret Zouche, a nun of Wilton pensioned shortly after,[3] was probably a relative. Many of the nuns in the Shaftesbury pension list, with names such as Zouche, Mayo, Horsey, Gerard, Lovell, Champneys, Ashley, Rogers, Ashe, and Bisse came from prominent and wealthy families in the south-west, a number of whom ironically were to benefit considerably from the suppression of the religious houses and the distribution of their estates.[4]

227 Amys (Agnes) Ball, occ. 22 March 1539;[5] alive 1553.[6]

228 Alice (Alicia) Payne, occ. 22 March 1539 (when described as 'sicke and lame').[7]

229 Joan (Johanna) Longford (Langford), occ. 22 March 1539;[8] alive 1553.[9]

230 Edith (Edithe) Kemer, occ. 22 March 1539.[10]

---

1   *Monasticon* 2, 485b–486b.

2   Ibid., 474 n. q; Bettey 1989, 180–1 (Appendix I).

3   Wilton Abbey was surrendered by its last abbess Cecily Bodenham on 25 March 1539 (*VCH Wiltshire* 3, 240b), with pensions awarded to the nuns the following day (*Monasticon* 2, 329b). Cecily was granted £100 yearly, in addition to which she received houses at Fovant (Wilts), together with their gardens, orchards, meadow and pasture, and a weekly load of firewood. Much of this property, however, which had been leased by Cecily to friends and relatives, was promptly retrieved by the Crown three days later, though she was allowed to retain one of the houses (*VCH Wiltshire* 3, 240b).

4   Bettey 1989, 180–1 (Appendix I), at 180.

5   *Monasticon* 2, 486a.

6   Ibid., 474 n. q; Bettey 1989, 180–1 (Appendix I), at 180.

7   *Monasticon* 2, 486a.

8   Ibid.

9   Ibid., 474 n. q.

10 Ibid., 486a.

231 Joan (Johanna) Benbury (Benburie), occ. 22 March 1539;[1] alive 1553.[2]

232 Jane Percevall, occ. 22 March 1539.[3]

233 Margaret (Margareta) Mewe (Mahoo, May, Mayo, Mayowe), occ. 22 March 1539,[4] 1547-8;[5] alive 1553;[6] presumed dead by 1573-4.[7] Recorded (as Margareta May), with Edith Magdalen (**243**), in a survey of the nunnery site 1547-8 as renting one of two adjacent tenements next to the former abbey burial ground (*unum tenementum juxta cimiterium Abbatie*) in the parish of Holy Trinity.[8]

234 Anne Audley (Awdeley, Awdley), occ. *c.*1505+, 22 March 1539;[9] alive 1553.[10] Niece of Edmund Audley, bishop of Salisbury (1502-24),[11] who presented her with a finely decorated manual psalter with Sarum *kalendarium*,[12] probably when she became a nun after 25

1   *Monasticon* 2, 486a.

2   Ibid., 474 n. q; Bettey 1989, 180–1 (Appendix I), at 180.

3   *Monasticon* 2, 486a.

4   Ibid.; Bettey 1989, 180–1 (Appendix I), at 180.

5   Straton 2, 492.

6   *Monasticon* 2, 474 n. q; Bettey 1989, 180–1 (Appendix I), at 180.

7   The rental and extent of 1573–4 (see *supra* p. 36 n. 5) mention the two adjacent tenements formerly leased by Margaret and Edith (… *ij Tenementa insimul jacentia juxta Cemiterium predictum sub redditu utrumque eorum xxj[s] iiij[d] sic olim arentata Margarete Mayowe & Edythe Mawdlen*: Straton 2, 516). The cemetery, or nuns' burial ground, which lay between Holy Trinity churchyard and the north side of the abbey church, was known as 'the Abbey lytten' (ibid.). The rent for each tenement, originally 10*s* 8*d* (ibid., 492), had clearly doubled since 1547–8.

8   Straton 2, 492.

9   *Monasticon* 2, 486a.

10 Ibid., 474 n. q; Bettey 1989, 180–1 (Appendix I), at 180.

11 For Audley, see Hughes, 'Audley'.

12 *Llp* MS 3285 (formerly at Steyning (West Sussex), *penes* Sir Arthur Howard, and Wellington (Somerset), *penes* J. Hasson: Ker, *MLGB*, 177, with supplement (ed. Watson, 1987), 62), dated *s.*xv (*c.*1430–1440), with contemporary and later (*s.*xvi,[1]) annotations (Bell 1995, 166 no. 6; Scott 1, 76 n. 30, 378–9 (Table I, *Pictorial Subjects in Selected English Psalters, c.1400–1500*), at 379; Pfaff 2009, 345 n. 12; Luxford, 48, with n. 123 and Plate 29).

June 1505.[1] Evidence of donation and ownership on fol. 191r ('liber iste pertinet domine Anne / Awdeley moniali monasterii . Shaston'. / Ex dono Reueren[di] domini domini [*sic*] Ed / mundi Awdeley Sar' ep*iscopi* ac / Auunculi predicte domine.'[2]) is supplemented by Anne's signature (*Anne Awdeley*) on fol. 1r, above which is inscribed 'Anna Awdley est domina / mea t*este.* Joanne Bonde'. If Joanne was not an abbey servant, she may have been a lately admitted novice under Anne's tutelage (perhaps related to Alice Bonde, **253**), which may explain her absence from the 1539 pension list.

    235 Alice Pecocke, occ. 22 March 1539.[3]

    236 Maria Cressett, occ. 22 March 1539;[4] alive 1553.[5]

    237 Julyan Burdeauxe, occ. 22 March 1539.[6]

    238 Joan (Johanna) Towse (Fowsey), occ. 23 September 1536- 22 March 1539;[7] alive 1553.[8] One of two nuns (see also **262**) of Cannington Priory (Somerset),[9] who transferred to Shaftesbury on the dissolution of their house in 1536.[10] A third, Radegund Tilley, went to Polsloe Priory (Devons), remaining there until its suppression in 1538, and was apparently still alive in 1560.[11]

    239 Anne Philpott (Philpotte), occ. 22 March 1539;[12] alive

---

1   Anne does not appear in the list of nuns, both fully professed (*expresse professe*) and awaiting profession (*tacite professe*), present at the election of Dame Elizabeth Shelford as abbess on 25 June 1505 (*Reg. Audley*, fol. 126v), and presumably entered the convent at a later date.

2   This inscription (dated *s.*xvi, first quarter) is reproduced by Luxford, Plate 29).

3   *Monasticon* 2, 486a.

4   Ibid.; Bettey 1989, 180–1 (Appendix I), at 180.

5   *Monasticon* 2, 474 n. q; Bettey 1989, 180–1 (Appendix I), at 180.

6   *Monasticon* 2, 486a.

7   Ibid.; Bettey 1989, 180; Dunning, 137.

8   *Monasticon* 2, 474 n. q; Bettey 1989, 180–1 (Appendix I), at 180.

9   For Cannington Priory, see *VCH Somerset* 2, 109–11; Dunning, 38, 42–3, 53, 123, 125 *et passim*.

10 Dunning, 137.

11 Ibid.

12 *Monasticon* 2, 486a.

1553.[1]

240 Margaret (Maria) Butsett (Buttehead), occ. 22 March 1539;[2] alive 1553.[3]

241 Elizabeth Ayssheley (Ashley, Assheley), occ. 22 March 1539;[4] alive 1553.[5]

242 Christine (Cristian, Christiana) Weston, occ. 22 March 1539;[6] alive 1553.[7]

243 Edith (Editha, Edithe) Magdalen (Mawdeleyn, Mawdlen), occ. 22 March 1539,[8] 1547-8,[9] 1553;[10] presumed dead by 1573-4.[11] Recorded (as Editha Magdalen), with Margaret Mewe (**233**) in a survey of the nunnery site 1547-8 as renting one of two adjacent tenements next to the former abbey burial ground in the parish of Holy Trinity.[12]

244 Elizabeth Horsey, occ. 22 March 1539;[13] alive 1553.[14]

245 Margaret (Margareta, Margarete) Nuton (Newton), occ. 22 March 1539;[15] alive 1553.[16]

1 *Monasticon* 2, 474 n. q; Bettey 1989, 180–1 (Appendix I), at 180.

2 *Monasticon* 2, 486a.

3 Ibid., 474 n. q; Bettey 1939, 180–1 (Appendix I), at 180.

4 *Monasticon* 2, 486b.

5 Ibid., 474 n. q; Bettey 1989, 180–1 (Appendix I), at 180.

6 *Monasticon* 2, 486b.

7 Ibid., 474 n. q; Bettey 1989, 180–1 (Appendix I), at 180.

8 *Monasticon* 2, 486b.

9 Straton 2, 492.

10 *Monasticon* 2, 474 n. q; Bettey 1989, 180–1 (Appendix I), at 181.

11 Straton 2, 516.

12 Ibid., 492.

13 *Monasticon* 2, 486b.

14 Ibid., 474 n. q; Bettey 1989, 180–1 (Appendix I), at 181.

15 *Monasticon* 2, 486b.

16 Ibid., 474 n. q; Bettey 1989, 180–1 (Appendix I), at 181.

246 Alice Gerard, occ. 22 March 1539;[1] alive 1553.[2]

247 Ursula Johnson, occ. 22 March 1539;[3] alive 1553.[4]

248 Elizabeth Larder, occ. 22 March 1539;[5] alive 1553.[6]

249 Alice Rogers, occ. 22 March 1539;[7] alive 1553.[8]

250 Dorothy (Dorothe) Clansey (Clancey), occ. 22 March 1539;[9] alive 1553.[10] Dorothy was the illegitimate daughter of Cardinal Thomas Wolsey and Mistress (Joan?) Lock (or Larke), an innkeeper's daughter of Thetford in Norfolk, who adopted the name Clansey (or Clancey) before being compelled to become a nun of Shaftesbury at the age of twenty four.[11] On the suppression of the monastery she was awarded a modest pension of £4 13s 4d.[12]

251 Anne Bodenham (Bodenhame), occ. 22 March 1539;[13] alive 1553.[14] Perhaps related to Cecily Bodenham,[15] last abbess of Wilton, 1534-9.

252 Elizabeth Denham (Denhame), occ. 22 March 1539;[16] alive 1553.[17]

1   *Monasticon* 2, 486b.

2   Ibid., 474 n. q; Bettey 1989, 180–1 (Appendix I), at 181.

3   *Monasticon* 2, 486b.

4   Ibid., 474 n. q; Bettey 1989, 180–1 (Appendix I), at 181.

5   *Monasticon* 2, 486b.

6   Ibid., 474 n. q; Bettey 1989, 180–1 (Appendix I), at 181.

7   *Monasticon* 2, 486b.

8   Ibid., 474 n. q; Bettey 1989, 180–1 (Appendix I), at 181.

9   *Monasticon* 2, 486b.

10 Ibid., 474 n. q; Bettey 1989, 180–1 (Appendix I), at 181.

11 *Monasticon* 2, 486b; Bettey 1989, 18, 50–2, 181; Bettey 1992, 5–7, with n. 7; Chandler, 94; Jack, 'Wolsey', under *Early life*. The name also occurs as Clausey or Clusey (so *Monasticon* 2, 474 n. q, Bettey and Chandler).

12 *Monasticon* 2, 486b.

13 Ibid.

14 Ibid., 474 n. q; Bettey 1989, 180–1 (Appendix I), at 181.

15 *Monasticon* 2, 330b; Youings, 80–1; Bettey 1989, 108, 115.

16 *Monasticon* 2, 486b.

17 Ibid., 474 n. q; Bettey 1989, 180–1 (Appendix I), at 181.

253 Alice Bonde, occ. 22 March 1539;[1] alive 1553.[2]

254 Elizabeth Wortheton (Wroughton), occ. 22 March 1539;[3] alive 1553.[4]

255 Margaret Keylewaye (Keylway), occ. 22 March 1539;[5] alive 1553.[6] Perhaps related to Dorothy Kelwaye,[7] a nun of Wilton pensioned shortly after.

256 Margaret Aysshe, occ. 22 March 1539.[8] Perhaps related to Anne Asshe,[9] a nun of Wilton pensioned shortly after.

257 Jane Weste, occ. 22 March 1539; [10] alive 1553.[11]

258 Katherine (Katheryn) Hayward, occ. 22 March 1539;[12] alive 1553.[13]

259 Margaret Lovell, occ. 22 March 1539;[14] alive 1553.[15]

260 Elizabeth Babington, occ. 22 March 1539; [16] alive 1553.[17]

261 Margaret Frye, occ. 22 March 1539;[18] alive 1553.[19]

262 Alice Bysse (Bisse), occ. 23 September 1536-22 March

---

1   *Monasticon* 2, 486b.

2   Ibid., 474 n. q; Bettey 1989, 180–1 (Appendix I), at 181.

3   *Monasticon* 2, 486b.

4   Ibid., 474 n. q; Bettey 1989, 180–1 (Appendix I), at 181.

5   *Monasticon* 2, 486b.

6   Ibid., 474 n. q.

7   *Monasticon* 2, 330b.

8   Ibid., 486b.

9   Ibid., 330b.

10   Ibid., 486b.

11   Ibid., 474 n. q; Bettey 1989, 180–1 (Appendix I), at 181.

12   *Monasticon* 2, 486b.

13   Ibid., 474 n. q; Bettey 1989, 180–1 (Appendix I), at 181.

14   *Monasticon* 2, 486b.

15   Ibid., 474 n. q; Bettey 1989, 180–1 (Appendix I), at 181.

16   *Monasticon* 2, 486b.

17   Ibid., 474 n. q; Bettey 1989, 180–1 (Appendix I), at 181.

18   *Monasticon* 2, 486b.

19   Ibid., 474 n. q; Bettey 1989, 180–1 (Appendix I), at 181.

1539; presumed dead by 1553. One of two nuns (see also **238**) of Cannington Priory (Somerset),[1] who transferred to Shaftesbury on the dissolution of their house in 1536.[2]

1   See *supra* p. 108 n. 9.

2   Dunning, 137.

BIBLIOGRAPHY

1 PRIMARY SOURCES (ORIGINAL)

Manuscripts

Great Britain

The prefix GB- is omitted from citations of sources in British libraries and archives

Cambridge, Corpus Christi College (*GB-Ccc*)
        042
Cambridge, Fitzwilliam Museum (*GB-Cfm*)
        2-1957
Cambridge, University Library (*GB-Cu*)
        Ii. 6. 40
London, British Library (*GB-Lbl*)
        Cotton Charter viii. 38
        Cotton Cleopatra C. x
        Cotton Nero C. iv
        Egerton 3098
        Egerton 3135
        Harley 61
        Harley 433
        Lansdowne 383
London, Lambeth Palace Library (*GB-Llp*)
        3285
Oxford, Bodleian Library (*GB-Ob*)
        French e. 22

United States

Dallas, Southern Methodist University, Bridwell Library (*US-DAubl*)
        Special Collections 9

Archives

Great Britain

Chippenham, Wiltshire and Swindon History Centre (*GB-CHIhc*)
D1/2/3, *The Register of Robert de Wyville, bishop of Salisbury, 1330–75*, in
2 parts [*Reg. Wyville*].
D1/2/6, *The Registers of Richard Mitford, bishop of Salisbury, 1395–1407,
and Nicholas Bubwith, 1407* [*Reg. Mitford* only cited].
D1/2/8, *The Register of John Chandler, bishop of Salisbury, 1417–26* [*Reg.
Chandler*].
D1/2/10, *The Register of William Aiscough, bishop of Salisbury, 1438–50*
[*Reg. Aiscough*].
D1/2/11, *The Register of Richard Beauchamp, bishop of Salisbury, 1450–
81*, in 2 parts [*Reg. Beauchamp*].
D1/2/14, *The Register of Edmund Audley, bishop of Salisbury, 1502–24*
[*Reg. Audley*].
Salisbury Cathedral, Dean & Chapter Archives (*GB-SBca*)
Press I, Box 17, Shaftesbury/1–3, 128.
Taunton, Somerset Record Office (*GB-TAr*)
D/D/cd/4

2 PRIMARY SOURCES (PRINTED)

AA. SS.   *Acta Sanctorum quotquot toto orbe coluntur*, ed. J. Bolland *et al.*, 64
vols. (Antwerp, Tongerloo, Paris, and Brussels, 1643 ff.).

Æthelweard   Alistair Campbell (ed. and translated by), *The Chronicle of
Æthelweard*, Nelson's Medieval Texts (London: Thomas Nelson
& Sons Ltd, 1961).

AM   H. R. Luard (ed.), *Annales Monastici*, 5 vols. (London: Longman,
Green, Longman, Roberts, & Green, 1864–9): I *Annales de
Margam* (A.D. 1066–1232); *Annales de Theokesberia* (A.D. 1066-
1263; *Annales de Burton* (A.D. 1004–1263); II *Annales monasterii
de Wintonia* (A.D. 519–1277); *Annales monasterii de Waverleia*
(A.D. 1–1291); III *Annales prioratus de Dunstaplia* (A.D.
1–1297); *Annales monasterii de Bermundeseia* (A.D. 1042–1432);
IV *Annales monasterii de Oseneia* (A.D. 1016–1347); *Chronicon
vulgo dictum Chronicon Thomæ Wykes* (A.D. 1066–1289); *Annales
prioratus de Wigornia* (A.D. 1–1377); V Index and glossary.

A-NL   M. Dominica Legge, (ed.), *Anglo-Norman Letters and Petitions
from All Souls MS 182*, Anglo-Norman Texts 3, Anglo-Norman
Text Society (Oxford: Basil Blackwell, 1941).

Anselmi opera   F. S. Schmitt (ed.) *Anselmi Cantuariensis archiepiscopi opera omnia*, 6 vols., 1938–61: I (1938, Seckau, reprinted 1946, Edinburgh: Thomas Nelson & Sons Ltd), II–III (1946), IV (1949), V (1951), VI (1961), Edinburgh: Thomas Nelson & Sons Ltd.

ASC   *The Anglo-Saxon Chronicle, a collaborative edition, a semi-diplomatic edition with introduction and indices*, general editors David Dumville and Simon Keynes (Cambridge UK: D. S. Brewer, 1983 ff.): vols. 1, Facsimile of MS F, the Domitian bilingual, ed. David Dumville; 3 (MS A), ed. Janet M. Bately; 4 (MS B), ed. Simon Taylor; 5 (MS C), ed. Katherine O'Brien O'Keeffe; 6 (MS D), ed. G. P. Cubbin; 7 (MS E), ed. Susan Irvine; 8 (MS F), ed. Peter S. Baker; 10, *The Abingdon Chronicle, A.D. 956–1066* (a reconstructed edition of MS C, with reference to MSS B, D, E), ed. Patrick W. Connor; 17, *The Annals of St Neots* with *Vita prima Sancti Neoti*, ed. David Dumville and Michael Lapidge [cited by MS and year].

Asser   W. H. Stevenson (ed.), *Asser's Life of King Alfred, together with the Annals of St Neots erroneously ascribed to Asser* (Oxford: The Clarendon Press, 1904), new impression with introduction by Dorothy Whitelock discussing recent work on Asser's *Life of Alfred* (Oxford: The Clarendon Press, 1959, reprinted by Sandpiper Books Ltd, 1998).

ASW   Dorothy Whitelock (ed. and translated by), *Anglo-Saxon Wills* (Cambridge: Cambridge University Press, 1930).

BHL   *Bibliotheca Hagiographica Latina Antiquæ et Mediæ Ætatis*, Société des Bollandistes, Subsidia Hagiographica 6, 2 vols. (Brussels, 1898, 1901), with supplements, 1911 and 1986.

Birch   Walter de Gray Birch (ed.), *Liber Vitae: Register and Martyrology of New Minster and Hyde Abbey, Winchester*, Hampshire Record Society (London: Simpkin & Co. Ltd, and Winchester: Warren & Son, 1892).

Brompton   *Chronicon Johannis Bromton ... ab Anno Domini 588, quo S. Augustinus venit in Angliam usque mortem regis Ricardi I, scilicet Anno Domini ... 1198 ...* in Sir Roger Twysden, *Historiæ Anglicanæ Scriptores ... nunc primum in lucem editi. Adjectis variis lectionibus, glossario, indiceque copioso ...* vol. 10 (London: Sumptibus Cornelii Bee, 1652).

CCR   *Calendar of the Close Rolls preserved in the Public Record Office printed under the superintendence of the Deputy Keeper of the records,* ed. H.C. Maxwell Lyte *et al.* (London: HMSO, 1900 ff.).

CM   H. R. Luard (ed.), *Matthæi Parisiensis, monachi Sancti Albani, Chronica Majora,* 7 vols., Rerum Britannicarum Medii Ævi, or Chronicles and Memorials of Great Britain and Ireland during the Middle Ages [Rolls Series] (London, 1872–83): 1 (*The Creation to A.D. 1066*).

Councils & Synods   F. M. Powicke and Christopher R. Cheney (eds.), *Councils and Synods with other documents relating to the English Church* 2 *1205–1313,* pt. 1 *1205–65* (Oxford: The Clarendon Press, 1964).

CPL   *Calendar of Entries in the Papal Registers relating to Great Britain and Ireland [Calendar of Papal Letters],* ed. W. H. Bliss, C. Johnson, J. A. Twemlow *et al.* (London: HMSO, 1893 ff.).

CPR   *Calendar of the Patent Rolls preserved in the Public Record Office printed under the superintendence of the Deputy Keeper of the records,* ed. H. C. Maxwell Lyte *et al.* (London: HMSO, 1901 ff.).

CRR   *Curia Regis Rolls ... preserved in the Public Record Office printed under the superintendence of the Deputy Keeper of the Records,* ed. C. T. Flower *et al.* (London: HMSO, 1922 ff.).

Delisle 1866   *Rouleaux des morts du neuvième au quinzième siècle, recueillis et publiés pour la Société de l'Histoire de France, par Léopold Delisle* (Paris: Veuve Jules Renouard, 1866, reprinted New York: Johnson Reprint, 1968).

Delisle 1909   *Rouleau mortuaire du bienheureux Vital, abbé de Savigni, contenant 207 titres écrits en 1122–1123 dans différentes églises de France et d'Angleterre,* Édition phototypique avec introduction par Léopold Delisle (Paris: Philippe Renouard, Librairie H. Champion, 1909).

EDB   *Exeter Domesday Book.*

EEA Salisbury   Brian R. Kemp (ed.), *English Episcopal Acta* 18 (*Salisbury 1078–1217*), 19 (*Salisbury 1217–28*), 36 (*Salisbury 1229–62*) and 37 (*Salisbury 1263–97*) (Oxford: Oxford University Press for The British Academy, 1999, 2000, 2010).

EETS   Early English Text Society publications (Oxford: Oxford University Press, 1864 ff.): Original Series, 1864 ff.; Extra

Series, 1867–1921 (issues for 1922–69 continuing as part of the Original Series); Supplementary Series, 1970 ff.).

EEW   F. J. Furnivall (ed.), *The Fifty Earliest English Wills in the Court of Probate, London, AD 1387–1439, with a priest's of 1454, copied and edited from the original registers in Somerset House* ... London: EETS, Original Series 78, 1882, reprinted 1964.

EKM   Christine E. Fell, *Edward King and Martyr*, Leeds Texts and Monographs New Series, The University of Leeds School of English (Menston (Yorks): The Scolar Press Ltd, 1971).

ELW   A. Gibbons (ed.), *Early Lincoln Wills, An Abstract of all the Wills and Administrations recorded in the Episcopal Registers of the old Diocese of Lincoln ... 1280–1547* (Lincoln: James Williamson, 1888).

Fœdera   Thomas Rymer and Robert Sanderson (eds.), *Fœdera, conventiones, litteræ, et cujuscunque generis Acta publica, inter Reges Angliæ, et alios quosvis Imperatores, Reges, Pontifices, Principes, vel Communitates, ... ab anno 1101, ad nostra usque tempora, habita aut tractata; ex autographis, infra secretiores Archivorum Regiorum thesaurarias ... fideliter exscripta ...* 2nd edition revised and supplemented by George Holmes, 20 vols. (London: Jacob Tonson, 1704–32).

GDB   *Great Domesday Book.*

GP   William of Malmesbury, *Gesta Pontificum Anglorum*, ed. and translated by M. Winterbottom & R. M. Thomson, *William of Malmesbury, Gesta Pontificum Anglorum, The History of the English Bishops*, Oxford Medieval Texts, 2 vols. (I Text and Translation, II Commentary), Oxford University Press, 2007.

GR   William of Malmesbury, *Gesta regum Anglorum*, ed. and translated by R. A. B. Mynors, R. M. Thomson & M. Winterbottom, *William of Malmesbury, Gesta Regum Anglorum, The History of the English Kings*, Oxford Medieval Texts, 2 vols. (I Text and Translation, II Commentary), Oxford University Press, 1998.

Horrox & Hammond   Rosemary Horrox and P. W. Hammond (eds.), *British Library Harleian Manuscript 433*, 4 vols. (Gloucester: Alan Sutton Publishing Ltd for the Richard III Society, 1979–83): 1 *Register of grants for the reigns of Edward V and Richard III.*

Horstmann   C. Horstmann (ed.), *S. Editha, sive Chronicon Vilodunense im*

Wiltshire Dialekt aus MS. Cotton Faustina B III ... (Heilbronn: Verlag von Gebrüder Henninger, 1883).

Hunter   J. Hunter (ed.), *Magnum Rotulum Scaccarii vel Magnum Rotulum Pipæ* [Pipe Roll] *de anno tricesimo-primo regni Henrici primi; quem plurimi hactenus laudarunt pro rotulo quinti anni Stephani regis ...* (London: Record Commission, 1833).

John of Worcester, *Chronicle*   R. R. Darlington and Patrick McGurk (eds.), with translations by Jennifer Bray and Patrick McGurk, *The Chronicle of John of Worcester*, vols. 2 and 3 only published (2 *The Annals from 450 to 1066*, 3 *The Annals from 1067 to 1140 with the Gloucester Interpolations and the Continuation to* 1141), Oxford Medieval Texts (Oxford: The Clarendon Press, 1995, 1998).

Kelly   S. E. Kelly (ed.), *Charters of Shaftesbury Abbey*, Anglo-Saxon Charters V, Oxford University Press for The British Academy, 1996 [includes references to Sawyer, *Anglo-Saxon Charters*, 1968].

Keynes 1996   S. Keynes (ed.), *The Liber Vitae of the New Minster and Hyde Abbey, Winchester: British Library Stowe 944, together with leaves from British Library Cotton Vespasian A. VIII and British Library Cotton Titus D. XXVII*, Early English Manuscripts in Facsimile, edited by Geoffrey Harlow, Peter Clemoes and Fred C. Robinson, XXVI (Copenhagen: Rosenkilde & Bagger, 1996).

Keynes & Lapidge Simon Keynes and Michael Lapidge (ed. and translated by) *Alfred the Great: Asser's Life of King Alfred and other contemporary sources* (Harmondsworth: Penguin Classics, 1983).

Lapidge   Michael Lapidge (ed.), *Anglo-Saxon Litanies of the Saints*, Henry Bradshaw Society 106 (London: The Boydell Press, 1991).

Legg   J. Wickham Legg (ed.), *The Sarum Missal edited from three early manuscripts* (Oxford: The Clarendon Press, 1916, reprinted 1969).

L & P Henry VIII   *Letters and Papers, Foreign and Domestic, of the Reign of Henry VIII preserved in the Public Record Office, the British Museum, and elsewhere in England*, ed. J. S. Brewer *et al.* (London: HMSO, 1862 ff.).

Liebermann   F. Liebermann (ed.), *Die Heiligen Englands* (Hanover: Hahn'sche Buchhandlung, 1889).

LMH   Edward Edwards (ed.), The *Liber de monasterii de Hyda*, Rerum Britannicarum Medii Ævi, or Chronicles and Memorials of Great Britain and Ireland during the Middle Ages [Rolls Series] (London: Longmans, Green, Reader & Dyer, 1866).

Millet 2005–6   Bella Millet (ed.), *Ancrene Wisse, a corrected edition of the text in Cambridge, Corpus Christi College MS 402, with variants from other manuscripts*, 2 vols., EETS Original Series 325–6 (Oxford: Oxford University Press, 2005–6).

Millet 2009   *Ancrene Wisse, Guide for Anchoresses: a translation based on Cambridge, Corpus Christi College MS 402*, by Bella Millet, Exeter Medieval Texts and Studies (Exeter: University of Exeter Press, 2009).

Monasticon   *Monasticon Anglicanum, or, the History of the Ancient Abbies, and other Monasteries, Hospitals, Cathedral and Collegiate Churches in England and Wales ... collected and published in Latin by Sir W. D.* [William Dugdale], *and now epitomised in English* [by J. Wright], revised by H. Caley, H. Ellis and B. Bandinel, 6 vols. in 8 (London, 1817–46).

Morgan   Nigel J. Morgan (ed.), *English Monastic Litanies of the Saints after 1100*, II (Pontefract–York), Henry Bradshaw Society (Woodbridge: Boydell & Brewer, 2013).

PL   *Patrologia Latina cursus completus*, ed. J.-P. Migne, 217 vols. with index, 4 vols. (Paris, 1844–64).

RB   *Rule of St Benedict* [the version of the *Rule* cited throughout this work is *RB 1980* (*The Rule of St Benedict in Latin and English, with notes*), edited by Timothy Fry, OSB, *et al.*, and published by The Liturgical Press, Collegeville, Minnesota, 1980].

Reg. Blyth   D. Wright (ed.), *The Register of John Blyth, Bishop of Salisbury, 1493–1499*, Wiltshire Record Society 68 (Chippenham, 2015).

Reg. Gainsborough   J. W. Willis Bund (ed.) *The Register of Bishop William Gainsborough, Bishop of Worcester, 1303–1307*, Worcester Historical Society (Oxford: James Parker & Co., 1907).

Reg. Ghent   C. T. Flower and M. C. B. Dawes (eds.), *The Register of Simon of Ghent, Bishop of Salisbury, 1297–1315, Registrum Simonis de Gandavo* [*Ghent*], *diocesis Saresberiensis, A. D. 1297–1315*, 2 vols., The Canterbury and York Society XL–XLI (London, 1934).

Reg. Hallum Joyce M. Horne (ed.), *The Register of Robert Hallum, Bishop of Salisbury, 1407–17*, The Canterbury and York Society LXXII (Torquay: The Devonshire Press, 1982).

Reg. Langton D. P. Wright (ed.), *The Register of Thomas Langton, Bishop of Salisbury, 1485–93*, The Canterbury and York Society LXXIV (London, 1985).

Reg. Martival *The Registers of Roger Martival, Bishop of Salisbury, 1315–1330*: I, ed. K. Edwards, The Canterbury and York Society LV–LVI, 1959–60; II (in two parts), ed. C. R. Elrington, The Canterbury and York Society LVII–LVIII, 1963, 1972; III, ed. S. Reynolds, The Canterbury and York Society LIX, 1965; IV, ed. D. M. Owen, with general introduction by K. Edwards, The Canterbury and York Society LXVIII, 1975.

Reg. Waltham T. C. B. Timmins (ed.), *The Register of John Waltham, Bishop of Salisbury, 1388–1395*, The Canterbury and York Society LXXX (Woodbridge: The Boydell Press, 1994).

Regularis Concordia T. Symons (ed. and translated by), *The Regularis Concordia, the monastic agreement of the monks and nuns of the English nation*, Nelson's Medieval Texts (London: Thomas Nelson & Sons Ltd, 1953).

Rhys Olwen Rhys (ed.), *An Anglo-Norman Rhymed Apocalypse with Commentary: from the Giffard MS. formerly in the possession of Sir John Fox and now in the Bodleian*, with introduction by Sir John Fox, Anglo-Norman Text Society 6 (Oxford: Basil Blackwell, 1946).

RRA-N *Regesta Regum Anglo-Normannorum, 1066–1154*, 3 vols., 1913–68: I *Regesta Willelmi Conquestoris et Willelmi Rufi, 1066–1100*, ed. H. W. C. Davis (Oxford: The Clarendon Press, 1913); II *Regesta Henrici Primi, 1100–1135*, ed. C. Johnson & H. A. Cronne (Oxford: The Clarendon Press, 1956); III *Regesta Regis Stephani ac Mathildis Imperatricis ac Gaufridi et Henrici Ducum Normannorum*, ed. H. A. Cronne & R. H. C. Davis (Oxford: The Clarendon Press, 1968).

Rushforth 2008 Rebecca Rushforth (ed.), *Saints in English Kalendars before A. D. 1100*, Henry Bradshaw Society 117 (London: The Boydell Press, 2008).

Salu *The Ancrene Riwle*, (The Corpus MS: *Ancrene Wisse*), translated by M. B. Salu, with introduction by Dom Gerard Sitwell, OSB, and preface by J. R. R. Tolkien (London: Burns & Oates, 1955).

Simeon of Durham   T. Arnold (ed.), *Symeonis monachi opera*, 2 vols., Rerum Britannicarum Medii Ævi, or Chronicles and Memorials of Great Britain and Ireland during the Middle Ages [Rolls Series] (London, 1882, 1885).

SMW (1383–1500) F. W. Weaver (ed.), *Somerset Medieval Wills (First Series), 1383–1500*, Somerset Record Society 16, 1901.

SMW (1501–1530) F. W. Weaver (ed.), *Somerset Medieval Wills (Second Series), 1501–1530*, Somerset Record Society 19, 1903.

Southern 1972 R. W. Southern (ed.), *The Life of St Anselm, Archbishop of Canterbury*, by Eadmer (*Eadmeri Vita Sancti Anselmi*), Nelson's Medieval Texts, Thomas Nelson & Sons Ltd, London, 1962, revised and reprinted, Oxford Medieval Texts (Oxford: The Clarendon Press, 1972).

Stacy   N. E. Stacy (ed.), *Charters and Custumals of Shaftesbury Abbey, 1089–1216*, Records of Social and Economic History, New Series, Oxford University Press for the British Academy, 2006.

Statutes & Customs Christopher Wordsworth and Douglas Macleane (eds.), *Statutes and Customs of the Cathedral Church of the Blessed Virgin Mary of Salisbury* (London: William Clowes & Sons Ltd, 1915).

Straton   C. R. Straton (ed.), *Survey of the Lands of William, first Earl of Pembroke, transcribed from vellum rolls in the possession of the Earl of Pembroke and Montgomery. With an introduction [by the editor] ... and a preface by the Earl of Pembroke and Montgomery*, 2 vols., Roxburghe Club (Oxford: privately printed at the University Press by Horace Hart, 1909).

Tolkien   J. R. R. Tolkien (ed.), *The English Text of the Ancrene Riwle: Ancrene Wisse, edited from MS Corpus Christi College, Cambridge 402*, with introduction by Neil R. Ker, EETS 249 (Oxford: Oxford University Press, 1962).

Wilkins, *Concilia*   D. Wilkins (ed.), *Concilia Magnæ Britanniæ et Hiberniæ, A Synodo Verolamiensi A. D. CCCCXLVI ad Londinensem A.D. [MDCCXVII]. Accedunt constitutiones et alia ad historiam Ecclesiæ Anglicanæ spectantia*, 4 vols. (London, 1737).

Wormald 1934 F. Wormald, *English Kalendars before A. D. 1100*, Henry Bradshaw Society 72 (London, 1934).

3 Secondary sources (Books, articles, catalogues, dictionaries, and other reference works)

1 Printed

Abels   R. Abels, *Alfred the Great: War, Kingship and Culture in Anglo-Saxon England*, The Medieval World (London & New York: Longman Ltd, 1998).

André 1844   L'Abbe André, *Cours alphabétique et méthodique de droit canon mis en rapport avec le droit civil ecclésiastique, ancien et moderne ... (Encyclopédie théologique ou série de dictionnaires sur toutes les parties de la science religieuse, offrant en français, la plus claire, la plus facile, la plus commode, la plus variée et la plus complète des théologies,* 9), publiée par J.-P. Migne 2 vols. (Paris: Petit Montrouge, Ateliers catholiques, 1844).

André 1892   J. L. André, 'Widows and vowesses', *Archæological Journal* 49 (1892), 69–82.

Arenberg MSS Illuminated manuscripts (11th century through to the 16th century) from the Bibliothèque of their Highnesses the Dukes d'Arenberg (New York: Jacques Seligmann & Co. 1952).

Astill, 'Berkshire'   G. Astill, 'The towns of Berkshire', in Haslam 1984, 53–86 (Ch. 3).

Aston, 'Somerset'   M. Aston, 'The towns of Somerset', in Haslam 1984, 167–201 (Ch. 5).

Barker *et al.*   K. Barker, D. A. Hinton and A. Hunt (eds.), *St Wulfsige of Sherborne: Essays to Celebrate the Millennium of the Benedictine Abbey, 998–1998* (Oxford: Oxbow, 2005).

Bell 1933   H. I. Bell, 'A Register of Deeds from Shaftesbury Abbey', *The British Museum Quarterly* 8, 1 (July 1933), 18–22.

Bell 1995   D. N. Bell, *What Nuns Read: Books & Libraries in Medieval English Nunneries*, Cistercian Studies Series 158, Cistercian Publications (Kalamazoo: Michigan, Spencer: Massachusetts, 1995).

Bellenger   'Benedictine life and influence then and now', in Keen 1999, 117–29.

Bettey 1989   J. H. Bettey, *The Suppression of the Monasteries in the West Country*

(Gloucester: Alan Sutton Publishing Ltd, 1989).

Bettey 1992 J. H. Bettey, 'The suppression of the Benedictine nunnery at Shaftesbury in 1539', *The Hatcher Review* 4, 34 (1992), 3–11.

Biddle   Martin Biddle, '*Felix Urbs Winthonia*: Winchester in the Age of Monastic Reform', in Parsons, 123–40 (Ch. 10).

Bishop   Edmund Bishop, 'On the origins of the feast of the Conception of the Blessed Virgin Mary', in Edmund Bishop, *Liturgica Historica, papers on the liturgy and religious life of the Western Church*, edited by Dom R. H. Connolly and K. Sisam (Oxford: The Clarendon Press, 1918, reprinted 1962), 238–59.

Blair   John Blair, 'A handlist of Anglo-Saxon saints', in A. T. Thacker and R. Sharpe (eds.), *Local Saints and Local Churches in the Early Medieval West* (Oxford: Oxford University Press, 2002), 495–565.

Brenner   Elmer Brenner, *Leprosy and Charity in Medieval Rouen*, Royal Historical Society Studies in History, New Series (Woodbridge: Boydell & Brewer, 2015).

Bruder   J. S. Bruder, *The Mariology of St Anselm of Canterbury* (Dayton, Ohio: St John's Press, 1939).

Bullock-Davies Constance Bullock-Davies, 'Marie, abbess of Shaftesbury and her brothers', *English Historical Review* 80 (April 1965): 314–22.

Bullough   D. A. Bullough, 'The Continental Background of the Reform', in Parsons, 20–36 (Ch. 3).

Campbell-Kease   J. Campbell-Kease, 'The medieval family of Forsey, an essay in local history, genealogy and heraldry', *PDNHAS* 109 (1987), 21–4.

Chandler   J. Chandler, *A Higher Reality, The History of Shaftesbury's Royal Nunnery* (East Knoyle: The Hobnob Press, 2003).

Cheney   C. R. Cheney, *English Bishops' Chanceries, 1100–1250* (Manchester: Manchester University Press, 1950).

Coldicott   Diana K. Coldicott, *Hampshire Nunneries* (Chichester: Phillimore & Co. Ltd, 1989).

Cooke 1990 Kathleen Cooke, 'Donors and daughters: Shaftesbury Abbey's benefactors, endowments and nuns *c.*1083–1130', *Anglo-Norman Studies* 12 (1990), 29–45.

Cooke 1996 Kathleen Cooke, 'The English nuns and the Dissolution', in J. Blair and B. Golding (eds.), *The Cloister and the World: Essays in Medieval History in Honour of Barbara Harvey*, Ch. 13 (Oxford: The Clarendon Press, 1996).

Coulstock P. H. Coulstock, *The Collegiate Church of Wimborne Minster*, Studies in the History of Medieval Religion 5 (Woodbridge: The Boydell Press, 1993).

Cox & Jones *et al.* Peter W. Cox and Paul Jones, with contributions by Kate Brayne, Emma Firth and Laurence Keen, 'The west end of Shaftesbury Abbey church, archaeological investigations at Abbey House, Shaftesbury', *PDNHAS* 139 (2018), 199–207.

Cubitt C. Cubitt, 'The tenth-century Benedictine reform in England', *Early Medieval Europe* 6 (1997), 77–94.

Davis *et al.* G. R. C. Davis, *Medieval Cartularies of Great Britain and Ireland*, edited by Claire Breay, Julian Harrison and David M. Smith (London: British Library, 2010).

DNB Leslie Stephen and Sydney Lee (eds.), *Dictionary of National Biography*, 22 vols. (Oxford: Oxford University Press, 1968).

Dobson E. J. Dobson, *The Origins of Ancrene Wisse* (Oxford: The Clarendon Press, 1976).

DTC A. Vacant, E. Mangenot and É. Amman (eds.), *Dictionnaire Théologie Catholique*, publié sous la direction de A. Vacant ... avec le concours d'un grand nombre de collaborateurs, 15 vols. (Paris: Letouzey & Ané, 1899–1950).

Dunning R. Dunning, *Somerset Monasteries* (Stroud: Tempus Publishing Ltd, 2001).

Elkins Sharon K. Elkins, *Holy Women of Twelfth-Century England* (Chapel Hill and London: University of North Carolina Press, 1988).

Emden A. B. Emden, *Medieval Decorated Tiles in Dorset* (London & Chichester: Phillimore & Co Ltd, 1977).

Farmer D. H. Farmer, 'The Progress of the Monastic Revival', in Parsons, 10–19 (Ch. 1).

Fell   Christine E. Fell, 'Edward King and Martyr and the Anglo-Saxon hagiographic tradition', in D. Hill (ed.), *Ethelred the Unready: papers from the millenary conference*, British Archaeological Reports, British Series 59 (Oxford: 1978), 1–13.

Foot 2000   Sarah Foot, *Veiled Women, Female Religious Communities in England, 871–1066*, 2 vols. (Aldershot: Ashgate, 2000).

Foot 2011   Sarah Foot, *Æthelstan: The First King of England* (New Haven, Connecticut: Yale University Press, 2011).

Fox 1910   J. C. Fox, 'Marie de France', *English Historical Review* 25 (1910), 303–6.

Fox 1911   J. C. Fox, 'Mary, abbess of Shaftesbury', *English Historical Review* 26 (1911), 317–26.

Fox 1913   J. C. Fox, 'An Anglo-Norman Apocalypse from Shaftesbury Abbey', *Modern Language Review* 8 (1913), 338–51.

Freeman   E. A. Freeman, *The History of the Norman Conquest of England, its causes and results*, 2nd edition, 4 vols. (Oxford: The Clarendon Press, 1867–79).

Freise   Edgar Freise, 'Mathilde II' ['Mathilde, Äbtissin von Essen'], *Neue Deutsche Biographie* 16 (Berlin: Duncker & Humblot, 1990).

Gasquet & Bishop   [F. A.] Gasquet and E. Bishop, *The Bosworth Psalter, An Account of a Manuscript formerly belonging to O. Turville-Petre esq. of Bosworth Hall, now Additional MS 37517 at the British Museum* (London: George Bell & Sons, 1908).

Gill   Miriam Gill, 'Female Piety and Impiety–selected images in wall paintings in England after 1300', in Samantha J. E. Riches and Sarah Salih (eds.), *Gender and Holiness: Men, Women and Saints in Late Medieval Europe* (London & New York: Routledge, 2002), 101 ff (Ch. 7).

Gneuss & Lapidge   H. Gneuss and M. Lapidge, *Anglo-Saxon Manuscripts, A Bibliographical Handlist of Manuscripts and Manuscript Fragments Written or Owned in England up to 1100*, Toronto Anglo-Saxon Series 15 (Toronto, Buffalo, London: University of Toronto Press, 2015, reprinted in paperback, 2016).

Grierson & Blackburn   P. Grierson and M. Blackburn, *Medieval European Coinage, with a Catalogue of the Coins in the Fitzwilliam Museum, Cambridge,* 1 *The Early Middle Ages: 5th–10th centuries* (Cambridge: Cambridge University Press, 1986), 326–41 (Appendix 1, *Gold pennies of the Carolingian and early feudal period*).

Haney 1980 K. E. Haney, 'The provenance of the psalter of Henry of Blois', *Manuscripta* 24, 1 (March 1980), 40–4.

Haney 1986 K. E. Haney, *The Winchester Psalter: An Iconographic Study* (Leicester: Leicester University Press, 1986).

Harleian Manuscripts A *Catalogue of the Harleian Manuscripts in the British Museum,* 4 vols. (London: British Museum, 1808–12).

Harris   Barbara J. Harris, 'A new look at the Reformation: aristocratic women and nunneries, 1450–1540', *Journal of British Studies* 32, 2 (April 1993), 89–113.

Haslam 1984   J. Haslam (ed.), *Anglo-Saxon Towns in Southern England* (London & Chichester, Phillimore & Co. Ltd, 1984).

Haslam, 'Devon'   J. Haslam, 'The towns of Devon', in Haslam 1984, 249–83 (Ch. 8).

Haslam, 'Wiltshire' J. Haslam, 'The towns of Wiltshire', in Haslam 1984, 87–147 (Ch. 4).

Heslop   T. A. Heslop, 'The Canterbury Calendars and the Norman Conquest', in R. Eales and R. Sharpe (eds.), *Canterbury and the Norman Conquest: Churches, Saints and Scholars, 1066–1109* (London & Rio Grande, The Hambledon Press, 1995), 53–85.

History of Parliament   J. S. Roskell, L. Clark and C. Rawcliffe (eds.), *The History of Parliament: the House of Commons, 1386– 1421* (Woodbridge: Boydell & Brewer, 1993).

HMSO   His/Her Majesty's Stationery Office.

Hopton   F. C. Hopton, 'The buildings of Shaftesbury Abbey in the mid-sixteenth century', *PDNHAS* 115 (1994), 1–13.

House of Stourton   The History of the Noble House of Stourton, of Stourton, in the County of Wilts, compiled from original official documents, and other additional sources, under the instruction and supervision of Charles Botolph Joseph, Lord Mowbray, Segrave and Stourton, 2 vols.

(London: Privately Printed, Elliot Stock, 1899).

HRH   *The Heads of Religious Houses, England and Wales, 940–1540*, 3
               vols. (Cambridge: Cambridge University Press, 1972–2008): 1
               (940–1216), ed. D. Knowles, C. N. L. Brooke and Vera C. M.
               London, 1972; 2 (1216–1377), ed. D. M. Smith and Vera C. M.
               London, 2001; 3 (1377–1540), ed. D. M. Smith, 2008.

Hutchins 1774 J. Hutchins *The History and Antiquities of the County of Dorset
               ... with a copy of Domesday Book, and the Inquisitio Gheldi for the
               County ... some remarkable particulars of natural history ... a map,
               etc.*, edited by Richard Gough, 2 vols. (London: W. Bowyer & J.
               Nichols, 1774).

Hutchins 1868 J. Hutchins, *The History and Antiquities of the County of Dorset ...
               1774*, revised and reissued in four volumes edited by W. Shipp
               & J. W. Hodson, 3rd edn. (Westminster: John Bowyer Nichols &
               Sons, 1861–73): 3 (1868).

Janaro   J. Janaro, 'Saint Anselm and the development of the doctrine
               of the Immaculate Conception: historical and theological
               perspectives', *The Saint Anselm Journal* 3, 2 (Spring 2006), 48–
               56.

Jones & Underwood   M. K. Jones and M. G. Underwood, *The King's Mother,
               Lady Margaret Beaufort, Countess of Richmond and Derby* (Cambridge:
               Cambridge University Press, 1992, reprinted 1995).

Kauffmann 1975   C. M. Kauffmann, *Romanesque Manuscripts 1066–1190*,
               Survey of Manuscripts Illuminated in the British Isles, General
               Editor, Jonathan J.G. Alexander, 3 (London: Harvey Miller
               Publishers, 1975).

Kauffmann 2001   C. M. Kauffmann, 'British Library, Lansdowne Ms. 383:
               the Shaftesbury Psalter?', in Paul Binski and William Noel
               (eds.), *New Offerings, Ancient Treasures: Studies in Medieval Art for
               George Henderson* (Stroud: Alan Sutton Publishing Ltd, 2001),
               256–79.

Keen, 'Dorset' L. Keen, 'The towns of Dorset', in Haslam 1984, 203–247
               (Ch. 7).

Keen 1999   L. Keen (ed.), *Studies in the Early History of Shaftesbury Abbey*,
               Dorset County Council Environmental Services (Dorchester,
               1999).

Ker, *MLGB*   N. R. Ker, *Medieval Libraries of Great Britain, A List of Surviving Books* (London, Royal Historical Society Guides and Handbooks 3, 2nd edition, 1964, with supplement by A. G. Watson, Royal Historical Society Guides and Handbooks 15, London, 1987).

Keynes 1999   Simon Keynes, 'King Alfred the Great and Shaftesbury Abbey', in Keen 1999, 1–72.

Keynes 2005   Simon Keynes, 'Wulfsige, monk of Glastonbury, abbot of Westminster (c.990–3), and bishop of Sherborne (993–1002)', in Barker *et al.*, 53–94.

Knowles 2004   David Knowles, *The Monastic Order in England, A History of its Development from the Times of St Dunstan to the Fourth Lateran Council, 940–1216,* 2nd edition (Cambridge: Cambridge University Press, 1963, reprinted 1966; first paperback edition, 2004).

Langham   A. and M. Langham, *Lundy*, The Island Series (Newton Abbot: David & Charles, 2nd edition, 1984).

Latham   R. E. Latham (ed.), *Revised Medieval Latin Word-List from British and Irish Sources* (Oxford: Oxford University Press for The British Academy, 1965).

Legge   M. Dominica Legge, *Anglo-Norman in the Cloisters, The Influence of the Orders upon Anglo-Norman Literature*, Edinburgh University Publications, Language and Literature 2 (Edinburgh: Edinburgh University Press, 1950).

Lemaire   Claudine Lemaire, 'La bibliothèque des Ducs d'Arenberg, une première approche', in Frans Vanwijngaerden *et al.* (eds.), *Liber Amicorum Herman Liebaers* (Brussels: 1984), 81–106.

Le Neve, *Salisbury*   Joyce M. Horn (ed.), J. Le Neve, *Fasti Ecclesiæ Anglicanæ, 1300–1541,* 3 *Salisbury diocese* (London: Institute of Historical Research, 1962).

Liveing   H. G. D. Liveing, *Records of Romsey Abbey, An Account of the Benedictine House of Nuns, with notes on the Parish Church and Town (A.D. 907–1558), compiled from Manuscript and Printed Records* (Winchester: Warren & Son Ltd, 1906).

Logan   F. D. Logan, *Runaway Religious in Medieval England, c.1240-1540* (Cambridge: Cambridge University Press, 1996).

Luxford   J. Luxford, *The Art and Architecture of English Benedictine Monasteries, 1300-1540: A Patronage History* (Woodbridge: Boydell, 2005, reprinted in paperback 2012).

McKisack   May McKisack, *The Fourteenth Century, 1307–99*, The Oxford History of England 5 (Oxford: The Clarendon Press, 1959, reprinted 1997).

Meyer 1977   M. A. Meyer, 'Women and the tenth-century English monastic reform', *Révue Bénédictine* 87 (1977), 34–61.

Meyer 1981   M. A. Meyer, 'Patronage of West Saxon royal nunneries in late Anglo-Saxon England', *Révue Bénédictine* 91 (1981), 332–58.

Millet 1992   Bella Millet, 'The origins of Ancrene Wisse: new answers, new questions', *Medium Aevum* 61 (1992), 206–28.

Murphy   Elinor Murphy, 'The nunnery that Alfred built at Shaftesbury', *The Hatcher Review* 4, 38 (1994), 40–53.

NQSD   *Notes & Queries for Somerset and Dorset*, Sherborne, 1890 ff.

O'Carroll   M. O'Carroll, *Theotokos, a Theological Encyclopedia of the Blessed Virgin Mary* (Eugene, Oregon: Wipf & Stock Publishers, 2000, a Michael Glazier Book originally published by The Liturgical Press, 1982).

ODCC   F. L. Cross and E. A. Livingstone (eds.), *The Oxford Dictionary of the Christian Church*, 3rd edition revised by E.A. Livingstone (Oxford: Oxford University Press, 2005).

ODS   D. H. Farmer, *The Oxford Dictionary of Saints*, 5th edition, Oxford Paperback Reference (Oxford: Oxford University Press, 2003).

Oestereich, 'Abbess'   T. Oestereich, 'Abbess', *The Catholic Encyclopedia* 1 (New York: Robert Appleton Company, 1907), 7–10.

Owen   Gale Owen, 'Wynflæd's wardrobe', *Anglo-Saxon England* 8 (1979), 195–222.

Parsons   David Parsons (ed. with introduction by), *Tenth-Century Studies: Essays in Commemoration of the Millennium of the Council of Winchester and Regularis Concordia* (London & Chichester: Phillimore & Co. Ltd, 1975).

Pächt & Alexander O. Pächt and J. J. G. Alexander, *Illuminated Manuscripts in the Bodleian Library, Oxford* 3 (Oxford: The Clarendon Press, 1973).

PDNHAS *Proceedings of the Dorset Natural History and Archaeological Society,* Dorchester, 1928 ff.

Pevsner & Cherry Nikolaus Pevsner, *The Buildings of England* (*Pevsner Architectural Guides*), *Wiltshire,* 2nd edition revised by Bridget Cherry (London: Penguin Books, 1975).

Pfaff 1998 R. W. Pfaff, 'Lanfranc's supposed purge of the Anglo-Saxon calendar', in *Liturgical Calenders, Saints, and Services in Medieval England,* Variorum Collected Studies Series 610, Aldershot (UK) & Brookfield (Vermont USA), Ashgate Publishing (1998), 95–108 (pt. III).

Pfaff 2009 R. W. Pfaff, *The Liturgy in Medieval England, A History* (Cambridge: Cambridge University Press, 2009).

Phillips John R. S. Phillips, *Aymer de Valence, Earl of Pembroke, 1307–1324: Baronial Politics in the Reign of Edward II* (Oxford: The Clarendon Press, 1972).

Pole Sir William Pole, *Collections towards a Description of the County of Devon, now first printed from the Autograph in the possession of his lineal descendant John-William de la Pole of Shute &c. in Devonshire* (London: J. Nichols, 1791).

Poole A. L. Poole, *From Domesday Book to Magna Carta,* The Oxford History of England 3 (Oxford: The Clarendon Press, 2nd edition, 1955, reprinted 1964).

Power Eileen Power, *Medieval English Nunneries, c.1275 to 1535* (Cambridge: Cambridge University Press, 1922).

Powicke F. M. Powicke, *Ways of Medieval Life and Thought, Essays and Addresses* (New York: Biblo & Tannen, 1967).

RCHME Dorset Royal Commission on Historical Monuments, England, *An Inventory of the Historical Monuments in the County of Dorset,* 5 vols. (2 in three parts, 3 in two) (London: HMSO, 1952–75).

RCHME Salisbury Royal Commission on Historical Monuments, England, *Ancient and Historical Monuments in the City of Salisbury* 1 (London: HMSO, 1980).

Reynolds   Brian K. Reynolds, *Gateway to Heaven: Marian Doctrine and Devotion, Image and Typology in the Patristic and Medieval Periods* (Hyde Park, New York: New City Press, 2012), 1 *Doctrine and Devotion.*

Ridyard   Susan J. Ridyard, *The Royal Saints of Anglo-Saxon England*, Cambridge Studies in Medieval Life and Thought, Fourth Series 9 (Cambridge: Cambridge University Press, 1988).

Rollason   D. W. Rollason, 'Lists of saints' resting-places in Anglo-Saxon England,' *Anglo-Saxon England* 7 (1978), 61–93.

Round, 'Adeliza'   J. H. Round, 'Adeliza of Louvain (*d.*1151)', *DNB* 1, 137b–138b.

Rushforth 2005 Rebecca Rushforth, 'The Writing and Spelling of Wulfsige's name,' in Barker *et al.*, 15–19.

Salih   Sarah Salih, *Versions of Virginity in Late Medieval England* (Cambridge: D. S. Brewer, 2001).

Sawyer   P. H. Sawyer, *Anglo-Saxon Charters: an annotated list and bibliography*, Royal Historical Society Guides and Handbooks 8 (London: 1968), revised and expanded as 'The Electronic Sawyer' (http://www.esawyer.org.uk/about/index.html).

Scott   Kathleen L. Scott, *Later Gothic Manuscripts, 1390–1490*, A Survey of Manuscripts Illuminated in the British Isles 6, General Editor, Jonathan J. G. Alexander, 2 vols. (London: Harvey Miller Publishers, 1996): 1 *Text and Illustrations*, 2 *Catalogue and Indexes.*

Searle   W. G. Searle, *Ingulf and the Historia Croylandensis, An Investigation Attempted*, Cambridge Antiquarian Society Octavo Publications 27 (Cambridge, 1894).

Smith   W. Smith, 'Sceftonia: an early account of Shaftesbury and its abbey by William of Malmesbury,' *The Hatcher Review* 4, 32 (1991), 1–10.

Southern 1963   R. W. Southern, *Saint Anselm and his Biographer, A Study of Monastic Life and Thought, 1059–c.1130* (Cambridge: Cambridge University Press, 1963).

Southern 1990   R. W. Southern, *St Anselm, A Portrait in a Landscape*

(Cambridge: Cambridge University Press, 1990).

Stenton   F. M. Stenton, *Anglo-Saxon England*, The Oxford History of
              England 2 (Oxford: The Clarendon Press, 3rd edition, 1971,
              reprinted 1985).

Strickland, *Lives*   Agnes Strickland, *Lives of the Queens of England from the
              Norman Conquest, compiled from official records and other authentic
              documents, private as well as public ... preceded by a biographical
              introduction by John Foster Kirk*, 16 vols. with Plates (Philadelphia:
              George Barrie & Sons, 1902–3).

Sydenham   Laura Sydenham, *Shaftesbury and its Abbey* (Lingfield: Oakwood
              Press, 1959).

Symons   T. Symons, '*Regularis Concordia*: history and derivation', in
              Parsons, 37–59 (Ch. 4).

Taylor   H. Taylor, 'The Anglo-Saxon church at Bradford on Avon',
              Archæological Journal 130 (1973), 141–71.

Thompson   Sally Thompson, *Women Religious, The Founding of English
              Nunneries after the Norman Conquest* (Oxford: The Clarendon
              Press, 1991, reprinted for Sandpiper Books Ltd, 1996).

Thurlby   M. Thurlby, 'Aspects of Romanesque ecclesiastical architecture
              in Dorset', *PDNHAS* 122 (2001), 1–19.

Toy   J. Toy (ed.), *English Saints in the Medieval Litanies of Scandinavian
              Churches*, Henry Bradshaw Society, Subsidia VI (Woodbridge:
              The Boydell Press, 2009).

Vaughn   Sally N. Vaughn, *St Anselm and the Handmaidens of God, A Study
              of St Anselm's Correspondence with Women*, Utrecht Studies in
              Medieval Literacy 7 (Turnhout: Brepols Publishers nv, 2002).

VCH   *Victoria History of the Counties of England*, edited by William Page
              (London: Archibald Constable & Co. Ltd, 1899 ff., and online,
              http://www.british-history.ac.uk/subject.aspx?Subjectid=23).

Vermeersch, 'Profession' A. Vermeersch, 'Profession', *The Catholic
              Encyclopedia* 12 (New York: Robert Appleton Company, 1911),
              451b–453a.

Vernarde   Bruce L. Vernarde, *Women's Monasticism and Medieval Society:
              nunneries in France and England, 890–1215* (Ithaca and London:

Cornell University Press, 1997).

WANHM   *The Wiltshire Archaeological and Natural History Magazine*, Devizes,
            1854 ff.

Ward & Herbert   H. L. D. Ward and J. A. Herbert, *Catalogue of Romances in
            the Department of Manuscripts in the British Museum*, 3 vols., 1–2
            by Ward, 3 by Herbert (London: British Museum, 1883, 1893,
            1910).

Whitbread   L. Whitbread, 'Æthelweard and the Anglo-Saxon Chronicle,'
            English Historical Review 74 (1959), 577–89.

Williams   Ann Williams, 'The knights of Shaftesbury Abbey', *Anglo-
            Norman Studies* 8 (1985), 214–41.

Wordsworth C. Wordsworth, *Ceremonies and Processions of the Cathedral Church
            of Salisbury* (Cambridge: Cambridge University Press, 1901).

Wormald 1973 F. Wormald, *The Winchester Psalter* (London: Harvey Miller &
            Medcalf, 1973).

Wormald & Giles   F. Wormald and P. M. Giles (eds.), *A Descriptive Catalogue
            of Additional Illuminated Manuscripts in the Fitzwilliam Museum
            acquired between 1895 and 1979, excluding the McClean Collection*
            (Cambridge: Cambridge University Press, 1982).

Yorke 1988 Barbara Yorke (ed.), *Bishop Æthelwold, his career and influence*
            (Woodbridge: The Boydell Press, 1988).

Yorke 1999 Barbara Yorke, 'Edward, King and Martyr: a Saxon murder
            mystery', in Keen 1999, 99–113.

Yorke 2003 Barbara Yorke, *Nunneries and the Anglo-Saxon Royal Houses*
            (London: Continuum, 2003).

Youings   Joyce Youings, *The Dissolution of the Monasteries*, Historical
            Problems, Studies and Documents (London: George Allen &
            Unwin Ltd, New York: Barnes & Noble Inc., 1971).

2 ONLINE

Anon., 'Adeliza'   https://en.wikipedia.org/wiki/Adeliza of_Louvain

Costambeys, 'Ealhswith'   Marios Costambeys, 'Ealhswith (*d.* 902), consort
            of Alfred, king of the West Saxons from 871 and of the Anglo-

Saxons from 886', https://doi.org/10.1093/ref:odnb/39226

ESTC   London, British Library, *English Short Title Catalogue*, Catalogue
                 of works published between 1473 and 1800 mainly in Britain
                 and North America, and primarily in English, http://estc.
                 bl.uk/F/?func=file&filename=login-bl-estc

Hughes, 'Audley'   J. Hughes, 'Audley, Edmund (*c.*1439–1524), bishop of
                 Salisbury', http://www.oxforddnb.com/view/article/891

Huneycutt, 'Adeliza'   Lois L. Huneycutt, 'Adeliza [Adeliza of Louvain]
                 (*c.*1103–1151), queen of England, second consort of Henry I',
                 https://doi. org/10.1093/ref:odnb/165

Jack, 'Wolsey'   Sybil M. Jack, 'Wolsey, Thomas (1470/71–1530), royal
                 minister, archbishop of York, and cardinal', https://doi.org/
                 10.1093/ref:odnb/29854

Jones & Underwood,   M. K. Jones and M. G. Underwood, 'Beaufort,
                 Margaret [*known as* Lady Margaret Beaufort], countess of
                 Richmond and Derby (1443–1509)', https://doi.org/10.1093/
                 ref:odnb/1863

Kemp, 'Longespée'Brian R. Kemp, 'Longespée, Nicholas (*d.* 1297), bishop
                 of Salisbury', https://doi.org/10.1093/ref:odnb/95180

Lloyd, 'Longespée'   S. Lloyd, 'Longespée, Sir William (*c.*1209–1250),
                 magnate', https://doi.org/10.1093/ref:odnb/16984

Maddicott, 'Ferrers'   J. R. Maddicott, 'Ferrers, Robert de, sixth earl of
                 Derby (*c.*1239–1279), magnate and rebel', https://doi.
                 org/10.1093/ref:odnb/ 9366

ODNB   *Oxford Dictionary of National Biography*, 60 vols. (Oxford: Oxford,
                 University Press, 2004), http://www.oxforddnb.com

PASE   Prosopography of Anglo-Saxon England, http://www.pase.
                 ac.uk

Ridgeway, 'Bauzan'   H. W. Ridgeway, 'Bauzan, Sir Stephen (*b.* after 1210,
                 d. 1257), knight', https://doi.org/10.1093/ref:odnb/47235

Sawyer   Peter Sawyer, *Anglo-Saxon Charters* (London: 1968), http://
                 www.esawyer.org.uk/about/index.html

Stafford, 'Eadgifu'.   Pauline Stafford, 'Eadgifu (*b.* in or before 904, *d.* in or after 966), queen of the Anglo-Saxons, consort of Edward the Elder', https://doi.org/10.1093/ref:odnb/52307

Strickland, 'Longespée' Matthew Strickland, 'Longespée [Lungespée], William, third earl of Salisbury (*b*. in or before 1167, *d*. 1226)', https://doi.org/ 10.1093/ref:odnb/16983

White, 'Aubigny' Graeme White, 'Aubigny, William d' [William de Albini; *known as* William d'Aubigny Pincerna], first earl of Arundel (*d*. 1176), magnate', https://doi.org/10.1093/ref: odnb/282

Wormald, 'Æthelweard' Patrick Wormald, 'Æthelweard [Ethelwerd] (*d*. 998?), chronicler and magnate', https://doi.org/10.1093/ref:odnb/8918

Wormald, 'Alfred' Patrick Wormald, 'Alfred [Ælfred] (848/9–899), king of the West Saxons and of the Anglo-Saxons', https://doi.org/10.1093/ ref:odnb/183

Yorke, 'Æthelwold' Barbara Yorke, 'Æthelwold [St Æthelwold, Ethelwold] (904x9–984), abbot of Abingdon and bishop of Winchester', https:// doi.org/10.1093/ref:odnb/8920

Yorke, 'Eadburh' Barbara Yorke, 'Eadburh [St Eadburh, Eadburga] (921x4–951x 3), Benedictine nun', https://doi org/10.1093/ ref:odnb/49419

Name, Place and Subject Index

Abbesses, prioresses and other nuns are of Shaftesbury, unless otherwise indicated. References are to page numbers, not entries.

Abbas Combe (Somerset), Shaftesbury abbey estate at 52
Abbesses, *see* Shaftesbury I Abbey, abbesses
Abbot, Alice nun 99
Abingdon abbey (Ben.), Berks. 46n3
Abram (Abraham), Alice nun 90
Adelaisa nun 57
Adeliza nun 56
Adeliza of Louvain, second queen consort of Henry I 68; possible retirement to Wilton abbey 68; Shaftesbury Psalter (*Lbl* Lansdowne MS 383) possibly made for *see* Shaftesbury Psalter; Wilton leper hospital (*leprosarium*) founded by 68 with n1
Ælfflæd (Elffled) *see* Edward the Elder
Ælfgifu *see* St Ælfgifu
Ælfhere of Mercia ealdorman 44
Ælfsige abbot of Ely 51
Ælfsige abbot of New Minster, Winchester 51
Ælfthryth (Ælfðryðe), queen consort of King Edgar 4n2, 6on4; appointed patron of Wessex nunneries 4n2, 49; founder and first abbess of Wherwell abbey 6on4
Ælfthryth (Alfþriþ), religious woman associated with Shaftesbury abbey 45
Æthelflæd (Ælfflæd, Elfleda, Ethelfleda) *see* St Æthelflæd of Romsey
'Æthelfreda' (Æthelflæd?, Æthelthryth?), 'Alfrida' abbess 13, 50-1
Æthelgifu *see* Alfred (Ælfred), Alfred the Great king of Wessex

Æthelhild *see* Edward the Elder
Æthelred II ('Unræd') king of England 41-2, 44, 45, 51, 52n7; negative portrayal of by William of Malmesbury 42n1
Æthelstan, Athelstan king of the English 5n4, 6 with n5
Æthelweard chronicler 41n5, 42n4, 47n5
Æthelwold bishop of Winchester *see* St Æthelwold
Agnes prioress 31, 56
Agnes de Dorset nun 64
Agnes de Ferrers (de Ferrariis, Ferere, de la Ferere, Ferrere) abbess 24, 31, 32, 33, 59, 61-2
Agnes de la Ryver nun 74
Aileva (Æthelgifu, Elveva) nun 55, 56
Aiscough, William bishop of Salisbury 89
Aishtone, Alice nun 93
Aisshecombe, Alice nun 35, 84
Aisshekewe (Aiscough, Ascough, Ayscogh), Katherine nun 89
Alberton, Agnes nun 86
Alford, Isabel nun 103
Alfred (Ælfred), Alfred the Great king of Wessex 1, 4, 10-11, 39, 44; Asser's *Life* of 1, 2nn1, 4, 10-12, 39, 44n5; Æthelgifu, daughter of 1, 6-7, 12-13, 32, 39, 44; Athelney abbey founded by *see* Athelney abbey, founded by King Alfred; Ealshwith (Ealshþið) consort of 4, 6n8, 39, 46; Latin scholarship revived by 10; Psalter translated by 11; religious

life revived by 10; Shaftesbury abbey
founded by *see* Shaftesbury I Abbey,
founded by King Alfred; will of 13
Alice de Lavington (Lavynton,
Lavyngton) *alias* de Winchester
(Wyntonia) abbess 30, 68-9; as nun
64
Aluvena nun 56
Amberleighe (Amberley), Alice nun 85
Amesbury priory (Font.), Wilts, 64n7,
84
Amice nun 62
Amys (Ames), Joan nun 99-100
anchoresses 40 with n3
Ancrene Riwle (*Ancrene Wisse*), 'Rule' or
'Guide for Anchoresses' 40 with n3
Anger, Joan nun 83
Anger, Jonette nun 75
Anglo-Norman 22, 40n3, 66 with n2,
75, 80; spoken at Shaftesbury abbey
22 *see also* English
Anglo-Saxon, charters 13, 40, 41n5, 44,
45n3, 46, 47 with n2; language 4n2,
7n10, 10-11, 13, 47n5; manuscripts
41n3, 45n5 *see also Anglo-Saxon
Chronicle*; saints 19 with n4 *see also*
Sts Ælfgifu Æthelflæd, Æthelwold,
Cuthburh, Dunstan, Eadburh,
Edith, Edward the Martyr, Grimbald,
Merewenna, Wulfsige
Asser *see* Alfred (Ælfred), Alfred the
Great king of Wessex
Anglo-Saxon Chronicle 2, 4nn2-3, 7n10,
47 with n5, 50
Annales monastici 1n2, 53n2, 58n3
Arenberg, 9th duke, library of 79n1
Arundel castle (Sussex) 68nn2, 5
Arundell, Sir Thomas 36 with n5
Ashe (Asshe), Agnes nun 16, 35, 96-7,
100
Ashecombe (Aisshcombe,
Aysshecoombe), Joan nun 15, 35,
81, 87
Asser *see* Alfred (Ælfred), Alfred the
Great king of Wessex
Asshe, Anne nun of Wilton 111
Athelney (Somerset), *Æthelingæg* 9;
monastery founded by King Alfred 9
with nn1-4, 10, 12n1
Atworth (Wilts), Shaftesbury abbey

estate at 55
Aubrey (Albereda) prioress 31, 56
Aubrey (Albereda) de Bosco Rohardi
nun 55
Aucher (Auchier), Margaret abbess 30,
32, 67, 70
Audley (Awdeley, Awdley), Anne nun
107-8; psalter (*Llp* MS 3285) owned
by 107 with n12, 108
Audley, Edmund bishop of Salisbury
107
Aymer de Valence, 2nd earl of
Pembroke 70n8; Beatrice de
Clermont countess of Pembroke,
wife of 70n8
Aysshe, Margaret nun 35, 111
Ayssheley (Ashley, Assheley), Elizabeth
nun 109

Babington, Elizabeth nun 111
Baker, Alice nun 104
Balga, Grace (Gracia) nun 103 with n5
Ball, Amys (Agnes) nun 106
Barking abbey (Ben.), Essex, 24, 105n9
Barley, Dorothy abbess of Barking
105n9
Baryl, Christine nun, misdemeanours
of 69
Bauceyn, Stephen knight 63 with n1
Beatrice de Clermont countess of
Pembroke *see* Aymer de Valence
Beauchamp, Isabel nun 35, 93
Beauchamp, Sir John 3rd Baron
Beauchamp of Bletsoe (Beds) 93
Beauchamp, Margaret duchess of
Somerset 33, 92
Beaufort, Margaret countess of
Richmond and Derby 93; mother of
Henry VII 93
Bec abbey (Ben.), Normandy
(*département* Eure), liturgical use of
19n4
Becham (Beauchamp?), Elizabeth nun
35, 84
Bede, monk and historian 11n1
bede rolls *see* obituary (bede) rolls
Bekyngham, Elizabeth nun 87
bells, convent rung at elections of
abbesses 25 with n4, 26
Benbury (Benburie), Joan nun 107

Benigna nun 57
Berkeley (Glos) pre-Conquest nunnery at 49
Beyntham, Joan nun 35, 94
Beyntone (Beynton, Beyngtone), Isabel nun 35, 85; as election proctor (*procuratrix*) 27nn4-5, 83, 85, 86, 88
Bingham, Robert bishop of Salisbury 28n1
Black Death, economic effects of 29, 34
Blanford, Joan nun 104
Blessed Virgin Mary, feasts of *see* St Mary the Blessed Virgin
Blount, Thomasine nun of Romsey 75
Blunt, Denise nun 69
Blyth, John bishop of Salisbury 100
Bodenham (Bodenhame), Anne nun 110
Bodenham, Cecily abbess of Wilton 106n3
Boethius, *On the Consolation of Philosophy* translated by King Alfred 11, 11nn1, 2
Bollandists 53n4
Bonde, Alice nun 108, 111
Bonde, Joan (Joanne) nun(?) 108
Bonham, arms of 80n11
Bonham, Edith abbess 25, 27 with n4, 30, 31, 33, 34, 35, 78, 79, 80n11, 81-2, 85, 86
Bonham, Philippa nun 35, 93; as scrutineer (*scrutatrix*) of chapter votes 88, 93, 97
Boniface IX pope 76n8
Boore, Edith nun 83
Bosc-le-Hard, Normandy (*département* Seine- Maritime), 55
Boucicaut Master of Paris, manuscript illuminator 78-9
Bradeleigh (Bradeley), Anastasia nun 35, 84
Bradeleighe (Bradley), Constance nun 35, 87
Bradeleygh (Bradeleigh, Bradley), Eleanor (Alianora, Alienora) nun 35, 88
Bradford-on-Avon (Wilts) 55; *cœnobium* with estate 44 with n4, 51; church of St Laurence 44n4
Bramley (Hants), parish church 101

Brent (Brente), Alice (Alicia, Avice) nun 102
Bridport (Dorset) 78
Brombelegh, Catherine nun 15, 77
Brome, Margaret nun 86, 93
Bromehill priory (Aug.), Norfolk, 62n6
Broughton Gifford (Wilts) 71n9; Shaftesbury abbey estate with church (*capella*) at 55
Brown, Margaret nun 93
Bryther (Brethyr, Bruyther), Elizabeth (Elisabeth) nun 15, 94-5
Bulstrode (Bulstroode), Joan nun 98-9
Bulwarden (Bulwardyn), Joyce (Jocosa, Jocia) nun 35, 97; as scrutineer (*scrutatrix*) of chapter votes 88, 93, 97
Bulwardyne, Joan nun, 35; as election proctor (*procuratrix*) 27n5, 83, 85, 88
Burdeauxe, Julyan nun 108
Burghal Hidage 8nn1-2, 12n2
Bury St Edmunds abbey (Ben.), Suffolk, 20n1
Butsett (Buttehead), Margaret (Maria) nun 109
Bysse (Bisse), Alice nun, formerly of Cannington priory 111-12

calendars (*kalendaria*), liturgical 19 with n3, 20n1, 43 with n1, 53nn3, 4, 67, 70n5, 78n7, 79, 95n11, 101n3, 107; *see also* Lanfranc, archbishop of Canterbury, liturgical calendar reforms of
Cambridge, Fitzwilliam Museum 101
Candover (Hants), royal estates at 13
Cann (Dorset), parish priest of *see* Marshall, Richard rector of Cann
Cannington priory (Ben.), Somerset, 35, 108, 112
canon law, lawyers 26
Canterbury, cathedral priory (Ben.) 19, 20n1, 43
Carolingian era 10
cartularies *see* Shaftesbury I Abbey, cartularies
Cary (Care), Elizabeth nun 104
Cater (Katour), Alexander lay sacristan of Shaftesbury abbey 96 with n7;

floorslab memorial 96n7
Catesby (Cattisby), Philippa nun 100
Catherine of Aragon 103n5
Cecilia nun 56
Cecilia de Lavington abbess of Wherwell 69
Cecily abbess 23, 32, 57-8
Cecily de Basynges nun 66
Champnys (Champeney, Champeneys, Champnes), Alice nun 102-3; Shelford horæ (Cfm MS 2- 1957) owned by 101n8, 102-3
chancery, royal 33 see also writs, royal
chantries see Shaftesbury I Abbey, chantries
Chaper alias Nicolls, John of Fontmell (Dorset) 102
chaplains see Shaftesbury I Abbey, chaplains
charters, royal 29, 54, 55, 57, 73, 76; see also Anglo-Saxon, charters
Chaundose, Alice nun 25, 27n4, 82
Cheselbourne (Dorset), Shaftesbury abbey estate at 40
Chichestere, Felice nun 84
Cholsey abbey (Berks, now Oxon), founded by King Æthelred II 52n7
Church, Augustine bishop of Lydda (Palestine) 95n11
Christine de Bampton nun 66
Chynham, Maud nun 75
Clansey (Clancey, Clausey?, Clusey?), Dorothy nun, natural daughter of Cardinal Thomas Wolsey 110
Clare earls of Gloucester, arms of 80n11
Clarice de Mere nun 59
Clauerynge, Isabel nun 83
Clemence (Clementia) Russell nun 64
Clowes, Amice nun 83
Clyvedon, Richard of Somerset 74
Cnut king of England, Denmark and Norway 7n9
Coke (Cocks), Margaret nun 100
Cokkyng, Eleanor nun of Wilton 77
Combe, Margaret nun 91
commoniales 97, 102n11
coniux/coniunx regis, regia coniux/coniunx as equivalent of regina 4n2, 45, 46
conversae, lay sisters 16
Corff alias Remston, Robert canon of

Wells cathedral (Somerset), rector of Corfe (Dorset), will of 80
Cosyn (Cosin), Christine nun 86
Cosyn, William chaplain (capellanus) of Shaftesbury abbey 60-1, 63
Council of Canterbury 1328 20n2
Council of Chalcedon 451 19
Council of Ephesus 431 19
Council, Lateran 1215 (Fourth Lateran Council) 26n1
Council of Oxford 1222 30n2
Council of Winchester 973 48n4
Cressett, Maria nun 108
Cressy, Agnes nun (of Shaftesbury?) 79
Croft, Anne nun 104
Cros, Joan nun 75
Crouke, Joan sub-prioress 82
Crowland abbey (Ben.), Lincs, 47
Culmer, Anne nun 84
Cusin (Cosyn?), Wimark (Wimarka) nun 60-1

Danegeld 57
Danelaw 4n2
De intendendo, royal writ of 27-8, 28
Denham (Denhame), Elizabeth nun 110
Denise (Dionisia, Dionysia) la Blunde (Blounde, Blount?, Blunt?) abbess 15, 31, 69n12, 71
Denise (Dionysia) de Maundevile (Mandeville) nun 63
Derby, earls of see Ferrers
devotae 46
Deynton (Dentoy), Anne nun 98
Domesday Book 13, 24n2, 45, 46, 51-2, 55, 56
domina, 'Dame', as style for nun 33, 66n5, 75, 79, 101, 103
dominus, 'Dom' ('Sir'), as style for priest 67n2
Donhead (Wilts), Shaftesbury abbey estate at 55
Dover priory (Ben.), Kent, Vitæ sanctorum from 54n3
Downside abbey (Ben.), Stratton-on-the Fosse (Somerset) 38n3
Druell, Master John bishop's official 81n12
Duket (Dukett), Joan abbess 30, 72; as

nun 69-70

Duns Scotus, Johannes scholastic
theologian 21

Durneford, Joan nun 24, 76

Durneford, Katherine (nun of
Shaftesbury?) 76

Eadburh see St Eadburh (Edburga)

Eadflæd see Edward the Elder

Eadgifu see Edward the Elder

Eadmer of Canterbury 20n3, 21;
Tractatus de conceptione S. Mariæ of
20n3

Eadmund I king of the English 40, 41,
45; Ælfgifu first consort of see St
Ælfgifu

Eadred king of the English 45, 46, 47

Eadwig king of England 41

Ealshwith (Ealshþið) see Alfred (Ælfred),
Alfred the Great king of Wessex

earls of Arundel see William d'Aubigny

earls of Derby see Ferrers earls of Derby

earls of Gloucester see Clare earls of
Gloucester

earls of Pembroke see Aymer de Valence;
Herbert, [Henry], William

earls of Salisbury see Longespée,
Montacute

Edgar king of England 4n2, 5, 40, 41,
46, 47

Edith (Editha, Eadgitha, Eadgiða) nun
57

Edith of Wilton see St Edith of Wilton

Ediva (Eadgifu) nun 57

Edward I king of England 65n7;
Eleanor of Castile first queen
consort of 65n7; Mary of Woodstock
daughter of 65n7

Edward II king of England 69

Edward III king of England 72; Philippa
of Hainault queen consort of 72

Edward the Elder king of the Anglo-
Saxons 3, 45; Ælfflæd second
consort of 5-6; Æthelhild daughter
of 6; Eadburh daughter of see St
Eadburh (Edburga); Eadflæd
daughter of 5-6; Eadgifu third
consort of 13, 42, 45-7

Edward the Martyr king of England see
St Edward the Martyr

Edyngdone, Joan nun 83

Egbert (Ecgberht) king of Wessex 3

Egelina de Counteville (Countvylle,
Countevile, Countevyle) abbess 29
with n1, 31, 33, 75-6

Eldeva (Ælfgifu?, Elgiva/Elfgiva?) nun
57

Eleanor of Castile see Edward I

Eleanor de Clare see Hugh le Despenser
the younger, 1st Lord Despenser

Eliot, Eleanor (Alienora) nun 15, 100-1

Elizabeth I queen regnant of England
23n1, 37

Elizabeth de Favenham nun 24, 70

Elizabeth de Hulle nun (of
Shaftesbury?)

Elstow abbey (Ben.), Beds, 25n2

Ely abbot of see Ælfsige

Emma abbess 14, 55, 57

Emma de Portibus (de la Porte) nun 61

English, spoken at Shaftesbury abbey
22; used at elections of abbesses 25,
26n1 see also Anglo-Norman, Latin

Eufemia nun 62

Eulalia (Eularia) abbess 14, 22, 23, 28,
53-5, 56n9; abbey church rebuilt by
17; receives letters from St Anselm
16-17; regeneration of royal cults
by 23

Exeter, minster church (cathedral),
relics of Sts Ælfgifu and Edward the
Martyr at 43

Faringdon (Farrendon), Joan nun 102
with n11

Felawe *called* 'Congesbury', William
clerk, rector of Portishead
(Somerset) 78

Felpham (Sussex), Shaftesbury abbey
estate at 46

Ferrers earls of Derby, William V, Robert
VI 61 with n10

fitz Hamon, Robert lord of Gloucester
and Glamorgan 57

Fitzherberde, Lucy prioress 24, 30, 33,
74

Florey (fflorey), Katherine nun 35, 94

Florey (fflorey), Maria nun 35; as
election proctor (*procuratrix*) 27n5,
83, 85, 86; as prioress 30-1

Fontmell (Dorset), Shaftesbury abbey estate at 6n5

Formage (Firmage, Furmage), Joan abbess 24, 28, 29, 30, 32, 33, 73-4, 76; abbey charters confirmed by king during rule of 29; will made by 24, 73

Formage, William probable relative of Joan Formage abbess 73

Forsey family of Bridport 78

Fourth Lateran Council see Council, Lateran 1215

Fovant (Wilts), Shaftesbury abbey estate at 77

Fovent, Cecily abbess 15n2, 31, 77, 79

Fox (Foxe), Richard, bishop of Winchester, translation of Rule of St Benedict by 50n1

Frauntleroy (ffrauntleroy, Fanntelaroy), Brigid (Brigett) nun 103

Frye, Margaret nun 111

Fyherse? (Forsey?), Lucy nun (of Shaftesbury?) 78-9

Geoffrey V (Plantagenet) count of Anjou 58

Gerard, Alice nun 110

Gerard of Brogne, Lotharingian monastic reformer 48n2

Gibbes (Gibbis, Gibbys, Gybbes, Kybbys), Alice abbess 31-2, 88, 92, 95

Giffard, Godfrey bishop of Worcester 65, 70

Giffard, Mabel abbess 24, 28, 31, 32, 65-6

Giffard, Walter archbishop of York 65

Giffard, Master William, chaplain (capellanus) of Shaftesbury abbey 66

Giles de Bridport bishop of Salisbury 62n6, 64

Glastonbury abbey 5n2

Godewyn, Margaret nun 35, 86

Goodwyne (Godwyn, Goodewyne), Elizabeth nun 35, 100

Goscelin of Canterbury, hagiographer 3n3; Life of St Edith of Wilton by 3n3; Passio of St Edward the Martyr attributed to 18, 50

Goviz, Eleanor (Alianora) nun 84

Graunte, Alice nun 82

Grene, Isolde (Isota, Isolda) nun 94

Grimbald [of Saint-Bertin] see St Grimbald [of Saint-Bertin]

Gyles (Gelise), Katherine nun 104

Halle, Agnes nun 35, 102

Halle (Hall), Katherine nun 35, 99; as prioress 31, 99, 105

Hallum, Robert bishop of Salisbury 77

Hanleighe (Hanlegh), Joan nun 82, 83

Hardguylle, Edward 94

Hardyng, Alice nun 93

Hardyng, Amice, nun 83, 93

Hartley Witney priory (Cist. nuns), Hants, 50n1

Hastings, Hæstingaceaster (Sussex) burh 8

Hawise abbess of Wilton 58

Hayward, Katherine nun 111

Hemmerford (Hymerford, Hymmerford), Margaret nun 99

Henry I king of England 52, 55, 57, 68

Henry II king of England 58

Henry III king of England 23n1, 33, 63

Henry V king of England 1n4, 78

Henry VI king of England 15, 81; as Henri II king of France 81n3

Henry VII king of England 35, 92

Henry VIII king of England 23n1, 103n5

Henry de la Ryver of Gloucestershire 'chivaler' 74

[Herbert, Henry 2nd earl of Pembroke], rental and extent of 36n5, 37n1, 107 with n7

Herbert, William 1st earl of Pembroke 36 with n5, 37 with note 2; survey, rental and extent of 36-7, with 36n5

Herelufu, Herleva abbess 13, 23, 39, 52; as possible monastic reformer 48-50; obit in Anglo-Saxon Chronicle, 47, 50; witness to charter 47

Herman, bishop of Sherborne, (from 1075) bishop of Salisbury (Old Sarum) 18n2

Holy Rule see St Benedict of Nursia, Rule (the Holy Rule) of

Honorius III pope 14

horarium, monastic 49

Horsey, Elizabeth nun 109

Horton (Dorset) pre-Conquest nunnery at 49

Hosy (Hoosey, Husy, Hussey), Thomesine (Thomesina, Thomesyn) nun 97

Howchyn (Huchyne), Edith nun 91

Hugh le Despenser the younger, 1st Lord Despenser 71; Eleanor de Clare wife of 71

Hugh le Despenser, 2nd Baron le Despenser 71

Humfray, Elizabeth nun 90, 93

Hussey, Alice nun of Wilton 97-8

Hutchins, John, Dorset historian 18, 73n11

Hyde abbey, Winchester *see* Winchester, New Minster and Hyde abbey

Ine king of Wessex 2

Isle of Purbeck (Dorset), Shaftesbury abbey estate at 45

'J.' (Johanna, Joan) abbess 23, 27, 30, 58

Jakes, Alice (Alicia, Elise) nun 102 with n11

Joan le Blount prioress of Acornbury (Aug.), Herefs, 71

Joan de Bridport abbess 28, 29, 30, 32, 64-5

Joan le Despenser nun 71

Joan de Eketon (Oketon) nun of Wilton 74

Joan de Leueryngton nun (of Shaftesbury?) 79

John of Brompton, Cistercian chronicler 50n2, 51

John de Lavynton (Lavyntone) clerk 69

John de Leukenore household steward of Queen Philippa of Hainault 72 with n15

Johnson, Ursula nun 110

John of Worcester monk and chronicler 1n2, 4nn2-3, 5n1, 7n12, 8n2, 44n5, 47n1, 52n6

Jordan, Agnes abbess of Syon 105n9

Juliana almoner (*elemosinaria*) of Shaftesbury abbey 57

Juliana de Bauceyn (Bauscan, Bauzan, Bauzeyn) abbess 24, 28, 31, 32, 60, 62-3

Juliana la Despenser, Shaftesbury abbey corrodian 71

Kameys (Kemer), Parnel (Perinoi, Petronilla) nun 91

Katour, Alexander *see* Cater (Katour), Alexander

Kelly (Kelley, Kellie), Joan nun 104

Kelwaye, Dorothy nun of Wilton 111

Kemer, Edith nun 35, 106

Kemer, Parnel nun 35

Kemer (Kymer), Thomesine (Thomesia, Thomesina) nun 35, 88; as prioress 31, 89

Keylewaye (Keylway), Margaret nun 111

Kingsclere (Hants), royal estates at 13

Kingston (Dorset), Shaftesbury abbey manor and estate at 45

Kington St Michael priory (Ben.), Wilts, 90

knight-service (*servitium debitum*) 24, 61, 62 with n1

Landaffe (Landaff), Margaret nun 86

Lanfranc, archbishop of Canterbury, liturgical calendar reforms of 19 with n4

Larder, Elizabeth nun 110

Latin, used at elections of abbesses 25, 26n1 *see also* English

Laurence (Laurance), Agnes nun 97

Laurentia de Muscegros (Mucegros) abbess 31, 63-4

Lavington, Felise abbess of Wilton 69

Lavington, Market and West (Wilts) 69

Lawrence, Alice prioress of Kington St Michael 91

lay sisters, see *conversae*

Legbourne (Lincs), church of All Hallows 67n2

Leigh, Isabel nun 83

Leofrun abbess of Reading *see* Reading

Leominster (Herefs), pre-Conquest nunnery at 52

Leukenore (Lewknor) family 72 with n15

Leversheg (Leversey), Alice nun 91

Leveva (Leueua, Leofgifu?) abbess 13-14, 51-3; named in Domesday Book

13
'Liber vitæ' of New Minster and Hyde Abbey, Winchester 45 with n5, 47 with nn3, 4, 50, 51, 52 with n4; *nomina feminarum illustrium* in 47 with nn3, 4
litanies of the saints 43 with n2, 67-8
Litton Cheney (Dorset), rectory of 66
Llywelyn ap Gruffudd prince of Wales 62, 63
Longecote, Alice nun 70
Longespée (Longespee, Lungespe, Lungespee), Agnes abbess 27, 28, 29, 31, 32, 33, 59, 60
Longespée earls of Salisbury, William I, II, III 60 with n8
Longespée, Nicholas treasurer of Salisbury cathedral 60 with n9
Longford (Langford), Joan nun 106
Lotharingia, monastic reforms in 48n2 *see also* Gerard of Brogne, Lotharingian monastic reformer
Lovell, Margaret nun 111
Lundy Island 33, 61n4
Lyng (Somerset), Alfredian *burh* 8, 9n3

Mabel (Mabilia) countess of Gloucester 58
Magdalen (Mawdeleyn, Mawdlen), Edith nun 107, 109
major et sanior pars capituli mandatory at elections of abbesses 26
mancus, mancusa, gold coin or measure of gold 45 with n2
manuscripts 17n2, 20n1, 54nn2, 3, 61n8, 62 with note 8, 63, 66 with nn2, 5, 67-8, 77n6, 78, 79 with nn1, 3, 4, 80, 85-6, 94n13, 96 with n7, 101 with nn3, 5, 8, 103 with n4, 107 with n7, 108; see also *Anglo-Saxon Chronicle*
Margaret de Columbariis (du Colombier?) nun 63, 65
Margaret de Leukenore (Lewknor) abbess 27, 31, 32, 72
Margaret St John abbess 15n2, 24, 27, 28, 31, 32, 33, 34, 35, 82, 83, 85, 88, 89, 92-3
Margery de London nun 59
Marie de France poet 58

Marsh (de Marisco, Mariscis), William 33, 61 with n2
Marshall, Richard rector of Cann (Dorset) 103
Martival, Robert bishop of Salisbury 28n1; threatens to excommunicate abbess and prioress 34n2
Mary abbess 23, 28, 32, 58
Mary queen regnant of England 36-7, 95, 106
Mary de Hastinges nun 59
Mary of Woodstock nun of Amesbury *see* Edward I king of England
Mathilde II abbess of Essen 47n5
Matilda (Mathilde) abbess of Caen, Normandy (*département* Calvados) 22; obituary roll of 22, 53 with n2
Maud (Matillis) de Baillol' (Balliol) nun 59
Maud (Matilda) de Gurnay nun 63
Maunshill (Maunshyll), Joan nun 100
Mawes, Isabel nun 90
Melbury Abbas (Dorset), church of 69
Merewenna (Mærwenna, Mærþynn, Mærwynn, Merewenna, Merwinna) *see* St Merewenna of Romsey
Merwyn, Maria nun 104
Mewe (Mahoo, May, Mayo, Mayowe), Margaret nun 107, 109
minsters 4n3, 12, 43, 45, 52
mints, royal 6n6
Moghtheres, Joan nun 70
Moleyns, Adam dean of Salisbury 91-2; (from 1446) bishop of Chichester 91-2
Moleyns, Katherine nun 91; prioress (from 1492) of Kington St Michael 91-2
Momperson (Mompesson, Mounpessone, Mumpson), Elizabeth nun 89-90
monacha, consecrated nun 55, 66n5
monialis, consecrated nun 40, 66n5; as equivalent of Anglo-Saxon *mynecenu* 40; see also *mynchyne*
moniales expresse professe 31 with n3 34, 81, 87, 88, 89, 90, 91, 92, 99, 100, 101, 102, 105; *tacite professe* 31 with n3, 34, 81, 82, 87, 88, 89, 90, 92, 99, 100, 102, 103, 104-5

Monmouth (Monmouthe), Elizabeth (Elisabeth) sub-prioress 98, 105
Montacute earls of Salisbury, arms of 80n11
More, John of Hereford *see* Shelford, Elizabeth (Elisabeth) abbess
Mouresleyghe (Morsley), Joan nun 85; book owned by 85-6
Mousbury (Musbury), Isabel nun 86
mynchyne (Middle English form of Anglo-Saxon *mynecenu*), consecrated nun 94n12
mynecenu see *monialis*

Nicholas V pope 92n9
nomina feminarum illustrium see 'Liber vitæ' of New Minster and Hyde Abbey
nunne (*nonna*) 40, 46, 66 with n5; definition of 40
nuns *see* Romsey abbey, nuns; Shaftesbury I Abbey, nuns
nunscrude, nuns' clothing 41
Nuton (Newton), Margaret nun 109

obits, of Æthelred II 42n1, of Agnes Cressy nun (of Shaftesbury?) 79, of Elizabeth de Hulle nun (of Shaftesbury?) 66, of Herelufu abbess 47, of Joan Formage abbess 73n11, of Joan de Leueryngton nun (of Shaftesbury?), of Juliana de Bauceyn abbess 61, 63, of priests 67 with n2, of Stephen Bauceyn knight 63, of Wulfwynn abbess of Wareham 47
obituary (bede) rolls 22, 53n2, 56 with nn1-9, 57 with nn 1-7
Odo of Cluny *see* St Odo of Cluny
Oke, Alice nun 86
opus Dei 49
Ordere, Joan nun 75
Original sin, teachings of St Anselm 21-2, and St Augustine 21 on
Orosius 11n1
Orthodox Church 19n2
Osbert of Clare, *Life* of St Edburga by 5n6
Oscytel archbishop of York 47
Osegod *alias* Fovent, Robert of Fovent, Donhead St Mary (Wilts) member of

parliament 77
Otho I emperor 47n5

Panys, Elizabeth nun 35, 84
Panys, Isabel nun 35, 93
Paris, Matthew of St Albans (Ben.), monk and historian, *Chronica majora* of 42n6
PASE *see* Prosopography of Anglo-Saxon England
Payn (Payne), Margaret nun 35, 99
Payne, Alice nun 35, 102n8, 106
Payne (Payn), Maria nun 35, 97
Payne (Pame), Ursula nun 35, 102
Pecocke, Alice nun 108
Pembroke earls of, *see* Aymer de Valence, Herbert, [Henry], William
pensions assigned to nuns *see* Shaftesbury I Abbey, nuns, pensions assigned to at Dissolution
Percevall, Jane nun 107
Pevesy (Pewsy), Alice nun 98
Philippa [of Hainault] *see* Edward III
Philpott (Philpotte), Anne nun 108-9
Piddletrenthide (Dorset), Shaftesbury abbey estate at 40
pilgrims 17
Pilton, *Pilletune* (Devons) *burh* 8
Pius IX pope 22
Pokeswell, Christine nun 87-8; as election proctor (*procuratrix*) 27n5; as scrutineer (*scrutatrix*) of chapter votes 83, 85, 88, 93, 97
Polsloe priory (Ben.), Devons, 108
Poney (Powne), Agnes nun 15, 24, 77-8
Poore (Poor), Richard bishop of Salisbury 24
Pounde, Alice nun 84
Pourestock, Agnes nun 83
Poynes, Elizabeth nun 35, 90
Poynes (Pownys), Ellen (Elena) nun 35, 90
prebendaries *see* chaplains
prioresses 25, 30-1
procuratrix, procuratrices, proctor(s) at elections of abbesses 26-7
Prosopography of Anglo-Saxon England (PASE) 39nn2, 5, 41n5, 45nn1, 3, 5, 47nn1, 5
Prynce, Agnes nun 94

Pulter, Eleanor (Alienora, Elianora)
    nun 99
Purry (Pury, Pyry), Alice nun 97
Pytney, Alice nun 35, 94
Pytney (Pytteney), Christine nun 35, 91

Quarel, Isabel nun 71
Quia propter canonical statute of 26 with
    n1

Ralph de Codeford proctor of
    Shaftesbury abbey 73
Raynold, Bartholomia nun 104-5
Reading, abbey (Clun.), Berks, 20n1,
    52; pre- Conquest nunnery at 52,
    Leofrun abbess of 52
recluses, women 6, 40
Regularis Concordia 4n2, 48, 49; Anglo-
    Saxon translations of 50 with n1
relics 42nn6-7, 43, 44 *see also* St Ælfgifu,
    St Edward the Martyr
religious women 13, 39-47 *see also*
    vowesses
Rempston (Ramstone), Edith nun 35,
    88
Rempston, Ellen (Elena) nun 35, 87
Richard II king of England 15, 74
Richard III king of England 15, 94 with
    n13
Richard Rolle of Hampole, works of 85
Robert de Bingham bishop of Salisbury
    24
Robert de Hull priest and proctor of
    Shaftesbury abbey 67
Roderford (Rotherford), Emma nun 98
Rogers, Alice nun 110
Romanesque architecture 17, 37
Romsey abbey (Ben.), Hants, 47;
    abbesses 47 with n4, 50n1; *see also*
    Sts Æthelflæd and Merewenna;
    foundation attributed to Edward the
    Elder 5n1, to King Edgar 5; nuns
    6n2, 30n2, 75
Rotza nun 56
Rous, Ellen nun 72
royal assent (*assensus regius*) to election
    of abbess 25, 26-7, 95n9
royal licence to elect abbess (*licencia
    regia, litteras de licencia eligendi
    abbatissam*) 27

Rule of St Benedict (Holy Rule) *see* St
    Benedict of Nursia, *Rule*
Russell, Alice nun of Wilton 64
Russell, Amice abbess 30, 32, 35, 58-9,
    62n1, 64; as sacristan 30, 59
Russell, Clemence nun 35

saints, royal cult of 17, 23, 42, 43 with
    n6, 44 *see also* Sts Ælfgifu, Eadburh,
    Edith of Wilton, Edward the Martyr
St Ælfgifu first consort of Eadmund I
    13, 41, 45; buried at Shaftesbury
    42; compassion and generosity of
    43; confused with Æthelgifu 44 with
    nn4-5; cult, English 17, 42, 43-4, 67-
    8, and Scandinavian 43; feasts 42, 67
    with n4; metrical *Life* of attributed to
    William of Malmesbury 42; miracles
    42; prophetic powers 43; relics 42,
    43
St Æthelflæd (Ælfflæd, Elfleda,
    Ethelfleda) of Romsey 47n4
St Æthelwold 4n3, 7n11, 46, 47, 48,
    50n1
St Aldhelm 44n4
St Anne (Agia Anne) 19n2; abbey
    chantry dedicated to 61
St Anselm archbishop of Canterbury,
    Cur deus homo 21, *De conceptu
    virginali et de originali peccato* 21,
    Meditatio redemptionis humanæ 21n2;
    dedication of Shaftesbury abbey
    church by 17-18, 22; letters to nuns
    of Shaftesbury and Wilton 16-17;
    Mariology of 20-2
St Augustine, *Soliloquies* translated by
    King Alfred 11 with n1
St Benedict of Aniane 48
St Benedict of Nursia, *Rule* (*known also
    as* the Holy Rule) of 27n2, 32, 49,
    59n4; Anglo-Saxon and later English
    translations of 50 with n1
St Cuthburh (Cuþburh, Cuðburh,
    Cuthburg, Cuthburga) of Wimborne
    2
St Dunstan 7n11, 46, 47, 48
St Eadburh (Edburga), daughter of
    Edward the Elder and Eadgifu 5, 45,
    46; feast of 5n6
St Edith of Wilton 42, 67, 68

St Edward the Martyr 41, 42n1, 47n5, 52n7, 60n4; cult 17n3, 41n6; feasts 17n2, 67, 78n7; relics 43-4

St Eulalia of Barcelona 53n4, of Merida 53

St Faith (Foy) 77

St George (Seint Georg, Seintiorge), Margaret nun 90-1

St Giles, Wilton leper hospital (*leprosarium*) dedicated to 68 with n1

St Gregory the Great, *Pastoral Care* translated by King Alfred 10 with n7, 11n1

St Grimbald [of Saint-Bertin] 10

St John of Damascus 19

St John (Seint John, Seynt John), Margaret abbess 92-3; chantry endowed by 93

St John (Saynt John), Margery (Margeria, Margareta) nun 35, 98

St John, Sir Oliver of Bletsoe (Beds), Spelsbury (Oxon) and Lydiard Tregoze (Wilts) 92

St Katherine 77

St Margaret 77

St Mary the Blessed Virgin, feasts of the Assumption 17-19, 20nn1-2, Conception 19-20, Immaculate Conception 20-2, Nativity 19; miracles of 54n3

St Mary of Egypt 54n2

St Merewenna (Mærwenna, Mærpynn, Mærwynn, Merewenna, Merwinna) of Romsey 5n1, 43n2, 47 with nn2, 4; witness to charter 47n2

St Odo of Cluny 47n5

St Osmund bishop of Salisbury 18

St Pauls church, London 20n2, 67n2

St Rumbold's church, Cann (Dorset) 36n5, 103; rector of 103

St Stephen protomartyr 67

St Swithun's Psalter *see* Winchester, Psalter (St Swithun's Psalter)

St Thomas Aquinas 21

St Thomas the Martyr 101n5

St Wulfsige (Wlsige, Wulfsin, Wulsin) bishop of Sherborne 51

Salisbury, cathedral, consecration of abbesses at 28, 62n5, obits endowed at 73n11; earls of *see* Longespée,

Montacute; Old Sarum (*Searbyrig, Sorviodunum*) 7, 18, 54; see of 24

Sampson, Joan nun 87

Sarah (Sarra) de Meriet nun 65

Sarum rite 20n2, 54, 78 with n7, 107

Saunzaver, Constance nun 33, 59-60, 61

Savage, Alice nun 84

Savage, Eleanor (nun of Shaftesbury?) 84

Savia nun 57

Scholastic theologians 21

scrutatrix, scrutatrices, scrutineer(s) at elections of abbesses 26

Searbyrig see Salisbury, Old Sarum

Selgrave, Margaret prioress 31, 79

Sempringham, Gilbertine priory (Lincs) 71

servitium debitum see knight-service

Shaftesbury I Abbey, abbesses (Æthelgifu (*see* Alfred (Ælfred), Alfred the Great king of Wessex), Herelufu, 'Æthelfreda', Leveva, Eulalia, Emma, Cecily, Mary, 'J.' [Joan], Amice Russell, Agnes Longespée, Agnes de Ferrers Juliana de Bauceyn, Laurentia de Muscegros, Joan de Bridport, Mabel Giffard, Alice de Lavington, Margaret Aucher, Denise la Blunde, Joan Duket, Margaret de Leukenore, Joan Formage, Egelina de Counteville, Cecily Fovent, Margaret Stourton, Edith Bonham, Margaret St John, Alice Gibbes, Margery Twyneo, Elizabeth Shelford, Elizabeth Zouche), elections of 25-33, 75 (*see also* bells, *major et sanior pars capituli*, royal assent (*assensus regius*) to election of abbess, royal licence to elect abbess, *Quia propter, Te deum laudamus, Veni creator spiritus*), feudal obligations of 24-5; archaeology 11-12, 17n2, 18, 36n4; burial ground 36n5, 107 with n7, 109; cartularies 13 with n6, 24n2, 77n6, 96 with n7; chantries 60, 61, 63, 77 with n6, 93; chaplains (*capellani*) *known also as* prebendaries 27, 60, 61 with n1, 93; chapter house 25-6; church, rebuilt by abbess Eulalia 17 with n2, dedicated by St Anselm 17-18, 22; convent buildings 36, 37 with n1, 80 with n11; crenellation 29; estates (*see* Abbas Combe, Atworth, Bradford-on-Avon, Broughton Gifford, Cheselbourne, Donhead, Felpham, Fontmell, Fovant, Isle of Purbeck, Kingston, Piddletrenthide, Tarrant Hinton, Tisbury, Winterbourne Tomson); founded by King Alfred 1, 9-10, 12; garden 37n1; heraldic tiles 80 with n11, 81; infirmary 82; as *locus sanctus* 44; nuns (*see* Index *passim*), pensions assigned to at Dissolution 31, 36, 94n14, 97, 105 with n9, 106, profession of 31n3, 34, 81 (see also *moniales expresse professe, tacite professe*), prohibited from visiting town 69, social backgrounds of 14-15, 55; sacristy 37n1; shrines 17, 42, 44; site of 7, 11-12; spiritual life of 16; suppression 1, 105, and destruction of 17n2, 36-8

II *Burh* and town 6-8, abbey stone used for building in town 36 with n4; fortifications 7-8; foundation recorded by William of Malmesbury 7; Gold Hill 29n5; parish churches, Holy Trinity 36n5, 95n11, 109, St James 93n1

Shaftesbury Abbey museum 17n2, 36n2, 81

Shaftesbury Psalter (*Lbl* Lansdowne MS 383) 20n1, 54n2, 66-8; calendar 20n1 66-8, 79; litany 67-8; obits 66-7, 79; possibly made for Adeliza of Louvain 67-8; of possible Wilton origin 68

Shakespeare 38 with n2

Sheen (Surrey), Carthusian priory 2n4

Shelford, Agnes nun 35, 85, 101

Shelford, Elizabeth (Elisabeth) abbess 15n2, 31, 32, 34, 35, 68, 96, 101-2; arms of 101n7; *horæ* (*Cfm* MS 2-1957) owned by 17n2, 42nn1, 95n11, 103 with n4; parents of: John More of Hereford and Gwen his wife 101, memorial to latter 101; party to land purchased at Hindon (Wilts)

102; rebus of 101n8

Sherborne abbey (Ben.), Dorset, 42

Simeon of Durham monk and historian 1n2

Simon of Ghent (*de Gandavo*) bishop of Salisbury 23

Skyllyng, Margaret nun 103

Slo, Katherine prioress 24, 31, 78

Sorviodunum see Salisbury, Old Sarum

Southampton, *Hamtun* (Hants) *burh* 8

Spartygrane, Martha nun 35, 93

Spertegrane (Spartygrane), Margery nun 35, 83

Stanburne (Staynburn), Margaret prioress of Stamford (Ben.), Lincs, 50n1

Stephen king of England 54, 57, 68n2

Stokes, Joan nun 98

Stourton, Anastasia nun 24, 35, 80

Stourton, arms of 80

Stourton, John I of Preston Plucknett (Somerset), member of parliament 80

Stourton, Sir John of Preston Plucknett and Brimpton, 1st Baron Stourton 82

Stourton Margaret abbess 15n2, 31, 35, 79-81

Stourton, Mary nun 35, 80, 81

Susanna nun 56

Swein Forkbeard (*Tjúguskegg*) king of Denmark 7; attacks and destroys Wilton 7

Swyneffelde, Christine nun 83

Sybil de Bruere nun 65

Syon abbey (Brig.), Middx, 1n1, 105n9

Tarrant Hinton (Dorset), Shaftesbury abbey estate at 6n5

Tarrant Keyneston abbey (Cist. nuns), Dorset, 59, 79, 84

Te deum laudamus, hymn sung at elections of abbesses 26

Tewkesbury abbey (Ben.), Glos, foundation of 57

'Theotokos' (Θεοτόκος, *Deipara*), title of the Blessed Virgin Mary 19

Thornhylle (Thornuell), Katherine nun 98

Tilley, Radegund nun of Polsloe,

Devons, formerly of Cannington priory 108
Tisbury (Wilts), Shaftesbury abbey estate at 45; abbey stone from 17; parish church, roof bosses with arms of Elizabeth Shelford abbess 101n7
Torre abbey (Prem.), Devons, 63
Towse (Fowsey), Joan nun, formerly of Cannington priory 108
Tracy, Margaret nun 15, 74
Turbevill, Agnes nun 15, 72
Twyneo, Christopher seneschal (steward) of Shaftesbury abbey 96; (from 1507 to 1509) archdeacon of Berkshire 96
Twyneo (Twinhoe, Twinyhoe, Twyneho, Twynyho), Margery (or Margaret) abbess 15n2, 32, 34, 88, 94, 95-6, 102
Twynyho, George of Keyford, Frome (Somerset) gentleman, buried in Shaftesbury abbey church 96; will of 96
Tychebourne, Juliana nun 83

Uppehauyne, Isabel (Isabella) nun 82
Usschere (Ussher), Jonette nun 75

Veni creator spiritus, hymn sung at elections of abbesses 25
Vikings 6-8, 10, 12n2, 52n5
Vinfrey, Elizabeth nun 93
Vitalis abbot of Savigny, Normandy (département Manche), 22; obituary roll of 22, 53 with n2
vowesses 13, 39-47 (see Wynflæd, Ælfgifu, Ælfthryth, Eadgifu)

Wadesworth, Anne nun 83
Walbertone (Warberton), Joan nun 90
Wales 62-3
Walker, Alice nun 103
Wallingford (Oxon), Viking depredations of 52n5
Walter de la Wyle bishop of Salisbury 23
Waltham, John bishop of Salisbury 30n2
Wareham (Dorset), abbess of see Wulfwynn; fortified settlement (castellum) 2, 12; nunnery (monasterium sanctimonialium) 2, 47,

49; parish church of Lady St Mary 2n4; priory 2n4; relics of St Edward the Martyr removed to Shaftesbury from 44; Viking occupation of 12n2
Watton, Gilbertine priory, Yorks 71
Werlonde (Warlond), Katherine nun 89
Wessex 8-9, 30, 49
West, Lady Alice of Hinton Martel (Dorset) 75
Weste, Jane nun 111
Westeleighe, Isabel (Isabella) nun 85
Weston, Christine (Cristian, Christiana) nun 109
West Saxons, ruling dynasty 43n6, 44; nobility 12
Wherwell, abbey of Holy Cross and St Peter (Ben.), Hants, 28, 49, 50n1, 59, 60 with n4; abbesses of see Ælfthryth (Ælfðryðe), Cecilia de Lavington
widows 7 with n11, 13 with n7, 46, 68n2
William II ('Rufus') king of England 54
William d'Aubigny 1st earl of Arundel 68n2
William de la Corner bishop of Salisbury 63n10
William of Malmesbury, monk and historian 3n3, 5, 7, 11 with nn1-4, 42, 44, 46, 47n4, 52n6
William de la Rivere (de Ripariis), Master 64n10
wills, of King Alfred the Great 13, of Wynflæd 41 with nn3-4, of nuns 24, 30 with n2, 73-4, 76, 80; nuns as beneficiaries of 24, 41, 65-6, 70, 75, 76, 77, 78, 80
Wilton, abbey (Ben.), Wilts, 3, 16, 24, 49, 84, 106n3, abbesses see Bodenham, Cecily, and Lavington, Felise, archaeology 4n1; burh 3, 6, defeat of King Alfred by Vikings 6, fortified by King Alfred 6; house for religious women founded by King Egbert (Ecgberht) of Wessex 3, refounded by King Alfred 3, 12; leper hospital (leprosarium) see Adeliza of Louvain; royal palace 2; Wilton House 3-4
Wilton, Alice (Alicia) nun, pregnancy of 76

Wimborne (Dorset), college of secular
    canons 2n5; nunnery founded by
    St Cuthburh (Cuþburh, Cuðburh,
    Cuthburg, Cuthburga), sister of
    King Ine of Wessex 2
Winchester (Hants), Council of see
    Council of Winchester 973; New
    Minster and Hyde Abbey (Ben.) 19,
    42, 'Liber vitæ' of see 'Liber vitæ'
    of New Minster and Hyde Abbey;
    Nunnaminster (St Mary's Abbey) 4,
    5n2, 6, 24, 46, 49, 50n1, founded
    by Ealhswith (Ealshþið) consort of
    Alfred the Great 4, refounded by
    Æthelwold bishop of Winchester
    4n3; Old Minster 4n3; Psalter
    (Winchester, St Swithun's Psalter, Lbl
    Cotton Nero MS C. iv) 17n2, 62n8
Winterbourne Tomson (Dorset),
    Shaftesbury abbey estate at 40
Wodeford, Agnes nun 84-5
Wodehele (Wodehyll), Agnes nun 35,
    78, 86
Wodehill, Idony nun 15, 35, 78
Wolsey, Cardinal Thomas 110 with n11;

    natural daughter of see Clansey,
    Dorothy
Worcester, cathedral priory (Ben.) 19,
    20n1, 42
Wortheton (Wroughton), Elizabeth nun
    111
Wrangle (Lincs) 67n2
Wrangylle, Wrangle Richard priest 67n2
writs, royal 26 see also De intendendo
Wulfsige (Wlsige, Wulfsin, Wulsin)
    bishop of Sherborne see St Wulfsige
Wulfwynn (Wulfwyn, Wulfwin, Wulwina)
    abbess of Wareham 47 with nn2,5;
    obit in Anglo-Saxon Chronicle 47 with
    n5; witness to charter 47n2
Wynflæd (Wynnflæd, Wenflede,
    Winfled), religious woman
    associated with Shaftesbury abbey
    39-41, 42, 45n3; will of 41 with n3

Zouche (Souche, Zowch, Zowche,
    Zuche), Elizabeth (Elisabeth) abbess
    15n2, 27, 31, 32, 35, 96, 102, 105-6
Zouche, Margaret nun of Wilton 106

www.ingramcontent.com/pod-product-compliance
Lightning Source LLC
Chambersburg PA
CBHW060816100426
42813CB00004B/1099

9 781906 978921